Bringing Literacy to Life

Issues and Options in Adult ESL Literacy

Heide Spruck Wrigley

Gloria J. A. Guth

Aguirre International, San Mateo, CA
for the U.S. Department of Education
Office of Vocational and Adult Education

Published by Aguirre International, 411 Borel Avenue, Suite 402, San Mateo, CA 94402

Printed in the United States of America

This document was prepared for the U. S. Department of Education, Office of Vocational and Adult Education, with funding from the National English Literacy Demonstration Program for Adults of Limited English Proficiency, under contract number VN90002001. The opinions expressed in this document do not necessarily reflect the positions or policies of the department.

ISBN 0-9633702-0-0

This book is written in celebration of all the extraordinary learners and teachers who have joined together to bring literacy to life.

Table of contents

Preface

Bringing Literacy to Life is the result of a two year research study funded under the National English Literacy Demonstration Program for Adults of Limited English Proficiency.[1] Under this program, the U.S. Department of Education commissioned a national research study to "identify effective and innovative instructional approaches, methods, and technologies used to provide literacy instruction for adult English as a Second Language literacy students." The contract was awarded to Aguirre International of San Mateo, California, whose staff conducted the research: Gloria J. A. Guth directed the project; Heide Spruck Wrigley served as the specialist for language, literacy, and learning; and Anabel Adler and Kristin Helland provided research assistance.

The project was conducted in three stages:

- During the first stage, we conducted an extensive review of the literature on adult learning, second language teaching, and literacy education and examined curricula available for adult ESL literacy. We also sought input and advice from members of our working group (listed in the Acknowledgements) and other scholars in the field. After designing a profile that outlined the features of an educationally sound adult ESL literacy program, we requested nominations of programs that matched that profile. One hundred and twenty-three program nominations were received.

- During the second stage, we reviewed the program descriptions that were submitted and selected nine programs for further study. We then visited nine programs to find out more about their literacy work. We observed classes and asked teachers, learners, and administrators to talk about program issues and discuss the language and literacy practices that had proven to be effective in their particular context. Many of these ideas found their way into this handbook in the form of "Cases in Point" and "Promising Practices."

- During the final stage of the project, we interpreted and analyzed the information from previous phases and prepared two final documents, a technical report and this handbook on adult ESL literacy education. The technical report includes the methodology used in the study, major

---

[1]Authorized in Section 372(d) (1) of the U.S. Adult Education Act, P.L. 100-297, as amended.

findings and recommendations, and full site reports on the innovative programs we visited. The technical report serves as a companion piece to this handbook and is available from the U.S. Department of Education. The nine sites are listed below.

This handbook is based on the information gathered during the study and represents a synthesis of ideas derived from various sources. It includes insights by the scholars, teachers, and learners involved directly in the project, as well as ideas derived from the many writers who have written about language and literacy education. The opinions expressed in the book are our own.

Adult ESL Literacy Project Sites

El Barrio Popular Education Program
218 East 106 Street
5th Floor
New York, NY 10029

Refugee Women's Alliance (ReWA)
3004 S. Alaska
Seattle, WA 98108

Haitian Multi-Service Center (HMSC)
Adult Basic Education Program
12 Bicknell Street
Dorchester, MA 02125

International Institute of Rhode Island (IIRI)
Literacy/ESL Program
375 Broad Street
Providence, Rhode Island 02907

Lao Family Community of Minnesota
Family English Literacy Program
976 West Minnehaha Avenue
St. Paul, MN 55104

Project Workplace Literacy Partners for the
Manufacturing Industry in Cook County
Adult Learning Resource Center
1855 Mt. Prospect Road
Des Plaines, IL 60018

Arlington Education and Employment Program (REEP)
Wilson Adult Center
1601 Wilson Blvd
Arlington, VA 22209

Literacy Education Action (LEA)
Small Group Instruction Program
El Paso Community College
P.O. Box 20500
El Paso, TX 79998

UAW/Chrysler Tech Prep Academy
Eastern Michigan University
Corporate Services
3075 Washtenaw
Ypsilanti, MI 48197

About this book

This book is for all those who care about adult ESL literacy. It was written to help programs provide a rich educational program for the many adults who may speak some English but are not yet comfortable with literacy. It is a combination of background information, advice for teachers, and examples of good teaching. A blend of theory and practice, this book is meant to help practitioners and programs make informed decisions about teaching literacy in their own particular context. The ten curriculum modules, written by teachers in the field, are meant to illustrate some of the best practices that adult ESL literacy has to offer.

The book supports the basic assumption that in adult ESL literacy "one size does not fit all." It is, therefore, not written as a how-to guide for teachers without any background in teaching or as a blueprint for "what to do on Monday morning." Rather, it is meant as a resource for teachers who have some experience in teaching but are new to ESL literacy. It can also be used to provide guidance to teachers who want to teach language minority adults in the future.

How to use this book

This book contains some sections and components that appear in several chapters, each designed to meet different information needs. Except for "State of the Art" and "Curriculum Modules," each chapter is divided into three sections:

Background, Practice, and Reflections. You, as the reader, can decide what interests you the most.

Background

If you want to know more about the issues that are debated in the adult ESL literacy field, or, if you are interested in theories, the "Background" section is for you.

Practice

If you are looking for teaching strategies or want examples from actual programs, read the section called "Practice." Within this section, "Tips for Teachers" tell you what to do; "Cases in Point" show how innovative programs deal with an issue; and "Promising Practices" contain ideas that can be adapted for many different kinds of teaching contexts. Don't forget to also consult the ten curriculum modules in chapter 9 for ideas on what to do in the classroom.

Reflections

If you like to think of ways of making your own teaching more effective, or, if you would like to work with others to make your program more responsive to the needs of your students, consult the section entitled "Reflections."

This book contains nine chapters.

1. **"Adult ESL Literacy: State of the Art"** discusses some of the special features of adult ESL literacy: a focus on reading and writing, an emphasis on active learning, an understanding of the social contexts that shape literacy, and a consideration of "learning how to learn." The chapter provides some working definitions of ESL literacy, discusses the multi-dimensional nature of literacy, and gives examples of the different kinds of literacy that programs focus on in their teaching.

2. **"Approaches and Materials"** maintains that meaning-based approaches show the greatest promise in helping adults develop full literacy. The chapter discusses the different ways in which literacy can be taught and explains current theories of reading and writing development. The chapter also includes strategies for teaching initial

literacy and provides "Tips for Teachers" who want to provide rich literacy experiences for their students.

3. **"Teaching Adult ESL Literacy in the Multilevel Classroom"** shows that group work is the most effective strategy for dealing with the multilevel classroom. The chapter discusses various ways of grouping students and provides strategies for using "themes" to take advantage of the different skills that learners have. The chapter also briefly discusses the dangers inherent in emphasizing individualized instruction with beginning ESL literacy learners.

4. **"Using Computer and Video Technology in Adult ESL Literacy"** discusses the pros and cons of using technology in ESL literacy teaching. It shows how computer and video technologies can be used effectively in supporting meaning-based literacy. The chapter includes a sample unit that describes how technology can be integrated with classroom teaching and presents a chart to help teachers link the needs of their learners with the features to look for in software programs.

5. **"Native Language Literacy"** demonstrates that using the native language of the learners is a viable approach to introducing literacy to adults who are not literate in their first language. The chapter also describes the various ways in which the native language can be used in the ESL classroom and provides some strategies for discussing with the learners the use of English and/or the native language in the literacy classroom.

6. **"Learner Assessment"** shows that program-based assessments are superior to standardized tests when it comes to assessing the progress of individual learners. The chapter describes the various functions of assessment and shows what counts as evidence of success in many adult ESL literacy programs. It includes examples of innovative alternative assessments used by literacy educators.

7. **"Curriculum"** demonstrates that curriculum decisions are value decisions that mirror a program's philosophy and reflect the broader individual and social goals the program supports. While the first part of the chapter outlines some common curriculum orientations, the second part discusses two approaches to curriculum development: (1) the conventional model which depends on pre-specified objectives and (2) the alternative model which allows curriculum to emerge out of discussions and interactions with the learners. Case studies illustrate both models.

8.   **"Staff Development and Program Issues"** holds that effective staff development in adult ESL literacy should seek to provide knowledge and understanding in three areas: (1) the social context of ESL literacy; (2) adult learning, second language acquisition, and literacy development; and (3) the teaching processes that support successful ESL literacy learning. The chapter discusses some of the barriers to effective teaching in adult ESL literacy programs and examines the related issues of professionalism and advocacy. It also outlines three models for delivering staff development, the "craft model," the "applied science model," and the "inquiry model."

9.   **"Curriculum Modules"** presents ten teaching units, written by teachers in the field who have experience in adult ESL literacy. These units demonstrate examples of meaning-based teaching that can be used in a variety of contexts, including workplace, family literacy, and community literacy. These units illustrate a variety of teaching strategies, including how to teach initial literacy, how to create and use learner-generated materials, how to link literacy with a discussion of social issues, how to conduct research in the community, how to integrate phonics into a meaning-based curriculum, and how to teach context-specific vocabulary and life skills. Two examples of teaching literacy in a bilingual context are also included.

It is our hope that this book will lead to a new appreciation of the hard work and creative efforts put forth by the learners, teachers, and administrators in innovative programs. Their collaborations serve as an example to the field.

Heide Spruck Wrigley
Gloria J. A. Guth
San Mateo
May 1992

Acknowledgments

This project would not have been possible without the time and contributions of many people. Aguirre International and the project staff would like to thank all who participated in this study, funded under the National English Literacy Demonstration Program for Adults of Limited English Proficiency.

We are deeply indebted to the members of our Working Group for devoting time to this study and for contributing insights and ideas. The group provided detailed feedback on various drafts of the handbook and the technical report, and many individuals made themselves available so we could exchange ideas and argue points. We greatly appreciate their contributions.

We are also grateful to those colleagues who were not part of the Working Group but nevertheless reviewed sections of the manuscript and shared ideas and insights. Thanks in particular to Sandra Lee McKay, Gail Weinstein-Shr, and Pia Moriarty.

The Department of Education representatives gave us consistent support and excellent feedback throughout the study. In particular, our project officers, Laura Karl Messenger and Joyce Fowlkes Campbell, helped keep us on track and provided thoughtful comments at every step. We could not have asked for more responsive project officers.

Special thanks to all the programs that talked to us on the phone and those who invited us to study their programs. They provided the heart of this project, and the study would not have been possible without them. It was exciting to see such good work in action. We are grateful for the hospitality, trust, and openness the sites showed us, and we appreciated the opportunity to talk to learners face to face. We cherish all of their comments.

We wish also to thank the curriculum writers for the creative and interesting modules they prepared for this handbook. We believe that these modules will serve as an inspiration to both novice and experienced teachers. We applaud the writers.

We appreciate the hard work done by the two research assistants on the project, Anabel Adler and Kristin Helland. Both researched and reviewed articles and books, contributed insights and ideas, and provided assistance in editing. We want to thank Anabel Adler for the intelligence and charm she displayed in conducting phone interviews and for her efforts in helping to revise the manuscript. Her efforts in formatting and in managing the production of the final text helped to make this product a reality. We thank Kristin Helland for her contributions to the literature review, especially in the areas of Biliteracy and Language Experience. She maintained the bibliographic data base and took responsibility for the references in this handbook. We appreciate her thoroughness and her eye for detail. We also thank Cathy Davis for her contributions to the chapters on teaching ESL literacy in the multilevel classroom.

Working Group

Dr. Elsa Auerbach, Assistant Professor, Bilingual/ESL Graduate Program, University of Massachusetts, Boston, Massachusetts

Dr. JoAnn Crandall, Associate Professor, Department of Education, University of Maryland, Baltimore County, Baltimore, Maryland

Dr. Hanna Arlene Fingeret, Director, Literacy South, Raleigh, North Carolina

Mr. Bill Goodwin, Office of Job Training, Division of Seasonal Farmworker, Department of Labor, Washington, D.C.

Ms. Janet Isserlis, Literacy Specialist, The International Institute of Rhode Island, Providence, Rhode Island

Mr. Nick Kremer, Dean, Economic Development, Irvine College, Irvine, California

Dr. Richard Levy, Supervisor, Program Development, Bureau of Adult Education, Commonwealth of Massachusetts, Department of Education, Quincy, Massachusetts

Dr. Lynellyn Long, Senior Social Scientist, S&T/WID, Agency for International Development

Dr. Reynaldo Macias, Director, Center for Multilingual, Multicultural Research, School of Education, University of Southern California, Los Angeles, California

Dr. Wayne Pate, Division of Adult and Community Education, Texas Education Agency, Austin, Texas

Ms. Diane Pecararo, Adult Education Specialist, ESL, Minnesota Department of Education, St. Paul, Minnesota

Ms. K. Lynn Savage, ESL Specialist, Adult Education Unit, California Department of Education, Sacramento, California

Dr. Julia Spinthourakis, Operations and Management Consultant, HRS-OSRA, Tallahassee, Florida

Mr. Dennis Terdy, Adult Learning Resource Center/The Center, Des Plaines, Illinois

U.S. Department of Education Representatives

Laura Karl Messenger, Program Specialist, Office of Vocational and Adult Education, Washington, D.C.

Joyce Fowlkes Campbell, Program Specialist, Division of Adult Education and Literacy, Washington, D.C.

Susan Webster, Contract Officer, Washington, D.C.

List of Final Program Sites and Their Directors

El Barrio Popular Education Program, New York, NY:
Dr. Klaudia Rivera

El Paso Community College - Literacy Education Action, El Paso, TX:
Dr. Carol Clymer-Spradling

Haitian Multi-Service Center - Adult Basic Education Program, Dorchester, MA: Mr. Jean Marc Jean-Baptiste and Dr. Carol A. Chandler

International Institute of Rhode Island, Providence, Rhode Island:
Ms. Sara Smith, Ms. Francine Collignon, Ms. Janet Isserlis

Lao Family Community of Minnesota, Family English Literacy Program (FELP) St. Paul, MN: Mr. Geoffery Blanton

Project Workplace Literacy Partners for the Manufacturing Industry in Cook County, Adult Learning Resource Center, Des Plaines, IL: Ms. Linda Mrowicki

Arlington Education and Employment Program (REEP) - Wilson Adult Education Center, Arlington VA: Dr. Inaam Mansoor

Refugee Women's Alliance, Seattle, WA: Ms. Judy de Barros

UAW-Chrysler Tech Prep Academy/Eastern Michigan University Corporate Services, Ypsilanti, MI: Dr. Rena Soifer; Dr. Beth Voorhees

Other Sites Visited

Community College of San Francisco, Mission Campus, San Francisco, CA: Dr. Dian Verdugo

San Mateo Adult School, San Mateo, CA: Ms. Gloria Duber

YMCA Literacy School, San Francisco, CA: Ms. Nancy Larson O'Sullivan

Curriculum Writers

Ana Huerta-Macias	Janet Isserlis
Peggy Dean	Lynellyn Long
Deidre Freeman	Marilyn Gillespie
Gail Weinstein-Shr	Pat Rigg
Nancy Hampson	Maria E. Malagamba-Roddy
Laima Maria Schnell	Celestino Cotto Medina

Chapter 1

Adult ESL Literacy: State of the Art

Adult English as a Second Language (ESL) literacy is an exciting new field that holds great promise, not just for teaching literacy to language minority adults, but for adult basic education and mainstream ESL as well. The issues raised by literacy educators and the teaching practices used by innovative practitioners can serve as a starting point for discussion about learning and teaching in any context. At a time when the field is concerned about standards and accountability, innovative programs in ESL literacy offer examples of rigorous teaching that challenges students as well as teachers and meets the requirements for active learning.

This chapter provides an overview of the adult ESL literacy field, with a special focus on the innovative aspects of literacy teaching. The chapter is divided into two sections: "Background: History and Definitions" and "Practice: Dimensions of Literacy." The "Background" section provides a quick historical overview and then discusses some special features that reflect the state of the art of ESL literacy teaching. This section also shows how programs in the field deal with the thorny issue of defining literacy. The section on "Practice" looks at various aspects of learning and the dimensions of literacy they reflect. It also presents some features of adult ESL literacy that are commonly found in successful programs.

Background: History and definitions

For centuries, educators and scholars have examined various aspects of language and literacy. Literacy campaigns around the world have made countries aware of the importance of literacy and its power in shaping opportunities. Yet discussions about literacy in a second language have often assumed literacy in the first language, and studies about second language learners who are not literate in their native language are relatively new.

The United States government became concerned with English as a Second Language (ESL) literacy in the 1970s when the country experienced a large influx of refugees from Southeast Asia. Many of the refugees had very little experience with reading and writing and, in some cases, had never held a pencil before. For this reason, conventional ESL classes, where learners were expected to read and write the words and sentences they were studying, were no longer effective.

The second phase of ESL literacy awareness came in the late 1980s, during the implementation of the Immigration Reform and Control Act (IRCA). In order to fulfill IRCA's educational requirements needed to qualify for immigration "amnesty," thousands of undocumented, non-English speaking students flocked to classes. Educators soon realized that amnesty students, many of whom had only a few years of schooling in their home countries, could not possibly access the information contained in the textbooks mandated by the federal government unless they were given the opportunity to acquire literacy first.

As a result of this mismatch between what available curricula offered and what students needed to learn, practitioners began searching for appropriate models and techniques for teaching. While some adapted available ESL materials, others experimented with approaches originally developed for teaching literacy in the native language, such as whole language approaches, the Language Experience Approach, and Freirean pedagogy. In many areas, practitioner-based literacy efforts started to take hold and influence the way non-literate learners of English were taught. To a large extent, it has been these grassroots efforts that have helped shape the field and contributed to the experimentation and innovation that characterizes the field today.

Understanding adult ESL literacy

Adult ESL literacy is a relatively new field that draws ideas and practices from disciplines such as adult education, applied linguistics, anthropology, and the cognitive sciences. ESL literacy reflects the shifts that have taken place both in second language teaching and in literacy education during the last decade.

Focus on meaning in reading and writing

Just as second language teaching has moved away from a focus on grammar and toward a greater emphasis on communication, literacy has shifted from a focus on skills to a focus on meaning. Previously, literacy teaching concentrated on teaching learners the alphabet and providing practice in phonics before moving on to the kind of reading and writing adults practice in "real-life." This approach has been challenged extensively. There is now a growing consensus that "real-life" reading should be the starting point rather than the ending point of teaching initial literacy and that skills such as phonics should be used as a tool in helping learners understand the "print" they see around them.

Similarly, there is now an increased awareness that writing or composing need not wait until a person has mastered the entire alphabet or internalized the writing system.   Just as ESL learners are able to express ideas without having fully mastered the grammar and sound system of a language, literacy learners are able to write down ideas using their own approximation of letters and words, using what has been called "invented" or "experimental" writing. These two processes, understanding that written language carries meaning and turning thoughts into writing, are often called "meaning-making."

Social context of literacy

Adult ESL literacy reflects another shift in language and literacy teaching: a greater awareness of the fact that literacy is not an individual skill that exists in isolation. Rather, literacy occurs through interaction with and support from the world of people around us. Literacy, the literature now holds, is a social phenomenon that involves readers and writers who communicate through a process called "negotiating meaning." As a result of this awareness, scholars now try to find out more about the ways in which ESL learners use literacy in their lives, in their communities, at work, or in their interactions with the educational system.

Viewing literacy as a collective act rather than an individual achievement has led to a greater awareness of the social and cultural dimensions of literacy. Many scholars now hold that literacy is not only a social process, but it is defined by the economic and political realities of society as well. This view of literacy as culturally determined is referred to as the "ideological model,"[1] since it shows that a society's perspective on literacy is influenced by the values and ideologies its citizens espouse. The ideological model stands in contrast to the "autonomous model" of literacy, which holds that "skills are skills," regardless of context.

The recognition that literacy is not value free has lead to a greater awareness of the way literacy is influenced by issues of power and gender. In many adult ESL literacy programs, issues of power and gender have come to the forefront. For example, some programs serve women exclusively and try to support their traditions while others seek to share power by working collaboratively with learners. Some of these programs involve learners in decision making both in the classroom and in the program overall. Programs that deal with the social and political issues that shape literacy and work toward sharing the power between teachers and learners are often called "participatory programs."

Active learning

ESL adult literacy also reflects a greater awareness of how adults learn. There is now a strong body of research that shows that adults are active learners who use literacy to think and reflect, understand concepts, pose questions, and solve problems. Research has shown that learners do not passively take in information presented to them, but rather they construct their own knowledge and understanding and apply this knowledge in the world around them.

We now know that adult learners do not come to schools as empty vessels to be filled with knowledge. Rather they bring a wealth of information and experience with them that they can use in making sense out of the new knowledge and skills they are trying to acquire. As a result of the awareness of the cognitive abilities that adults have, we now see many programs that involve ESL literacy learners in complex tasks, such as jointly authoring a story or a text to be published, examining social issues that concern them, conducting interviews with friends and neighbors, and doing research in the community. (See the curriculum modules in chapter 9 for examples of literacy activities that take advantage of the learners' background knowledge.)

Learning to learn and language awareness

Along with a greater recognition of adults' problem solving or cognitive abilities comes an awareness of their metacognitive skills. Metacognition is the used for our ability to think about the way we learn or to reflect on the way we use language. These skills can be used to maximize the learning capabilities of adults, who may learn faster and better if they are consciously aware of the way they construct meaning for themselves.

In second language learning, this awareness is often extended to learning more about how language works, not just in terms of its grammar and structures, but in regard to its social functions as well. To foster and strengthen this awareness, many programs involve learners in examining the role that literacy plays in their lives and in exploring the many ways that language can be used. The ability to think about language is often called "language awareness."

Perceptions of literacy

The complex nature of literacy makes definitions difficult, and there is no consensus on what it means to be literate. There is even less agreement on what it means to be literate in a second language or in two or more languages simultaneously.[2] To be sure, a number of descriptions of "being literate" have been proposed. These range from grade level equivalents to being able "to fulfill self-determined objectives as family and community members, citizens, job holders, and members of social, religious, or other associations..."[3] The National Assessment of Educational Progress (NAEP) recognizes three distinct areas of knowledge and skills:

- prose literacy — understanding and using information from texts, such as newspapers, magazines, and books

- document literacy — locating and using information from documents, such as job application forms, bus schedules, maps, tables, and indexes

- quantitative literacy — applying numerical operations to information contained in printed materials, such as checkbooks, menus, order forms, and advertisements.

This definition has also been adopted by the National Adult Literacy Survey (NALS) project.[4]

Many literacies

Although there is no universally accepted definition of literacy, there is a growing consensus that to be literate means different things in different situations or social contexts. Thus, a person may be perfectly literate in a college library but feel illiterate when confronted with immigration forms. Similarly, a person who has gone to school in a rural area may feel quite overwhelmed by the literacy demands of a factory job.

Given these complexities, defining ESL literacy as merely "the ability to read and write in English" appears simplistic and reductionist and fails to provide guidance for literacy education. Recognizing that literacy contains social, political, and cultural dimensions, the field has come to see literacy in the following two ways:

1. as a plurality of literacies or "many literacies," shaped by social contexts and defined individually as well as collectively[5]

2. as a continuum that grows and expands as a person gains experience with different types of literacies, rather than as a dichotomy or "great divide" between literate and illiterate.[6]

When combined, these two perspectives show that nearly everyone who has grown up in a literate society will have experience with some form of literacy. The challenge for research then becomes to delineate these contexts and explore literacy uses within each. A second challenge will be to show to what extent literacy skills and practices transfer from one context to another and to determine whether there exists a threshold level that allows learners to access literacy independently in a variety of contexts.

The nature of ESL literacy is still more complex since it depends on literacy in two languages: the native language of the learner and English literacy. Since the degree of literacy in the first language can significantly influence the speed and depth of literacy development in the second language, the relationship between the two language systems needs to be taken into account. Since language and literacy are socially determined, ESL literacy is also influenced by two cultures: the learners' home culture and its literacy practices and the mainstream culture and its expectations of English literacy.

Working definitions of adult ESL literacy

Since no common definition of ESL literacy has been advanced, individual programs can define literacy in their own terms. While some see this lack of consensus as a situation to be remedied, others consider it a healthy sign. Clearly, any official determination of what counts as literacy would validate certain practices, perspectives, approaches, and outcomes and invalidate others. In the absence of a single definition, programs are free to articulate their own views as to the nature of ESL literacy and the goals of ESL literacy education.

It appears that most programs in the field have set the larger definition issue aside and have chosen instead to define literacy in two ways:

1.   by the learners they serve

2.   by the type of program that they offer.

In many programs, ESL literacy students are those who have less than three years of schooling in the home country and have difficulty progressing in a regular ESL class. This definition is not used in all programs. In many workplace or family literacy programs, for example, all students, even those who can read and write at intermediate levels of literacy, are classified as literacy students.

While there may be no agreement in the field on what ESL literacy is (similar to Supreme Court Justice Potter Stewart in his definition of pornography, many teachers say "they know it when they see it"), there is a growing consensus on what it is not.

From the perspective of practice, ESL literacy is "not" about

- learning the alphabet and copying words, although these skills are useful when finding a pizza parlor in the phone book or writing down the name of a good dentist

- phonics and decoding, although phonics is helpful when trying to pronounce the items on a menu in a Mexican restaurant

- translating words from one language to another, although it may be fun to try to translate "Fahrvergnuegen" into Spanish

- focusing on grammar, spelling, punctuation, and capitalization, although these skills are critical when writing a resume

- reading paragraphs in a textbook and answering comprehension questions, although these skills are helpful when taking a reading test

- memorizing vocabulary lists, although keeping personal "word banks" may make students feel knowledgeable

- filling in workbook pages, although focused exercises can help students gain practice.

And finally, ESL literacy is "not just" about

- power and politics, although it is important to understand the political aspects of language

- functional literacy, although it helps to know how to read a paycheck

- storytelling, although personal stories can enrich and enlighten the individual learner.

While there is no one accepted definition of ESL literacy, ESL literacy *teaching* could be defined as supporting adults with little English and little formal education in their efforts to understand and use English in its many forms (oral and written, including prose, document, and quantitative literacy), in a variety of contexts (family, community, school, work), so that they can reach their fullest potential and achieve their own goals, whether these be personal, professional or academic.

Adult ESL literacy programs

ESL literacy programs can be defined as programs (or sections of programs) that put a special emphasis on fostering the literacy skills and practices of adults who have limited proficiency in English. While most ESL literacy programs teach only English literacy, others teach literacy in the mother tongue (or native language) as well. A number of programs use both English and the mother tongue of the learners in their ESL literacy classrooms.[7] Still others use only English in the classroom.

ESL literacy programs are highly diverse. They differ in size, from one-to-one tutoring to full classes. They differ in setting, from community colleges to local education agencies (LEAs) to community-based organizations (CBOs). The variety in program contexts includes "generic" literacy, family literacy, workplace literacy, and community literacy, and the variety in funding sources includes federal, state, private, and combinations of these. Programs also differ in their long term goals and educational orientations, along with the broader social goals they support.

While some programs are eclectic in their perspective on literacy (e.g., seeking to combine traditional life skills with problem posing), others have a clearly defined literacy framework that guides classroom practice, staff development, and assessment. (See chapter 2, "Approaches," for an example of a framework.)

Finally, programs vary in the way they conceptualize learner-centeredness and the degree to which they share control of the program. In most innovative programs, learners are involved in deciding what they wanted to learn and how. To a much lesser extent, learners help make decisions about course goals and assessment. In some participatory programs, learners are involved in the governance of the program itself and help make decisions regarding program direction and program aims.

Adult ESL literacy learners

Although there is no common definition of ESL literacy, there is some agreement as to the characteristics of ESL literacy learners. They tend to be adults who want to learn English and need to develop their reading and writing skills. Most have had only a few years of schooling. Some come from literate societies but have never been to school; others come from pre-literate societies where print is not in use. Still others may have some experience with reading but may not be familiar with the Roman alphabet. As literacy teachers have long known, those who have never been to school face challenges that are very different from those who have some basic knowledge of what reading and writing are all about. Conversely, learners who are literate in a non-Roman alphabet often acquire English literacy more quickly than learners who are not literate in any language. The programs we studied served a wide range of learners, including those who have had fewer than three years of education and others who were quite literate in their mother tongues but had little literacy in English.

ESL literacy students often face special challenges. Refugees may be traumatized by years of warfare or political unrest in their home countries, and undocumented students may live in constant fear of being deported. Older learners may have vision or hearing problems that make listening and reading comprehension difficult. Others may have learning difficulties and may need a great deal of time before they acquire language and literacy in a second language.

Literacy learners often have strong views of what language and literacy learning should be all about. To some learners, reading may mean reading aloud, writing may mean copying from the blackboard, and learning a language might mean memorizing grammar rules and studying vocabulary lists. Similarly, some students might resist the notion that learning literacy in their mother tongue will help them to learn English, especially if they see acquisition of English as their primary goal. Cognizant of divergent perspectives on literacy, some programs have made learner discussions about language and literacy a part of their ESL literacy program.

Strengths of adult ESL literacy learners

Increasingly, programs have come to recognize that ESL literacy students, in spite of being classified as limited English proficient (LEP), bring a wealth of experience and background knowledge to the classroom. They have found that immigrant adults have a great deal of knowledge about "the real world," possess their own kind of strategic and communicative competence, have established strong social networks, and have proven problem solving abilities. These strengths are evidenced by the fact that most students have managed to secure housing, enroll their children in school, build strong families, access social services, and find jobs. As the experience with amnesty programs has shown, thousands of ESL learners, classified as low-literate, have successfully filled out immigration papers and negotiated their way through the complex IRCA legalization process. Many successful ESL literacy programs have harnessed the strengths of their learners and instituted models that involve these adults in program decisions.

Goals of adult ESL literacy learners

Not surprisingly, literacy learners have varied reasons for wanting to attend ESL literacy programs. Often their goals change as they become more confident and start to explore possibilities. Why would an adult want to go (back) to school and learn to read and write in English? Interviews with learners point to the following reasons:

- to understand the United States and make it through the "system"; to defend themselves against unfair treatment;[8] to get along and fight back when necessary; to talk to authority figures; to explain a problem, such as a traffic accident or a welfare check that was cut off; to be treated better by others from the same culture who may look down on those who are not literate and not fully bilingual

- to become more independent; to not have to rely on friends and family to translate; to not be at the mercy of kids who "interpret" school notices and report cards creatively; to be able to go to appointments alone

- to gain access to "better jobs;" to help children succeed; to teach children how to make it through the school system

- to give something back to the community; to help others; to support the school by becoming a teacher or an aide

- to feel like "somebody" and get some respect; to have others realize that they are dealing with someone who is smart and has ideas; to avoid feeling that all communication breakdown is the fault of the speaker

- to be involved in education for its own sake; to do something worthwhile for oneself.

Practice: Dimensions of literacy

It is a truism in linguistics that language is complex and can neither be taught nor learned all at one time. Given the complexity of language and the multi-faceted character of literacy, the field is starting to "unpack literacy" and explore its various dimensions. These include (1) individual and interpersonal dimensions, (2) social and cultural dimensions, (3) political and economic dimensions, (4) affective and expressive dimensions, (5) linguistic and metalinguistic dimensions, (6) cognitive and metacognitive dimensions, and (7) perceptual and mechanical dimensions.

At any one point, literacy practices in the classroom may focus on one or more of these dimensions, creating a literacy mosaic in which various pieces interlock. While some programs may emphasize some dimensions and de-emphasize others, most innovative programs choose various combinations to provide learners with a broad range of literacy experiences. Such a combination helps ensure that a variety of learner needs are met and that different learning styles are taken into account as the teaching cycle progresses.

Innovative programs address these various dimensions by creating activities, experiences, and events that focus on different aspects of language, literacy, and learning. For example, a program might choose to introduce literacy by encouraging learners to compose stories about life in their home towns and to talk about the things there they miss. In doing so, they focus on the personal, interpersonal, and affective dimensions of literacy. In another program, learners may talk about education in their home countries, discussing who can afford to go to school for many years and who needs to leave school to go to work. In such a discussion, the political and economic dimensions of literacy are emphasized. In still another case, learners may discuss what happens in immigrant families as some family members become literate in English while others rely largely on their oral skills. Here the focus is on the social and cultural dimensions of literacy.

Quite often, a program may find it necessary to provide opportunities for skill enhancement so that learners get a chance to focus on details such as recognizing the different letters of the alphabet (e.g., b, d, q), holding a pencil and forming letters (in cursive or print), becoming familiar with particular sound combinations (e.g., "house", "mouse"), or learning the past tense in English. In this case, a program may emphasize the perceptual, mechanical or linguistic dimensions of literacy. In still other cases, the learners may want to discuss different ways of solving a math problem or may wonder how they can increase their reading speed or improve their listening comprehension. In this case the cognitive (i.e., thinking and problem solving) and the metacognitive (thinking about thinking or learning how to learn) dimensions will be emphasized.

How does this relationship between the dimensions of literacy and various learning opportunities manifest itself in innovative programs? The following taxonomy provides some examples.

Focus on (self-)expression

Affective and interpersonal dimensions are emphasized. Classroom events may include talking and writing about experiences, events, and thoughts; sharing ideas with others; reading learner-generated stories; and responding to ideas and feelings expressed in a story or other pieces of writing.

Focus on survival or life skills

The relationship between the individual learner and the literacy requirements of the larger society are emphasized. Activities often include reading signs, labels, prices, and directions; filling out forms, charts, and schedules; and understanding directions and instructions. In the workplace, where this focus is often referred to as "functional context literacy," activities may include understanding graphs and charts, interpreting symbols, and dealing with aspects of quantitative literacy. This emphasis is sometimes referred to as the "literacy as tasks"[9] perspective.

Focus on problem posing

The political, economic, and social dimensions of literacy are emphasized. Classroom events include talking or writing about critical issues in learners' lives; discussing common concerns; responding to provocative pictures, stories, and events; linking classroom activities to community concerns; and linking literacy and social action. These dimensions are often combined under the label of "critical literacy."

Focus on collaborations among learners

Social and interpersonal dimensions are emphasized. Classroom events may include discussing issues as a group; making joint decisions; acting as resources for one another and sharing information; working in multilevel groups to identify issues and respond to problems; and doing project work, such as creating yearbooks, generating class texts, or developing fotonovelas. Learners may also conduct their own research in the community.

Focus on learning how to learn

The cognitive and metacognitive dimensions of literacy are emphasized. Learners may focus on understanding connections between oral language and print; developing strategies for reading, writing, and oral communication, such as predicting meaning from context or sampling key words; using background information effectively; learning how to organize information before writing; and using one's knowledge of the world to derive meaning from print.

Focus on culture

The social and cultural dimensions of literacy are emphasized. Classroom events may focus on understanding the relationship between language, literacy, and culture; connecting with readers and writers from other cultures; making cross-cultural comparisons of attitudes and behaviors along with strategies for living in a multi-ethnic environment. Learners may discuss when, where, and how they use literacy in the native language/mother tongue and to when they use English. This emphasis is sometimes called "literacy as cultural practice."

Focus on language awareness

The social, linguistic and metalinguistic dimensions of literacy are emphasized. Classroom interactions may focus on understanding the functions and uses of language at home, work, and in the community; understanding the relationships between form and function (why we say things a certain way, in certain situations, and why a letter to a friend looks different than a letter to social services); understanding why a word might fit or not fit in a given sentence; understanding how language forms (present tense versus past tense) affect meaning. Learners may also compare words or grammar patterns across languages.

Focus on basic literacy

The individual dimension of literacy is emphasized and reading and writing is taught as a cognitive process without reference to a larger social context. Classroom interactions may include reading paragraphs and answering comprehension questions; copying information from books or from blackboards; guided writing; arranging vocabulary lists alphabetically; and skimming and scanning through selected texts. This emphasis is sometimes referred to as the "literacy as skills" perspective.

Focus on skill enhancement

Linguistic, perceptual, and mechanical dimensions are emphasized. Activities include memorizing the alphabet; learning about sound/symbol relationships (phonics); focusing on proper handwriting, printing, and capitalization; leaving spaces between words; practicing visual discrimination between letters and aural discrimination between sounds; and emphasizing correct grammar, correct pronunciation, and proper spelling. These kinds of skills are sometimes referred to as "subskills."

Biliteracy

Along with the various dimensions of literacy, many programs put a special emphasis on strategies for developing literacy in the native language along with ESL literacy. In these classes, the focus may be on discussions of the values and challenges inherent in biliteracy and an examination of how language and literacy in two languages are used by individuals in the home and in the community. Students may address the language challenges faced by "learners in transition" (i.e., families that move between two cultures and two languages) and may include comparison of linguistic and cultural patterns.

Teaching adult ESL literacy: innovative features

While innovative adult ESL literacy programs may focus on different dimensions of literacy, they share some common characteristics. The approaches they use focus on meaning and are responsive to the learner's goals, interests, and needs. In innovative programs, teaching processes:

- use the experience of the learners as a starting point for literacy and base teaching on the skills that adults possess, rather than on perceived deficits

- address the context in which literacy is used (family, community, workplace, school) and present language and literacy in light of that context

- provide opportunities for "meaning-making," that is, learners are asked to discuss what a text might mean or what they as authors are trying to say in their writing

- put a primary focus on "getting the message" by presenting new learners with "whole texts" from the start (e.g., signs, captioned photographs, name tags), rather than focusing on words and letters in isolation

- use grammar and phonics as tools for understanding and expressing ideas, not as ends in themselves

- recognize that there are "many literacies" and provide a wide range of literacy experiences (reading signs, labels, fotonovelas, TV guides; writing lists, notes, poems, letters; creating illustrated biographies)

- address the various dimensions of literacy (personal, social, cultural, political, economic) and support a multi-functional approach to literacy (e.g., literacy for self-expression, literacy for survival, literacy for social change, and literacy for problem solving)

- present activities that maintain the connection between oral language and written language by integrating listening, speaking, reading, and writing

- help learners to activate the background knowledge that they have so that they can use this knowledge in dealing with literacy tasks

- invite discussion about issues of concern to the learners, including issues such as gang activity in the neighborhoods, fear of AIDS, and concerns about teenagers becoming too "Americanized"

- provide access to information that learners need and want (e.g., crime protection, AIDS prevention, job strategies, support for their children's schooling)

- help learners to access resources and get help; help them to acquire strategies for using English and literacy to ask questions, challenge answers and solve problems; encourage adults to become independent learners.

Summary

Adult ESL literacy is an exciting new field that challenges traditional views of language, literacy, and learning. Most educators in the field are now aware that ESL literacy is much more complex than previously acknowledged and that literacy exists in a wide range of contexts. Definitions have moved away from narrowly defined school- or skill-based notions of literacy, and innovative programs now support the idea of many literacies. There is also greater recognition of the various dimensions of literacy and the aspects of learning that are tied to these dimensions.

The field has also come to realize that adult learners bring with them a variety of skills, interests, and abilities that help them to access literacy in its many forms and allow them to make decisions about their own learning. Meaning-based approaches that are responsive to the needs, goals, and interests of the learners show great promise in leading the field toward innovation and greater effectiveness.

The remaining chapters of this handbook will look more closely at some of the ideas and practices that define the field. We will examine current theories and discuss the many ways in which innovative teachers are bringing literacy to life.

Endnotes

1.   See Street, 1984.

2.   Beyond the complexity of language and literacy, there is a second reason why there may never be one agreed upon definition. In recent years, literacy has become politicized as educators have pointed to the relationship between power and literacy, showing that middle class definitions of literacy serve to validate certain types of knowledge, including literacy, over others.

3.   See Hunter & Harman, 1979.

4.   National Adult Literacy Survey brochure (Princeton, NJ: Educational Testing Service, n.d. [1990]).

5.   See *Many Literacies* by Marilyn Gillespie, 1990.

6.   See also "Issues in Adult Literacy Education" by JoAnn Crandall and Susan Imel (Crandall & Imel, 1991).

7. See the biliteracy chapter in this handbook. As explained in that chapter, the literature indicates that mother tongue literacy and/or native language support in learning English might be the best option for non-literate learners who are new to English and share a common language. Yet lack of bilingual staff, lack of funding for biliteracy programs, and lack of understanding of the relationship between first and second language literacy keep this model from being realized more widely.

8. Spanish speakers often used the term "para defenderse" to explain this goal. Similar sentiments, however, were used by learners from other cultures as well.

9. See Lytle & Wolf, 1989.

References

Canale, M., & Swain, M. (1980). Theoretical bases of communicative approaches to second language teaching and testing. *Applied Linguistics, 1*, 1-47.

Crandall, J., & Imel, S. (1991). Issues in adult literacy education. *The ERIC Review, 1*(2), 2-8.

Cummins, J. (1979). Linguistic interdependence and the educational development of bilingual children. *Bilingual education paper series, 3*(2). Los Angeles: California State University, Evaluation, Dissemination and Assessment Center.

Fingeret, A. (1983, Spring). Social network: A new perspective on independence and illiterate adults. *Adult Education Quarterly, 33*(3), 133-146.

Freire, P. (1980). *Education for critical consciousness.* New York: Continuum.

Gillespie, M. (1990). *Many literacies: Modules for training adult beginning readers and tutors.* Amherst, MA: University of Massachusetts, Center for International Education.

Heath, S. B. (1983). *Ways with words: Language, life, and work in communities and classrooms.* Cambridge: Cambridge University Press.

Hunter, C. St. J., & Harman, D. (1979). *Adult illiteracy in the United States.* New York: McGraw-Hill.

Knowles, M. (1980). *The modern practice of adult education: From pedagogy to andragogy.* Chicago, IL: Association Press/Follett.

Krashen, S. D. (1981). Bilingual cducation and second language acquisition theory. In California State Department of Education (Ed.), *Schooling and language minority students: A theoretical framework.* Los Angeles: Evaluation, Dissemination and Assessment Center.

Lytle, S. & Wolf, M. (1989). *Adult literacy education: Program evaluation and learner assessment.* Information series no. 338. Columbus, OH: ERIC Clearinghouse on Adult, Career and Vocational Education.

Schumann, J. H. (1978). The acculturation model for second-language acquisition. In R. C. Gingras (Ed.), *Second language acquisition and foreign language teaching* (pp. 27-50). Arlington, VA: Center for Applied Linguistics.

Smith, F. (1971). *Understanding reading: A psycholinguistic analysis of reading and learning to read.* New York: Holt, Rinehart and Winston.

Street, B. V. (1984). *Literacy in theory and practice.* Cambridge: Cambridge University Press.

Chapter 2

Approaches and Materials

As a reading teacher I was in a somewhat similar position to those primitive societies that perform ritual ceremonies to make the rain come. They know that pouring water on the ground won't really open the heavens, but they have to do something.

Michael Simons cited in Cambourne, 1979

Many ESL literacy teachers find themselves in a position similar to Michael Simons'. Feeling overwhelmed by the variety of approaches available for language and literacy teaching, they are no longer sure of what works. Yet, while there are many options for teaching language and literacy, the field is clear on one point: The most effective approaches are those that focus on meaning, are responsive to the needs and interests of the learners, provide opportunities for active learning, and foster collaboration. This chapter explores a number of meaning-based approaches and provides strategies for classroom teaching.

In the "Background" section, we discuss two models of literacy development and show how teachers can integrate phonics into meaningful, communicative literacy activities. We then outline seven approaches in teaching ESL and literacy and show what kind of student might benefit from a particular approach. Finally, we explain how various approaches can be linked through a program-based literacy framework.

In the "Practice" section, we provide strategies for teaching initial literacy. We show how learners can be introduced to reading and writing and how teachers can help their students develop a good sense of what literacy is all about. Finally we offer "Tips for Teachers" who want to provide a rich literacy experience for their students.

The "Reflections" section deals with selecting and developing appropriate literacy materials. We offer a series of questions designed to help teachers and coordinators think about the needs of their program. These questions are meant as decision making tools that allow programs to decide what kind of materials might best reflect their program focus and meet the needs of students and teachers.

Background: Contrasting approaches

Learning to read and write is not a simple process, especially for adults who are acquiring literacy in a second language and have had little or no previous experience with print.   Reading involves understanding what a text means, matching marks on the page with the meaning of words, connecting the message of a text with background knowledge and experience, and interpreting the overall purpose of a text.[1] Writing requires thought, the language necessary to express these thoughts, powers of organization, and the mechanical skills necessary to put ideas on paper.   Obviously, there can be no quick and easy way to acquire the knowledge, skills, and strategies needed for understanding and using written language and becoming what society considers a literate person.   There are, however, a number of approaches to teaching literacy that show promise in helping students become independent readers and writers.

Skills-based versus social-context models of literacy development

Practice reflects theory and there is nothing as practical as a good theory. The approaches teachers choose reflect their view of learning and their understanding of the way adults acquire literacy in a second language. Two models of reading and writing development are common in the literacy field: (1) a decontextualized skills-based model that claims that literacy develops in a linear fashion from letters to syllables and from syllables to words and on to sentences, and (2) a holistic, social context model that holds that literacy develops as learners use their minds to make sense out of the literacy materials found in real-life.   These models are sometimes combined in interactive approaches that integrate phonics into a meaningful context.

Advocates of the skills-based model claim that literacy is an individual accomplishment, consisting of a set of skills that exist independently of the context (setting, situation) in which they are used.   In literacy teaching, this model has been represented by a phonics-first approach to literacy that is evidenced in many basic literacy programs (particularly Laubach). Phonics-based approaches are sometimes called "bottom-up" approaches since they start at the bottom (the letters on the page).

Proponents of the social context model, on the other hand, hold that literacy develops out of the need of humans to communicate and share meaning. In this view, literacy encompasses a set of social practices influenced by individual goals, collective experiences, and societal values. This model is reflected in approaches that focus first and foremost on communication and meaning.

Approaches based on this model are sometimes called "top-down" approaches since they start with the top, that is, the background knowledge and experience that exists in the learner's mind. Literacy educators agree that real-life literacy, or reading and writing for a purpose other than classroom practice, always involves both top-down and bottom-up processes. The debate revolves around how much time should be spent on making meaning and understanding the "big picture" and how much should be spent on practicing letters and sounds. The recent literature supports an approach that puts meaning first, but helps learners to understand the relationship between meaning and structure at a point when such information becomes relevant and necessary (i.e., when learners repeatedly get stuck in similar patterns or when learners ask questions about grammar and sound/letter relationships).

We will now turn to a discussion of the phonics-based approaches and their limitations and explain the cognitive theories that form the basis for meaning-based approaches. We then show how "bottom-up skills" can become part of meaning-based teaching through an interactive approach.

Phonics-based approaches and their limitations

Phonics-based, bottom-up approaches reflect literacy as a process that is largely visual and technical, requiring that the new reader learn to associate letters with sounds before moving on to meaningful texts. In this view, the meaning of a word resides on the page, "outside" of the readers mind. This model holds that before a word can be understood as a unit, smaller parts, such as letters and syllables, need to be assembled and sounded out. This process is often referred to as "decoding."

In spite of their popularity in many basic skills programs, phonics-based approaches have many detractors. Phonics foes point out that teaching letters, syllables, and words out of context may not only be useless, they may even be counterproductive, since a focus on skills keeps learners from gaining what really counts, namely, meaning.[2] They claim that

- millions of students have learned to read not because of phonics, but in spite of it, and thousands of students have already failed phonics in school

- asking students to discriminate between similar shapes, letters, and numbers only serves to confuse, frustrate, and discourage learners unfamiliar with literacy

- phonics requires an understanding of the English sound system, knowledge that many ESL literacy students have not yet acquired

- since sound-symbol relationships in English are distressingly irregular (e.g., common words, such as "here," "there," and "were," cannot be sounded out), phonics provides a tool that has limited use in English

- phonics-based approaches start with what ESL students "don't" know (decoding), instead of what they "do" know (making sense out of things that appear unfamiliar)

- many, if not most, learners spend only a few weeks in phonics-based programs and leave before they get a chance to read or write anything they care about.

Thus, focusing primarily on phonics during the first few weeks of literacy teaching may frustrate ESL literacy learners and keep them from learning how to deal effectively with the literacy of their everyday lives.

Meaning-based approaches

In contrast, advocates of meaning-based approaches see reading and writing as a cognitive process through which the reader associates meaning with print. As readers study the print on a page, they simultaneously try to match their own background knowledge with the ideas that appear in front of them, "making meaning" in the process. For example, a person who is familiar with the culture of shopping in a U.S. supermarket will be able to use a store directory effectively, since she understands that the store will be laid out in aisles and that noodles, for example, will most likely be in the pasta section. On the other hand, someone who has only shopped at a farmer's market will find the directory confusing and overwhelming in spite of being able to read the individual food items.   The directory only makes sense to someone who has the cultural knowledge to interpret its meaning.

Meaning-based approaches that focus on meaning and context instead of letters and sounds are based on research in psycholinguistics and cognitive psychology.[3] They rely on studies in information processing strategies that show that good readers do not decode every word they read. If they did, it would take them a very long time to get to the end of a page. Rather, fluent readers check out words quickly (sometimes using phonics as an aid) and then match what they see on the page to their own knowledge of the world.   For example, a reader fluent in English will realize immediately that, in a news story, the sentence "the firemen pulled the horse from the fire truck" contains either a typographical error or an absurdity that deserves special attention.

In effect, rather than reading each word, efficient readers "predict" what a text might say. As they read, they continue to confirm their predictions by moving forward and backward in the text in an effort to make sense out of words and create meaning. Poor readers, on the other hand, often get stuck on the word level, fail to use their knowledge of the world, and may continue to apply/reapply various word attack skills instead of making use of other information in the text.

The theory holds that proficient writers use similar strategies as they compose a text. They jot down ideas and then move back and forth, revising and making changes as their ideas take shape. Good writers know that writing is an ongoing process that includes brainstorming ideas, tentatively putting ideas on paper, organizing and revising, and finally editing, which may lead to additional writing. While good writers focus on meaning first and only secondarily on form, poor writers tend to focus on spelling and mechanics and often plunge ahead with little consideration for how their ideas connect.

Proponents of meaning-based approaches maintain that the basic processes that are used in reading and writing are essentially the same for everyone — children, adults, native speakers, and second language learners. They hold that those new to literacy will learn best if they are taught the same strategies that proficient readers and writers use.

The role of background knowledge in meaning-based approaches

Studies in psycholinguistics and text processing focus heavily on the role of background knowledge in the development of reading and writing, an issue of particular interest in ESL literacy since non-native speakers often do not share the same experiences as native speakers. Cognitive theory now holds that, as we experience the world and as we read, our minds seek to integrate what we already know with the new ideas that we encounter. Experiences and knowledge become encoded in the form of cognitive structures. Since each cognitive structure is called a schema, approaches that link experience and literacy are also called "schema-theoretic approaches."

Schema theory suggests the following: in trying to understand or compose a text, learners select the appropriate background knowledge in their minds, activate the particular schema needed for comprehension, and try to make sense of the meaning encoded in the words on the page, a process sometimes called "reading from behind the eyes."[4]

In ESL literacy, the relationship between past experience and present reading deserves special consideration since much of what is written in the United States presumes a certain cultural and linguistic knowledge that the ESL learner does not (yet) have.

Based on research in schema theory, the literature now holds that literacy education will be most effective if discussions, activities, and materials take full advantage of the background knowledge and experience of the learners. Furthermore, connecting literacy activities in the classroom to learners' lives beyond the classroom will significantly strengthen literacy development.

Integrating skills into meaning-based approaches

To become independent readers and writers, all literacy learners need opportunities to use language for communication and read and write meaningful texts. Some ESL learners, however, may have difficulty understanding the meaning of a text. Their limited vocabulary and their unfamiliarity with the structure of the language may make it hard to see the connection between what they know and what they see on the page.[5] These learners may need special support in blending top-down (meaning and communication) and bottom-up (phonics and grammar) processes. (For examples on how to blend these processes, see the curriculum modules by Lynellyn Long and Marilyn Gillespie and by Peggy Dean.)

In recognition of the fact that ESL learners might need additional support in making meaning, some educators support an "interactive" approach that combines strategies for meaning-making with vocabulary development and word identification skills. This approach suggests that literacy lessons include activities that help students develop the skills needed to identify letters and words quickly and accurately so that they can develop the automatic processing skills necessary for fluent reading.[6] Choosing an approach that views literacy development as integrated and interactive, nevertheless, requires that literacy be kept "whole." To be effective, the primary focus must remain on meaningful self-expression and social communication.

There now is agreement in the literature, if not in the field, that meaning-based approaches that focus on communication and social interaction are more effective in supporting adults in their literacy development than approaches that put phonics first or teach skills out of context. We will now turn to a discussion of meaning-based approaches that are used in the field.

Examples of meaning-based approaches to teaching ESL and literacy

There are a number of meaning-based approaches that can be used effectively in the ESL literacy classroom. While some were developed by linguists focusing on second language acquisition (the communicative approach and the natural approach), others were developed by educators concerned about literacy development in general (whole language, language experience, the participatory approach). The ethnographic approach was developed out of collaborations between anthropologists, linguists, and educators.

Each approach tends to emphasize some dimensions of literacy, while de-emphasizing others, and thus may be more appropriate for some programs than for others. The seven approaches outlined are (1) the functional approach, (2) the natural approach, (3) the communicative approach, (4) the whole language approach, (5) the language experience approach, (6) the participatory approach, and (7) the ethnographic approach.

Functional approach

The functional approach as developed in the United States was designed to teach the life skills needed in everyday life and at the workplace. Teaching units and learner outcomes are often expressed in the forms of competencies.[7] Functional skills to be taught often derive from a needs analysis in a particular domain (workplace, for example) that outlines the contexts in which language and literacy are needed. Functional skills are outlined and prioritized for each context and appropriate instructional strategies are developed.

The approach is most common in programs that focus on workplace literacy or life skills and works well when students want to focus on everyday survival skills, such as reading a bus schedule, writing a check, or filling out an official form. As a rule, this approach focuses on "coping skills" and tends to neglect the expressive and creative functions of literacy. As used in most programs, it tends to shy away from controversial social issues, such as lack of affordable housing, discrimination, or poor working conditions.

Natural approach

The natural approach, popular in ESL classrooms in California and elsewhere, tries to teach languages and literacy the "natural way," that is, in a way that parallels the way young children learn their first language. Developed for students who speak little or no English, the approach stresses listening before speaking and reading before writing. Students who are new to English are believed to need a "silent period" in which they focus on listening before they speak and reading before they write.

Instruction is highly structured and follows a linear sequence, moving from non-verbal communication to single words, then to two and three word combinations, and, finally, on to sentences. The approach stresses communication but does not specify what kind of language or literacy is to be taught. Teachers try to provide a supportive environment so that learners won't fear making mistakes, and errors are not explicitly corrected as learners speak. Based on the principles of language acquisition popularized by Krashen,[8] the approach was developed in reaction to the traditional grammar-based model of ESL teaching.

The natural approach works well for students and teachers who prefer a meaning-based approach that is clearly sequenced. As originally developed, it de-emphasizes the socio-cultural and political dimensions of literacy, focusing instead on language as a tool for general, all-purpose communication. Aspects of the functional, communicative, and natural approach are found in chapter 9 of this handbook in the curriculum modules by Maria Malagamba-Roddy, Nancy Hampson, Gail Weinstein-Shr, and Laima Maria Schnell.

Communicative approach

The communicative approach, as developed in Europe, focuses on the socio-cultural aspects of language use and teaches students what to say, to whom, and under which circumstances. This approach places a special emphasis on cultural and linguistic appropriateness. Teaching units are presented as "notions" and "functions." Notions explain how abstract concepts, such as time, distance, and quantity, are expressed. Functions explain expression of communicative intent in ways that are appropriate for a given culture.

Examples of functions include apologizing (e.g., for being late or drinking the last beer), complaining (e.g., about slow service or bad weather), requesting (e.g., that one's teenage son turn down the music or that neighbors control their dog), and contradicting (e.g., the boss who maintains no overtime was worked or the spouse who claims that all housework is women's work). Popular in many beginning ESL classrooms, the communicative approach integrates socio-cultural norms with the vocabulary and language forms used to express ideas between native speakers.

This approach works well when students want to compare cultures and understand "how things are done" in English. Similar to its U.S. counterpart, the functional approach, the communicative approach tends to neglect literacy for self-expression and often ignores the creative and cognitive functions of literacy.

Whole language approach

The whole language approach, based on research in psycho- and socio-linguistics, also supports a natural way of learning language and literacy, but it does not support the idea of a linear sequence from listening to speaking and from reading to writing. Learners may be encouraged to speak right away, using a combination between the native language and whatever English words or phrases they may have "picked up." Learners may "write" before they read, composing stories orally and putting down approximations of print that they later "translate" back to the teacher or to the group. Whole language teachers do not move from words to phrases to sentences but provide a variety of oral and written messages and then watch carefully to see which students might need additional support and which students would benefit from greater challenges. The basic tenet of whole language is that language must be taught and learned as a whole. Any attempt to break it into parts (vocabulary lists, phonics patterns, grammar exercises) destroys the spirit of language. A second principle holds that the four language modes — speaking, writing, listening, and reading — support each other and must not be artificially separated.[9]

A beginning whole language class may listen to a song in English and give it a title based on the feeling expressed in the music or create a giant birthday card for a classmate expressing wishes through "invented spelling." Another class may explore themes, such as "people migrating to different places," "countries gaining independence," "families helping each other," or "the history of work in our community." Learners talk about ideas and concepts related to these themes, collect pictures and symbols, make timelines, tell their personal histories, and interview friends and family members to get their views. Information is collected, discussed, analyzed, categorized, and then put into book form (pages stapled together with illustrated cover pages) to be shared with others. (See the curriculum modules in chapter 9 by Ana Huerta-Macias, Pat Rigg, and Janet Isserlis for other examples of using aspects of whole language.)

The whole language approach focuses on the social and cognitive aspects of language, giving learners the opportunity to talk, read, and write together, and discuss their own way of learning (often in conferences with the teacher). A highly reflective approach, whole language uses demonstrations and group interactions to explore how people use language and literacy to express thoughts and interpret ideas, in the process building "language awareness."[10] Carefully planned, whole language activities often focus on particular strategies for reading and writing (brainstorming, predicting, and connecting one's personal experience to the experience of others) while providing learners with many options of what they want to read and write.

The approach works well with learners who want to develop a broad foundation for literacy. Teachers and learners who prefer "direct teaching" may initially find it difficult to fully implement all aspects of the whole language approach.

Language experience approach

The language experience approach (LEA), developed in part as a reaction to phonics-based reading, uses the language of the learner as a basis for literacy development. Although developed before the whole language movement, it is now often regarded as part of whole language. Since it lacks a strong theoretical foundation and learning philosophy, it is regarded by many as a method or technique and not a full-fledged approach.

As a rule, the language experience approach follows this process: learners discuss an experience or describe an event (either individually or as a group). The story the learners generate is transcribed by either a teacher, an aide, a volunteer, or a literate student. The "scribe" then reads the story together with those who have composed it. These learner-generated texts are then used as a basis for discussion, further reading and writing, and, where appropriate, focused language development activities.

In an ESL literacy classroom, an LEA story may derive from a common experience or an event (e.g., a Cinco de Mayo celebration, Chinese New Year, or an earthquake), from photographs that capture a feeling, or from videotapes and dramatizations of learner experiences. As a group, learners discuss ideas and later dictate the story to the teacher who negotiates with the students as to how the sentences are written down ("How do we want to start? What should the first sentence be?"). As a rule, the teacher writes down only sentences generated by the students and does not correct the grammar, since the point is not to write correct English sentences but rather to build an awareness that "whatever can be said can be written down." The process continues until learners end their story.

Next the teacher might read the story as dictated and then ask the group to read the story along with her several times. Learners will discuss the details of the story. Then, encouraged by the teacher ("Is there anything that is not quite clear? Where would you like to make changes?"), the group revises the text and reads the new version either orally or silently and alone or in pairs. Rereading increases the learners' speed, enabling beginning readers to practice fluent, efficient reading. If learners have a strong background in oral English, they may go on to suggest editing changes (fixing the grammar, correcting misspellings, etc.). Depending on the focus of the class, learners might spend some time on focused language and literacy activities, such as cloze exercises, putting paragraphs in sequence, or making flash cards for "favorite words."

To move the LEA stories beyond the personal, the group might relate their story to the experiences of others. The group might listen to a song or a jazz chant, read a simple poem, look at photographs, watch a video, and then compare experiences. This approach works especially well with students who are new to print but can express their ideas in oral English. LEA lacks the strong theoretical foundation of whole language and thus cannot be implemented across all program components.[11] (The curriculum modules by Gail Weinstein-Shr and Janet Isserlis illustrate aspects of the Language Experience Approach.)

Participatory approach

The participatory approach, originally developed by Paolo Freire in Brazil, emphasizes shared decision making and seeks to examine issues critical to learners' lives. The participatory approach focuses on problem posing and communal problem solving with the goal of developing the skills and strategies necessary to participate in a new culture and effectively confront problems. Unlike the functional approach, where life skills are taught for individual competence, a Freirean approach emphasizes collective knowledge.[12]

In a classroom using the participatory approach, the group may discuss themes that have a strong emotional content for the learners, such as the changing relationships between teenagers and their immigrant parents. Learners may respond to a picture, story, or dialogue that illustrates that theme, then discuss the differences in parent/child relationships in the home culture and in the United States, and talk about reasons for these differences. Learners then might describe their concerns about raising children in this country and discuss ways in which the community can support strong family relationships. As appropriate, the teacher might integrate language development activities with these discussions. (See the curriculum modules by Ana Huerta-Macias, Celestino Cotto Medina and Deidre Freeman, and Maria Malagamba-Roddy.)

Many programs that use the participatory approach include phonics to show students how words and word families are related. The class chooses a "key word" that has strong meaning for the group and, after discussing the concepts that underlie this word, breaks it into syllables. These syllables are then used to "generate" new words. (See the curriculum modules by Peggy Dean and

Lynellyn Long & Marilyn Gillespie.)   While this method has been used successfully with Romance languages, such as Portuguese, Spanish, and Creole, it is less effective with Germanic-based languages, such as English, where basic words (house, food, school, children) are not easily generated out of common syllables.

This approach works best with groups who share the characteristics of the people that Freire worked with: learners who share a common language and culture, and teachers and learners who both share concerns for fairness and justice and are willing to work toward social change. The approach is less effective with groups of learners who do not share the same language and who are not prepared to discuss social or political issues in English.

Ethnographic approach

The ethnographic approach draws its ideas from anthropology, education, and socio-linguistics. It is designed to develop linguistic and cultural awareness of the uses and functions of literacy in the society, particular communities, special settings, and in the learners' lives. When used in conjunction with a participatory approach, it often explores the power structures that validate or invalidate certain forms of literacy (e.g., standard English has greater prestige than non-standard variations).[13] The approach is often used by teachers to find out more about the "literacy practices" of their students.   Some teachers also use ethnographic strategies to explore how their non-literate, non-English speaking students negotiate meaning in a print rich, English speaking environment.[14]

In some classrooms, students learn to observe and investigate how English is used in their homes, at work, at the doctor's office, and in other places. For example, a workplace literacy group may decide to investigate what people do and say when a problem arises, such as someone's being late or a supervisor's accusing a worker of making a mistake. The group would then investigate (1) what kind of problems commonly occur at their work sites, (2) who is involved, (3) the language used to introduce and explain the problem, (4) why such problems occur in the first place, and (5) possible strategies for resolving such problems.

The ethnographic approach emphasizes the socio-cultural dimensions of literacy and is often part of both the communicative and the participatory approach. This approach works well with teachers and students who are interested in exploring cross-cultural issues or patterns of communication. It is also an excellent starting point for needs assessment and curriculum development. It is less effective in classrooms where learners come from different communities and do not yet have the oral language skills required to explore the social dimensions of language in

English. (For examples, see the modules by Celestino Medina and Deidre Freeman, Ana Huerta-Macias, and Maria Malagamba-Roddy.)

Effective practices

In addition to these major approaches, there are a number of effective literacy practices that innovative teachers are using in their classrooms. These include dialogue journals,[15] project work, using learner-generated materials (by their own students as well as by others),[16] cooperative learning activities, field trips, and neighborhood surveys. For examples of some of these practices, see "Tips for Teachers" at the end of this chapter and the promising practices in other parts of this handbook.

Whether an approach is used exclusively or in combination with others, successful literacy events in the classroom share some common characteristics. They provide opportunities for learners to

- interact with print in a meaningful way, using "whole" texts and not just isolated words and letters, and allow learners to explore the various dimensions of literacy

- engage in wide variety of literacy experiences through a broad range of reading and writing experiences that include not only functional materials but literature and "visual texts" as well

- use listening, speaking, reading, and writing throughout the program and examine the roles language and literacy play in their lives and in their community (in English as well as in the native language)

- negotiate meaning in interactions with others and discuss the strategies they use in reading and writing

- participate in making decisions about their own learning, including decisions about program structure, curriculum content, and learner/teacher interactions

- explore language and literacy in its many forms and gain a sense of the role that literacy can play in their lives and in the larger communities in which they participate

Choosing approaches

Exploring program goals, the nature of their communities, and the needs and interests of their students will help programs decide which approach might work best. Such explorations can also show whether a program is better served by implementing one particular approach or combining aspects of several meaning-based approaches. The discussion outlined here is designed to facilitate this decision making process.

Using one approach

Some programs support the "strong form" of an approach, implementing the philosophy that the approach is based on across various program components (needs assessment, curriculum, teaching, and evaluation) and adhering to the principles the approach spells out in all aspects of the program. Thus, a program adhering to a participatory approach may involve learners in decision making throughout the program while a whole language program may use only holistic assessment and teaching in its program. Choosing one approach and adhering to its principles often strengthens a program and brings staff and teachers together through a common philosophy. Such a program, however, is only effective if the goals and assumptions of the chosen approach are continuously examined to ensure that the approach continues to meet the needs of the students.

Combining approaches

Since it is difficult to implement a new literacy approach across all program components, most literacy programs have chosen to implement an "eclectic approach" instead. In these programs, teachers pick and choose from various approaches combining aspects of one with features of another. Eclecticism of this kind carries some dangers:

- there may be lack of consistency from day to day within a class as well as across the program

- an ad-hoc approach to teaching may place greater emphasis on what to do on Monday morning than on consistent literacy development

- assessment may become fragmented since each approach might require a different assessment strategy.

A framework for adult ESL literacy

In an effort to minimize the shortcomings of the eclectic approach and to benefit from its flexibility, some innovative programs have developed a literacy framework that links various approaches through a common understanding of what the program is all about. Elements of a framework for ESL literacy include:

- an educational philosophy that outlines the pedagogical principles a program holds dear and the social goals it supports

- a set of literacy definitions that explain the assumptions the program makes about the nature of language, literacy, and learning

- the dimensions of literacy that the program wants to emphasize as it tries to be responsive to the needs of learners

- a curriculum focus that spells out whether the program has a general focus or whether it wants to limit literacy to specific contexts (e.g., community literacy or workplace literacy)

- a perspective on biliteracy that examines the program's stance on using the native language of the learners in its literacy education

- assumptions about learner participation that discuss the role that learners play in the program regarding decision making, curriculum development, classroom interactions between teachers and learners, and assessment

- assumptions about teacher participation that discuss the role that teachers and staff play in the program in respect to decision making, curriculum development, classroom interactions between teachers and learners, and assessment.

A literacy framework of this kind forms the basis of a well-articulated literacy education program that can bring together various approaches in a coherent fashion.

Practice: Implementing meaning-based approaches

This section is designed for teachers and coordinators who want to know how to implement meaning-based approaches in the ESL literacy classroom. It is divided into three parts:

1. "Classroom Strategies" for introducing initial literacy (reading and writing) and for helping learners to develop a sense of the uses and functions of literacy

2. "Cases in Point" that illustrate how innovative programs in the field have operationalized various aspects of meaning-based literacy teaching

3. "Tips for Teachers" that give practical advice for developing meaningful literacy activities that can be used with any approach.

Classroom strategies

Teaching strategies that introduce learners to reading

Most teachers use "meaning making" activities along with pre-reading practice during the first few weeks of a beginning literacy class. If the students are pre-literate or have no familiarity with print, pre-reading practice may include activities that help learners associate real objects with pictures, tell certain shapes from other shapes, and build letter discrimination skills. Similarly, students who have never written anything before may benefit from pre-writing activities that develop the kinetic skills of holding a pencil and in forming letters with ease. Such activities include tracing letters and shapes in the air or on rough cloth before trying out letters on paper.[17]

The following teaching strategies are commonly used at the start of a beginning literacy class:

*   Teachers and learners share their names, countries of origin, and bring in pictures of their families. The group shares the names of the people in the pictures and discusses relationships. Learners may volunteer the ages of people in the pictures. As the class progresses, short stories about the families in the pictures may be developed using the language experience approach.

- The teacher writes large name cards for students to place in front of them. Name cards are collected and, at the beginning of each class, learners help each other find their name tags. At various times, learners may be asked to sit next to someone who has a "similar" name (similar can mean coming from the same language, sharing the same initial letter, or having a similar length). As the class progresses, learners are asked to focus on certain aspects of their names (initial letters, letters that reoccur, or similar sounds among the names in the group).

- Teachers and learners develop signs about their home countries and group them by some criteria, such as distance from the U.S. or common languages. Learners can match their names with the names of their countries or participate in other activities that require problem solving.

- Learners discuss how they came to the United States and who came with them. Some may also want to talk about the family members they left behind. Learners are encouraged to draw pictures depicting their journeys or bring in photographs and share them with the group. Again, language experience stories can follow these discussions.

- The group talks about how long they have been in the United States or discusses how long it took to come to this country. If appropriate, dates are introduced. The teacher may write "Today is Monday, May 3, 1993" on the board and with the group read the new date each day. Simple grids or charts may be introduced that show who came from which country and when.

- As the class progresses, the teacher highlights certain letters as they appear in the words that learners are most familiar with and shows that many words share the same sound combinations.[18] (See also the curriculum module by Lynellyn Long and Marilyn Gillespie.)

Most teachers have found that introducing a few key words that contain the same letters is more effective than drilling learners on the alphabet or teaching 26 letters in alphabetical sequence. In many classrooms, the alphabet is used as follows: written out in big bright letters, it serves as a reference point for students and reminds them that there is a finite set of letters to be learned. At the appropriate time, teachers show how the alphabet can be used to make life easier (e.g., to check words in the dictionary, to sort vocabulary cards, or to find a dentist in the phone book).

Teaching strategies that introduce learners to writing

In many classrooms, writing is introduced as students learn to read and express themselves in English.   As teachers discover which words their students can recognize (their names, most often), they focus on a few initial letters. Many use the following strategies:

- Learners write letters in the air or trace them on velvet, sandpaper, or on the surface of their desks before attempting to copy them on the blackboard. Some learners might trace their names a few times before attempting to write them freehand, and those who have never held a pencil may need a chance to develop small motor coordination by drawing loops and imaginary letters.

- Learners use big, brightly colored felt tip pens on butcher paper or large cardboard strips. As learners progress to writing their first and last names, paper or strips can be cut to show word boundaries.

- The teacher provides opportunities for learners to sign large birthday cards or draw pictures for a get well message. These messages are then posted in the classrooms as first examples of learners' "published writing." Language experience stories, typed up by the teacher (and possibly enlarged), are also collected, illustrated, shared, and made public.

As the class progresses, learners are encouraged to interview each other to find out more about their classmates' backgrounds, experiences, hopes, struggles, and their opinions of issues that interest the class. Teachers often develop grids and charts that allow learners to write down short answers to the questions they ask, answers that later on may turn into poems, plays, biographies, or opinion pieces.

Classroom strategies for developing print awareness

In addition to the reading and writing strategies outlined above, some educators now propose that teachers focus on helping students develop what is called "print awareness."   Under this model, students are encouraged to see, collect, and respond to the print that surrounds them and, thus, slowly develop a sense for the functions and uses of print. (See the curriculum module by Pat Rigg.)

At the print awareness level, students are not asked to read or write anything in the conventional sense. The teacher merely helps them to develop a sense of what print looks like, such as how it is different from a picture or the wallpaper, which merely exists as decoration. Students who are not familiar with the Roman alphabet may also need to develop a global sense of the shape and look of English writing before focusing on individual words and letters.

Some teachers help learners to move from print awareness to literacy by using realia that contain writing to help students see what they already know. This is illustrated in the following activity:

1. The teacher brings in food packages, a stop sign, a tube of toothpaste, a dollar bill, a pack of popular cigarettes, or some other common commercial item with print on the outside. Then, working together, learners discuss where the products may have come from or what they might be used for. As they try to guess what the print on the packet might say, the teacher supports good guesses (even if they don't correspond exactly to the print on the product) and encourages further hypothesizing. The teacher then marks the most obvious print on the product and the group, proud of their success in getting the general idea of the printed message, reads together.

2. In a follow-up activity, a teacher may ask students about the products they use most often. If members of the group mention that they like soft drinks, the teacher might bring in cans of Coca Cola or 7-Up and some food and have a mini-party. Students select what drink they want by "reading" the label on the appropriate can. These activities are then repeated with other items that learners can easily "read."

3. As the class progresses, the teacher will move from using realia to using only graphics, photographs, product labels, or pictures of store signs. Learners now discuss the pictures and try to guess what a label or sign might say. Again, learners should be encouraged to talk about the strategies they use in their guessing so that they can develop confidence in their own ability to interpret print.

4. Finally, the teacher copies the names of the most popular products and signs onto newsprint (e.g., Kent or Crest, arroz or soy sauce) and learners try to match the writing on the page with the actual product.

Similar activities can be developed around the print commonly found around classrooms, an area marked "DANGER," a door marked "EXIT," "911" tagged to the bulletin board, the word "LADIES" on a restroom door, or a "WALK/DON'T WALK" signal in front of the school.

These strategies are effective because they build on the knowledge that adults already possess. In showing adult learners that they can make sense of literacy the same way that they make sense of their environment every day, these types of literacy activities also build confidence and pride.

Cases in point

The following cases illustrate how programs in the field use variations of meaning-based approaches to support learners in their language and literacy development. We offer these examples as a starting point for discussions among teachers and among teachers and coordinators.

Providing a social context for literacy education

Many successful ESL programs have come to realize that literacy education is most effective if it is tied to the lives of the learners and reflects their experience as community members, parents, and workers.

♦ Case in point

El Barrio Popular Education Program in New York asks the men and women in the program to do research in the community and report their findings back to the group. When we visited, the participants had canvassed several streets in the neighborhood, counted the number of stores with bilingual signs, and interviewed the merchants to find out what language was used in their interactions with customers. Back in the classrooms, participants charted the information, showing a pattern of bilingual use in commercial interactions street by street. Later analysis and synthesis of the information led to a discussion of the benefits of bilingualism in various contexts (family, business, and trade). By using the community as a context for literacy, the program showed learners how to access, interpret, synthesize and analyze information in ways that spoke to the learners' reality and connected school-based learning with community experience. (See also the curriculum modules by Celestino Cotto Medina and Deidre Freeman.)

Learning through experience

ESL teachers have long known that linking verbal and non-verbal communication is an effective way of introducing language and literacy. To that end, they provide learners with the opportunity to participate in "purposeful literacy tasks," such as following directions for a VCR or on a subway ticket machine, building a model to specifications, or following a recipe. As learners gain confidence, such hands-on learning is often followed by "experiential learning" in which they work in groups to give a presentation, write a class story, develop a yearbook, generate "class rules" that the group wants to follow, or design a resource guide for other students.

◆ Case in point

At the YMCA literacy school in San Francisco, learners take a field trip using the city's bus and subway system. They take pictures of the ticket machines, the ticket purchasing instructions, and the large subway maps on the wall. Back in the classroom they use the photographs to study the subway maps. Then they discuss the problem solving strategies they used to get their tickets and find their way around.

◆ Case in point

Refugee Women's Alliance (ReWA) in Seattle publishes the stories that the women in the program have written as part of a class called Family Talk Time. These stories contain the women's remembrances about family celebrations, as in the stories "Nigisti's Wedding" and "New Year," and about special places as in "Torn's House in Laos" and "On the Mekong."[19] Illustrated by the women, the stories, many only a paragraph or two long, are stapled together with a bright cover showing the native languages of the group and shared with the community. (For examples of using learner-generated materials, see the curriculum module by Gail Weinstein-Shr.)

Linking communicative competence and language awareness

To find the proper balance between fluency and accuracy in English (especially in writing), most innovative programs put a primary focus on communication and a secondary focus on error correction. Yet, largely in response to learner requests for information on "what is correct," teachers often give simple explanation about sentence structure and word patterns. Many programs use process writing, a method that teaches students to focus on meaning during the "creative stage" and on form during the editing stage. Through process writing, students learn to edit what they have written, pay attention to certain language patterns as they read the text of others, and develop strategies for moving toward the use of standard spelling and grammar.

◆ *Case in point*

At IIRI in Rhode Island, learners work in small groups to develop stories based on sets of pictures distributed by the teacher. As the group develops ideas, students take notes. They then compose the story on newsprint. One student acts as a scribe and checks spelling and wording choices with the group. Since the group knows that the story will be shared with the rest of the class, editing becomes an important aspect of writing. The story is then brought to the front of the class where a member of the group reads it aloud using the picture to illustrate her point. Other learners then respond to the writing, asking questions such as "why is the girl smiling?" or making suggestions for improvement such as "the dress red is not right."

In innovative programs teachers often alternate between activities that involve listening and speaking and those that demand reading and writing; however, the major focus remains on meaning and communication. As they provide opportunities for using literacy in purposeful ways, these teachers are mindful of their learners. They watch closely to see what their strengths are, where their interests lie, where they might need further support, and where they could benefit from additional challenges. They have become classroom ethnographers.

Tips for ESL literacy teachers

How can teachers provide a rich literacy experience for their students? The following suggestions, based on the educational principles that shape rich language and literacy development, may provide some guidance. These guidelines are not meant as "teacher-proof" solutions to ESL literacy; rather they are meant as a basis for reflection and discussion.

☞ **Strive for genuine communication between yourself and your students.**

Design activities that tell you who your students are, what their experiences have been, what they care about, and what literacy means to them. Share information about yourself, your joys, and your sorrows, and invite your students to talk about themselves. Treat your student as you would any intelligent adult and do not spend a great deal of time asking questions to which you already know the answer. After you have just written the date on the board, saying "Su Ma, could you please read the date on the board?" is more respectful than asking "What's the date today?"

☞ **Make your classroom into a community of learners where everyone feels welcome and all views are respected.**

Provide opportunities for different groups to work together, share information, and be a resource for each other. Ask learners to read as a group, share their ideas about a piece they have read, and write collaboratively. Invite contributions that do not depend on language and literacy, such as illustrating a story the group has written. Provide opportunities for sharing experiences across cultures by asking learners to talk about their lives back home and share significant cultural customs (e.g., weddings, funerals, or births) and family traditions. Discuss differences in literacy practices as well as commonalities. Learn to be a facilitator who guides the group, instead of a general who controls all interactions.

☞ **Link literacy with visual information.**

Provide information in the forms of visuals and realia (objects such as phones, staplers, machines, food, and signs) to get a point across. Choose photographs, posters, slides, and videos whose message can be understood without language (e.g., Charlie Chaplin's "The Immigrant," the grape stomping scene from "I Love Lucy").[20] Use these visuals to create an atmosphere, illustrate a point, demonstrate a task, elicit a feeling, or pose a problem. Encourage learners to respond in many different ways, allowing them to smell, touch, and manipulate realia and to respond to visuals in both verbal and non-verbal ways (classifying signs or developing strip stories by moving pictures around). Provide opportunities for learners to illustrate their writings with illustrations and photographs and give them a chance to interact without having to depend on language and literacy (e.g., sharing food, organizing a potluck, dancing at end-of-cycle parties).

☞ **Publish your students' work.**

Make room for your students' writing on your walls and in the hallways. Involve them in making signs, labels, and posters. Write their ideas down on large newsprint, tape papers on the wall, and refer to them often. Involve the school in publishing end-of-semester yearbooks, autobiographies, and collections of student writings. Use hallways or places where students congregate as a gallery for displaying student work, photos, poems, etc. Encourage learners to invite family and friends to visit and admire their work.

☞ **Don't let learners get "mired in words."**

Instead, provide opportunities to get the "big picture." Ask learners to bring in literacy materials they find puzzling, have them explain the context, and enlist the group in guessing what the materials might say. Highlight key words and ask learners to fill in the rest using what they know about the real world. Watch an interesting video with the sound off and have learners create their own stories or predict what the actors might be saying. Turn on the sound and ask learners to repeat the phrases they catch. Talk about the way adults learn to listen and read in a second language by linking what they already know about the world with what they hear and see written.

☞ **Make literacy learning fun and focus on things that matter.**

Students learn best when they have something to say and a reason for paying attention to others. Present a variety of options and then let learners choose what interests them, so they will enjoy their work. Give them opportunities to respond in a variety of ways in class, such as quiet listening, group recitations, non-verbal reactions, and written responses. Encourage and support your students, but challenge them as well.

☞ **Focus on meaning while helping learners see how language works.**

Recognize that ESL students need opportunities to use language and literacy for their own purposes. Sometimes, that purpose includes understanding unusual phrases, idiosyncratic pronunciation, or simple grammar rules. At other times, students may wonder what language is appropriate in certain situations, such as what kind of note to write if a teacher's mother has died. Make room in your class for a language awareness session in which you answer questions about structure or assist learners in the editing process. Don't interrupt the flow of communication or authentic reading and writing with explanations about form, structure, or phonics. Keep your explanations simple and don't let the "grammar freaks" trap you into lengthy explanations, especially if you are not certain about the answers. Point curious students toward books or make an appointment for after class. Keep in mind that students learn to read by reading and that they learn to write by writing.

☞ **Trust the learners (and yourself).**

Even learners who don't talk or write much can tell you many things about themselves. They do so through the pictures and movies they like, the books they choose to look through, and the smiles they give you when they enjoy an activity. Several strategies can help you find out more about what learners want and need:

- Ask them. If you don't share a common language, find someone who does and ask that person to work with you in setting up periodic group discussions (two or three weeks into the session may be a good time to start).

- Provide choices. Present many different kinds of learning opportunities and watch what happens in your classroom.

- Celebrate learning (even small steps count) and encourage literacy experiments.

- Invite your students to assess their own progress and tell you about the challenges they face and the successes they have.

- Use the feedback you receive to make the class work for everyone.

☞ **Invite the community into your classroom.**

Bring in guests from the community and from social service agencies and encourage them to interact with your students. Choose speakers who have something important to say and brief them ahead of time. Ask them to bring in pictures, videos, pamphlets, and realia and to keep the literacy demands low. Develop activities that allow your students to understand key concepts and become familiar with key words before the speaker arrives. Ask groups of students to write down the topics that concern them and the questions they want to have answered. Let them predict what the speaker might say. Help your students make connections between what they know, what they are curious about, and the information they expect to receive. Ask your students to respond to the session and evaluate the speaker (e.g., what they liked and didn't like, understood and didn't understand, their favorite new words, etc.).

☞ **Connect literacy to life.**

Ask students to tell their stories, share their pictures, and recite their favorite poems or sayings. Give them the opportunity to observe literacy use in a variety of contexts and ask them to listen for interesting language wherever they go. Turn your students into researchers who ask family members, friends, and acquaintances about their experiences with schooling and learning. Ask them to find out about other people's views on language and culture and compare them to their own. Encourage learners to examine the role of literacy in their life and in their communities and help them see how literacy can be used to shape and alter the world.

☞ **Assess success.**

As you observe your learners, ask yourself "what is really going on here?" Find ways of recording "literacy incidents," events that show you whether your students are fully engaged in a particular activity or are just "going through the motions." Share your notes. Collaborate with others in your program (coordinators, teachers, and learners) and decide "what really counts." Define what you mean by success in language, literacy, and learning for the program and develop strategies for capturing small successes along the way. Categorize, analyze, and summarize until a rich picture of your literacy class emerges. Congratulate your students on their achievements. Share your success.

Reflections: Selecting and/or developing materials

How can a program successfully match its approach to teaching ESL literacy with materials that are comprehensible, interesting, and relevant to learner's lives? Much depends on

- the approach a program supports

- the preference of learners and teachers

- the availability of commercial materials suitable for the program's purposes

- the time, money, interest, and experience available to develop program-based materials.

Given the wide diversity of ESL literacy programs, it is not surprising that there is diversity in the kind of materials programs use.

Some programs rely largely on **learner-generated materials**, which may include language experience stories, student drawings, illustrations and photographs, environmental print collected in the classroom and in the community, and "found" materials, such as bills, letters, and notices that learners bring from home. As learners progress, these materials are often supplemented with "authentic stories," accounts written by writers for a general audience, not just for ESL learners.

In other programs, materials might largely consist of **"literacy kits"** that teachers have assembled over the years. These may include pictures, posters, movies, songs, stories, poems, magazines, and books which may be in both English and the learners' mother tongue.

Still others use **textbooks** they have found that learners and teachers enjoy. Most programs, however, use a combination of materials that are learner-generated, teacher-assembled, and commercially produced.

Questions for decision making

To help programs make informed decisions about materials to select or develop, we offer the following questions for reflection. Please keep in mind that not all questions will be applicable for all programs.

Need

1. Do we need textbooks and, if so, for what purposes?

2. Are our students better served with textbooks or should we develop a resource bank of materials that teachers can share?

3.   What is the best way to spend our limited dollars? Does it make more sense to spend funds on textbooks and prepared materials or should we invest in teacher time and expertise?

4.   Does it make sense to invest in technology? If so, should the focus be on commercially prepared videos and computer-based literacy programs or should we focus on buying equipment that allows students to produce their own materials (cameras, camcorders, word processors, printers)?[21]   Should we invest in equipment that allows learners to use literacy for telecommunication?

Linking ESL literacy to program focus

1.   Do the materials illustrate the varying perceptions that teachers and learners have of the reading and writing process? Is there a focus on meaning throughout?

2.   Are content, language, and exercises in the materials reflective of the program philosophy? If not, how would the materials fit into the orientation the program has chosen?

3.   Do the materials emphasize both accuracy and fluency in reading and writing? Does the balance between these skills support the program's view of the way literacy should be taught?

4.   Is the primary focus of the materials on the literacy area the program wants to emphasize (e.g., workplace, ESL civics, pre-employment, pre-academic, life skills, family literacy, self-actualization)?

Language and literacy

1.   Will students feel both successful and challenged doing the lessons?

2.   Do the materials try to link listening and speaking to reading and writing?

3.   Do the materials focus on meaningful reading and writing for a purpose (other than practice)? Are there enough opportunities for students to "try out" writing and express their ideas on paper?

4.   Do the activities present a good balance between word recognition skills and letter identification on the one hand and whole language activities on the other? Do the activities provide enough opportunities for global processing?

5.   Do the materials take advantage of the print environment that exists in the students' communities? Do they present opportunities to develop print awareness?

6.   Are the materials written at the appropriate level in regard to students' overall language proficiency, literacy background, familiarity with cultural concepts, and prior knowledge?

7.   Do the materials encourage students to make hypotheses while reading by asking students to guess the meaning of a word using context cues? Do the materials encourage students to take risks in their writing by going through a process of brainstorming with others, writing down ideas, composing several try-out drafts, and focusing on selected aspects of spelling, punctuation, and grammar in the final editing phase?

Linking text to student needs, goals, and experiences

Do the materials

1.   contain the kind of activities that respond to student needs and student goals?

2.   reflect the students' reality, their roles, lives, and aspirations?

3.   help students to link their own experience to the activities and tasks? Do they provide space for student contributions, such as learner-generated materials, student research, etc.?

4.   provide a link to the community, such as realistically reflecting issues that the community faces?

Extending the students´ background knowledge

Do the materials

1. help activate the background knowledge that students bring to class and call on the coping strategies that they have developed?

2. help students acquire new ideas by linking their experiences and ideas to larger issues in the community or the society?

3. contain opportunities to develop critical thinking and problem solving?

Cultural bias

1. Do the materials present positive images of immigrant groups in general and of the student group in particular? Do they avoid stereotyping according to age, gender, and ethnic group?

2. Do the materials stereotype by omission? Are women, the elderly, Asians, Latinos, Blacks, and other groups absent or do they appear only as tokens?

3. Is there an ethnocentric slant to the way cultural information is presented? Do the materials give the impression (or even insist) that there is one right way of doing things or do they explain options and choices?

4. Are the contributions of immigrants and minorities in general and the learners' groups in particular adequately represented in the readings?

5. Do the materials allow learners to present their own perspectives on life or do they simply show adults in their roles as model workers, model parents, or model community members?

Linking teacher experience and interest with the materials

1. Given the background of the teachers, do the materials look "teachable?" If not, can the program provide the support needed to make it so?

2. Would the materials be a joy to teach and fun to learn from? What activities can be used to "lighten up" literacy overload?

3. Does the content reflect the interests of both teachers and students?

4. Is it clear how teachers are meant to use these materials? How does the teaching approach the materials support fit into the focus of the program's staff development efforts?

Print accessibility

1. Is the print easily accessible? Is it large enough and is there enough white space?

2. Is print supported by context, such as pictures, photographs, charts, and headings?

3. Is there enough room for students to practice, scribble, and edit their writing?

Adaptability

1. Can the materials be adapted to various learning and teaching styles?

2. Are there enough different kinds of activities so all students can develop a range of skills?

3. Do the activities lend themselves to whole group discussions, small group work, pair activities, and individual reading and writing?

Assessment

1. Do the materials support both the curriculum and the assessments that the program is using (e.g., assessment of reading and writing processes)?

2. Can the activities be used as a basis for observing how students interact with print? Do they lend themselves to observing and evaluating literacy progress?

Endnotes

1. For a discussion of the reading and writing process, see Bell & Burnaby, 1984; Byrnes, 1987; Cambourne, 1979; Carrell, 1987; Eskey, 1988; Goodman et al., 1984; Hughes, 1986; Kern, 1989; Smith, 1982a; and Smith, 1988.

2. See Smith, 1986; Goodman, 1986; and Cambourne, 1979.

3. See Goodman, 1986; de Beaugrande, 1980; Flower & Hayes, 1981; Graves, 1983; Rumelhart, 1985; Smith, 1982; and Smith, 1988.

4. See Smith, 1982.

5. See Bell & Burnaby, 1984; Carrell & Eisterhold, 1988; Eskey, 1988; and Grabe, 1988.

6. See Eskey, 1988 and Grabe, 1988.

7. See also the discussion of a competency-based curriculum in the Curriculum chapter.

8. See *The natural approach* by Krashen & Terrell, 1983.

9. See Rigg & Kazemek, in press.

10. For a full discussion, see Crandall, in press; Goodman, 1986; Kazemek, 1989; Rigg & Kazemek, in press; and Soifer et al., 1990.

11. See also Dixon & Nessel, 1983; Rigg, 1990; and Taylor, in press.

12. See Wallerstein, 1983.

13. Sometimes learner investigation includes examining the values that are attached to certain ways of speaking or writing (e.g., attitudes toward accents or non-standard spelling), leading to a discussion of "correctness" as a concept that reflects middle class values. See also Auerbach, 1990.

14. See Fingeret, 1983 and Weinstein-Shr, 1990. See also the chapter on biliteracy in this handbook for ideas about which questions to ask.

15. See *Dialogueueueueue journal writing with nonnative English speakers* by Peyton & Reed, 1990.

16. See *Listening to students' voices: Publishing students' writing for other students to read* by Joy Kreeft Peyton, in press.

17. For examples of activities to use with pre-literate students, see Savage, 1984 and Bell & Burnaby, 1984.

18. There is no agreement on whether it is better to start with lower case or upper case letters and some confusion on the part of the learners is inevitable, as they try to figure out why the small "q" looks so different from the capital "Q." Since most literacy students have had

some experience with print, teachers often introduce the two sets simultaneously and then let the learners choose the type of letters they want to use, knowing that mix-ups will sort themselves out eventually.

19.   See ReWA, 1991.

20.   For more ideas, contact the video interest section of TESOL or Lenore Balliro of the Adult Learning Resource Center (ALRC) at Roxbury College in Boston.

21.   We want to thank Elsa Auerbach for suggesting this point.

References

Auerbach, E. R. (1990). *Making meaning, making change: A guide to participatory curriculum development for adult ESL and family literacy.* Boston: University of Massachusetts [in press (1992), Regents Prentice Hall/Center for Applied Linguistics].

Bell, J., & Burnaby, B. (1984). *A handbook for ESL literacy.* Toronto, Ontario: OISE Press.

Byrnes, H. (1987). Getting a better reading: Initiatives in foreign language reading instruction. In S. J. Savignon, & M. S. Berns (Ed.), *Initiatives in communicative language teaching II: A book of readings* (pp. 171-204). Reading, MA: Addison-Wesley.

Cambourne, B. (1979). How important is theory to the reading teacher? *Australian Journal of Reading*, 2(2), 78-90.

Carrell, P. (1987). Fostering interactive second language reading. In S. J. Savignon, & M. S. Berns (Eds.), *Initiatives in communicative language teaching II* (pp. 145-171). Reading, MA: Addison-Wesley.

Carrell, P. L., & Eisterhold, J. C. (1988). Schema theory and ESL reading. Cambridge, MA: Cambridge University Press.

Crandall, J. A. (Editor). (in press). *Approaches to adult ESL literacy instruction.* Englewood Cliffs, NJ: Prentice Hall Regents/Center for Applied Linguistics.

de Beaugrande, R. (1980). *Text, discourse, and process: Toward a multidisciplinary science of texts.* Norwood, NJ: Ablex.

Dixon, C. N., & Nessel, D. (1983). *Language experience approach to reading (and writing): LEA for ESL.* Hayward, CA: Alemany.

Eskey, D. E. (1988). Holding in the bottom: An interactive approach to the language problems of second language readers. In P. L. Carrell, J. Devine, & D. E. Eskey (Eds.), *Interactive approaches to second language reading* (pp. 93-100). Cambridge: Cambridge University Press.

Fingeret, A. (1983, Spring). Social network: A new perspective on independence and illiterate adults. *Adult Education Quarterly*, 33(3), 133-146.

Flower, L., & Hayes, J. (1981). A cognitive process theory of writing. *College Composition and Communication, 32*, 365-387.

Goodman, K. (1986). *What's whole in whole language?* Portsmouth, NH: Heinemann Educational Books.

Goodman, K., Goodman, Y., & Flores, B. (1984). *Reading in the bilingual classroom: Literacy and biliteracy.* Rosslyn, VA: National Clearinghouse for Bilingual Education.

Grabe, W. (1988). Reassessing the term "interactive" In P. L. Carrell, J. Devine, & D. E. Eskey (Eds.), *Interactive approaches to second language reading* (pp. 56-70). Cambridge: Cambridge University Press.

Graves, D. (1983). *Writing: Teachers and children at work.* Exeter, NH: Heinemann.

Hughes, J. (1986). Inside-out, outside-in: Which approach is best for the second language learner? *Australian Journal of Reading, 9*(3), 159-166.

Kazemek, F. E. (1989). Whole language and adult literacy education. *Information Update, 6*(2), 3-7. New York: Literacy Assistance Center.

Kern, R. (1989). Second language reading strategy instruction: Its effects on comprehension and word inference ability. *Modern Language Journal, 73*(2), 135-149.

Krashen, S. D., & Terrell, T. D. (1983). *The natural approach: Language acquisition in the classroom.* New York: Pergamon.

Peyton, J. K. (in press). Listening to students' voices: Publishing students' writing for other students to read. In J. A. Crandall (Ed.), *Approaches to adult ESL literacy instruction.* Englewood Cliffs, NJ: Prentice Hall Regents/Center for Applied Linguistics.

Peyton, J. K., & Reed, L. (1990). *Dialogue journal writing with nonnative English speakers: A handbook for teachers.* Alexander, VA: Teachers of English to Speakers of Other Languages (TESOL).

Refugee Women's Alliance (ReWA). (1991). *Family stories project: Spring quarter 1991.* Seattle, Washington: Author.

Rigg, P. (1990). Using the language experience approach with ESL adults. *TESL Talk, 20*(1), 188-200.

Rigg, P., & Kazemek, F. E. (in press). Whole language in adult education. In J. A. Crandall (Ed.), *Approaches to adult ESL literacy instruction.* Englewood Cliffs, NJ: Prentice Hall Regents/Center for Applied Linguistics.

Rumelhart, D. E. (1985). Toward an interactive model of reading. In H. Singer & R. B. Ruddell (Eds.), *Theoretical models and processes of reading* (pp. 722-750). Newark, DE: International Reading Association.

Savage, K. L. (1984, January). *Teaching strategies for developing literacy skills in non-native speakers of English.* Paper presented at the National Adult Literacy Conference, Washington, DC.

Smith, F. (1982). *Understanding reading.* New York: Holt, Rinehart, & Winston.

Smith, F. (1986). *Insult to intelligence: The bureaucratic invasion of our classrooms.* New York : Arbor House.

Smith, F. (1988). *Joining the literacy club.* Portsmouth, NH: Heinemann Educational Books.

Soifer, R., Irwin, M. E., Crumrine, B. M., Honzaki, E., Simmons, B. K., & Young, D. L. (1990). *The complete theory-to-practice handbook of adult literacy: Curriculum design and teaching approaches.* New York: Teachers College Press.

Taylor, M. L. (in press). The language experience approach. In J. A. Crandall (Ed.), *Approaches to adult ESL literacy instruction.* Englewood Cliffs, NJ: Prentice Hall Regents/Center for Applied Linguistics.

Wallerstein, N. (1983). The teaching approach of Paulo Freire. In J. W. Oller, & P. A. Richard-Amato (Eds.), *Methods that work: A smorgasbord of ideas for language teachers* (pp. 190-213). Rowley, MA: Newbury House.

Weinstein-Shr, G. (Preparer). (1990). *NCLE Q & A: Family and intergenerational literacy in multilingual families.* Washington, DC: Center for Applied Linguistics, National Clearinghouse on Literacy Education.

Chapter 3

Teaching Adult ESL Literacy in the Multilevel Classroom

Multilevel classrooms are a fact of life in adult education. Most classes are comprised of students from a variety of countries, educational experiences, and socio-economic backgrounds. Even classes that start with a homogeneous group may split into levels after a few sessions: some students may attend regularly while others do not, or some may make faster progress than the rest of the class. Other classes are heterogeneous from the beginning, either because the resources to offer different levels are not available or because students are not able to attend the classes designed for their individual levels due to family obligations or work constraints.[1] Thus, teaching a disparate group of students continues to be a challenge for all adult education teachers, especially for those who teach literacy to language minority adults.

This chapter is designed for teachers who need strategies for dealing with the multilevel classroom and would like to see examples of what multilevel classrooms look like. The chapter is divided into three sections.

The first section, "Background," outlines the factors to be considered when planning literacy activities and stresses the need to continuously assess both the progress that learners are making and the success of the literacy activities themselves.

The second section, "Practice," provides teaching strategies for the multilevel classroom, with a special emphasis on group activities. It also provides examples of effective literacy teaching in the form of "Promising Practices." These "Promising Practices" are based on the experiences of adult ESL literacy programs throughout the United States.

The third section, "Reflections," contains questions to help teachers know their students and suggests ways of designing activities to meet the variety of needs present in a multilevel classroom.

Background: Planning for the multilevel classroom

ESL literacy teachers face a special challenge: how to provide learning opportunities that support those who are still having difficulty "cracking the code" of literacy while providing enough challenges to those who are on their way to becoming independent readers and writers. In trying to meet the needs of all students, they often have to adapt the curriculum to fit the needs of the individual students while maintaining a cohesive classroom.

One factor to consider in setting up groups is whether the student is literate in her or his own language. This is relevant because a student with literacy skills has certain strategies which make learning a new language easier and less of a struggle. For example,

> If the student's educational background includes literacy skills, even if in a completely different script, they have developed a whole set of skills, such as the ability to predict or to draw information from physical context, that will transfer to the new language.[2]

Culture is another factor that plays a role in student expectations of the learning process. Some cultures expect students to act in a passive manner and not to question teachers. Learners from these cultures often expect to find a teacher-centered classroom and may need some time to get used to group work. Other cultures encourage students to ask questions, viewing questions and student verbal input as signs of interest in the subject matter. Care should be taken that these students don't dominate discussions and overwhelm other students who don't participate as actively.

Differences in student background with regard to politics, national pride, and gender roles can also lead to different student expectations. For example, learners from countries that have been at war with each other or that have vastly different political systems might initially be reluctant to work together or might want to use the classroom as a forum for political ideologies. Sometimes teachers find that some of their students have a tendency to stereotype and may harbor prejudices about other ethnic groups that should not go unchallenged.

Responses to these issues vary. Some teachers feel comfortable opening up a dialogue between various groups and try to facilitate discussions, while others find it necessary to establish ground rules that say that "politics are to be left outside the classroom door." Some teachers develop units or themes especially designed to address issues related to discrimination and prejudice. In exploring these issues with the group, they try to move the discussion from the personal to the political. In an effort to mediate conflict, some programs encourage members of the class to develop their own ground rules for handling disagreements over politics.

The important point is that teachers need to be aware of the potential conflicts that exist among the group and work with other teachers and with learners to develop strategies for addressing potentially divisive political issues.

In addition to these educational and cultural factors, individual factors, such as language ability, motivation, age, length of time in this country, and amount of study time also play a part in a successful learning experience. For example, older adults who have never studied another language and whose family responsibilities may keep them from studying may need to be in groups that value their experiences and ideas above their ability to process language quickly and accurately. Similarly, younger immigrants, although new to this country, may be very creative and have strong coping strategies. Younger learners often thrive in groups that take advantage of their problem solving skills and their ability to use language for specific purposes, such as obtaining a driver's license or getting a date. Differences in age and social status also need to be taken into account before setting up groups, since some learners will naturally defer to students they consider more prominent and some men will feel very uncomfortable in groups where women are the team leaders.

The solution lies in remaining responsive to learner needs by observing learners and their interactions and discussing cultural and personal differences in learning styles and interaction patterns.

Getting a sense of learner needs

In order to develop a curriculum that benefits students in multilevel classrooms, the program must be aware of learner and community needs. Some programs conduct a general needs assessment before classes start by spending time in the community, talking to community leaders, or getting input from other schools serving ESL literacy students. This needs assessment then feeds into a tentative literacy framework designed to help them make decisions about approaches that might work best with groups that have varying needs. (See chapter 1 for an ESL literacy framework.)

But a general needs assessment is not enough. To get a good sense of the learners' proficiency in literacy and oral English, along with their interests and goals, both an initial assessment and ongoing observation and evaluation are needed. ESL literacy teachers know that it is often difficult to find out what beginning learners already know, what they need to learn, and what their learning priorities are. Many teachers use assessment activities during the first few weeks of classes and then repeat these activities during various points of the teaching cycle to better understand their learners. Such activities may include

- one-on-one interviews between teachers and students or between peers

- group discussions

- supported reading and writing that captures the varied strengths of literacy students

- activities that allow individual learners to select the materials they want to read and write, such as postcards, notes, or pictures.

Such ongoing assessment should also evaluate the success of each literacy activity. Some teachers use check sheets to remember who seemed interested in a particular activity and who seemed overwhelmed. These teachers also take notes on the materials that strike a responsive chord in the learners and those that end up frustrating them. Teacher journals and evaluation grids, as discussed in the "Assessment" chapter, are other ways to evaluate the class so that appropriate teaching strategies can be developed.

In many cases, teachers develop activities that allow the learners to decide as a group which activities they found most worthwhile and why. Learner responses can also tell teachers more about the perceptions of language and literacy that learners hold dear. For example, some learners may think that copying letters on worksheets are better literacy activities than developing a language experience story. In cases where learner and teacher perceptions of sound literacy activities don't match, teachers may need to develop some activities that match the expectations of learners while continuing to provide other reading and writing experiences that learners find stimulating and interesting.

When modifications to the program are obviously needed, the problems must be clearly defined before they can be successfully resolved. Bell suggests that teachers might ask the following questions:[3]

- Are the activities not relevant to the students, or do they just need to be presented more clearly?

- Is the pace too quick, or do the students need time to adjust to the new method being used?

- Are the teacher's expectations too high, considering that the students have other adult responsibilities?

Answers to these questions can help teachers decide what changes they need to make to keep their lessons responsive to many different learner needs.

Key Point

A good sense of learners' backgrounds, needs, abilities, interests, and goals must form the foundation of all multilevel activities. Teachers can accomplish this by being sensitive to the learners' cultural backgrounds and their personal characteristics and by developing assessment activities that allow learners to showcase their strengths. It is also helpful to provide learners with different kinds of literacy activities that allow room for self-directed learning and to document learner responses to literacy tasks.

Practice: Multilevel teaching strategies

In the following section, we provide some teaching strategies to help teachers organize the multilevel classroom and present activities that are responsive to learner needs. Some of these strategies include setting up small groups, designing project work and shared tasks, and organizing the curriculum around themes. For programs that want to give their learners opportunities to work on basic literacy skills, we offer suggestions for setting up a literacy center. This section ends with examples of promising practices taken from innovative programs.

Homogeneous and heterogeneous groupings

One effective way for dealing with various levels of learners is by grouping them. There are essentially two ways of effectively grouping multilevel learners: in homogeneous groups and in heterogeneous groups.

Homogeneous groups

The class is divided into homogeneous groups according to their language and literacy levels. High proficiency learners are grouped with their peers, as are those who still need support.

This may be an effective approach for times when learners need practice in specific areas, such as reviewing vocabulary, and it may help learners who are intimidated by more proficient students. If the class is always grouped by proficiency levels, however, the grouping may have the effect of lessening the self-confidence of learners who have difficulties since they may feel stigmatized as "slow learners."

Non-literate students, especially, should never "get stuck" in a group where they do not get a chance to interact with others through rich literacy activities.

Heterogeneous groups

The class is divided into heterogeneous groups in which those who are quite comfortable reading and writing are grouped with those who are still having difficulties.

Many programs have found this to be a promising way to build a community of learners, especially if those who don't have strong literacy skills get the opportunity to shine in other ways, such as through oral storytelling, taking pictures, or drawing illustrations. At times, it may be important to present special challenges to the "better students" in the group so they won't start feeling "superior."

Alternating groups

Innovative teachers often alternate between setting up homogeneous and heterogeneous groups. Alternating grouping styles is an effective way of providing both special support when it may be needed and building group interactions across levels.

In many programs, the whole class stays together while the teacher tries to adjust her teaching to the proficiency level of various subgroups. This model is very difficult to accomplish in large classes, since teachers often teach "toward the middle," boring the more proficient learners while frustrating those who have difficulties. This technique almost always spells disaster in ESL classrooms where learners who are not literate in their native language are expected to catch up with those who are.

Working in a group, whether it is heterogeneous or homogeneous, can give all students a chance to work with literacy in ways that are relevant and challenging. Often, such group work provides an alternative to students who have been unsuccessful in the traditional learning environment. Shared activities involve students in language, literacy, and problem solving. We now turn to a discussion of the activities that small groups can become involved in.

Project work

Project work and other activities in which learners share tasks hold great promise in helping teachers meet the challenge of using appropriate materials for different levels while implementing sound literacy instruction for the class overall. Project work takes many forms and can include the following:

- planning a field trip to a place that many learners don't have opportunities to visit (one group chose the Six Flags amusement park over an "educational" outing)

- inviting a guest speaker to discuss issues of concerns in the community (a group of women in New York asked a female doctor to come and discuss breast cancer)

- writing a letter to a famous person or the city council (several groups in New York have written letters to City Hall and the Board of Education, addressing their need for literacy programs and protesting funding cuts)

- creating a poster that shows the history of some aspect of the community (jobs, changing demographics)

- making a list of community services or bilingual "hotlines" that can be used as a resource guide

- developing a "talent chart" that shows the special skills that class members have that could be shared or swapped (auto repair, childcare experience, special recipes)

- articulating "class rules" or a "students' bill of rights"

- creating a timeline that shows when different people in the class came to the United States and their countries of origin

- conducting research in the community, including language surveys that show who speaks what language in a particular neighborhood, whether there are bilingual signs and notices, and what the presence or absence of a language indicates.

Doing project work under the guidance of a facilitator involves learners in decision making. It allows learners to discuss who should do what and gives them the opportunity to volunteer for the tasks that take advantage of their talents and skills. During different times, students can work individually, in pairs, or as part of the whole group, as long as they plan the project and report the results jointly.

Using literacy themes

Organizing literacy activities around themes allows students to work together and to respond according to their own level of expertise. An example might be a unit on "Medicine: Folk versus Modern" in which each student is given a specific assignment.[4] During this project, more advanced students might read and report back on an article about the subject, while beginning learners might bring a traditional medicine from home and explain its use as a remedy.[5]

Collaborative learning tasks of this kind provide an opportunity for learners of different levels to work together. They support meaningful reading and writing activities by requiring that learners bring their knowledge of the world and their coping skills to each activity. They thus validate not only literacy ability but real world experience as well. Activities can be structured in such a way that each person contributes according to his or her interest and abilities. Since students are required to communicate as they share information, group activities of this kind also strengthen their speaking and listening skills.

For the teacher, developing projects, defining tasks, working out clear directions, and assessing progress is often difficult at first, but many teachers find it worth their time and effort in the long run. Programs can facilitate the teacher's job by setting up a materials resource bank and a picture file, providing opportunities for teacher sharing, facilitating the use of cameras and video equipment, and making funds available for incidentals, such as phone calls, materials, films, and postage.[6]

Literacy centers

Another way of dealing with different levels of language and literacy is to set up literacy centers where students can work on individual tasks geared towards their literacy level. Literacy centers can also be used for students who want to find materials and ideas for their joint projects.

Literacy centers could be reading corners where students can look through books, magazines, newspapers, catalogues, advertisements, television guides, food coupons, or interesting pictures to inspire a story or a poem. In addition, expressive posters, community art, or captioned photographs of the class, the school, and the surrounding community might decorate the walls.

Literacy centers can also contain picture files, articles, student texts, and activities arranged by themes, so that students who want to read or write about a particular topic can find information that piques their interest and matches their level of proficiency. Whenever possible, bilingual materials and dictionaries should be included.

Literacy centers have long been part of whole language classrooms where they are used to support group work and foster independent reading and writing. For example, learners might go to the center for information on topics such as immigration in our state or education in our community. Centers are also used to house magazines, calendars, photo-novels, books for adults, and books to read to children, both in English and in the learners' native languages. In many whole language classrooms, literacy learners use these centers to select materials to read or look at during periods of "silent reading."

Literacy centers can also be used to develop individual skills. The Center for Applied Linguistics (CAL) explains how literacy centers can become learning labs in which students can work individually on structured activities to improve their basic reading and writing skills. CAL suggests that these centers contain the following items for reading and writing.[7]

Reading

- Use vocabulary items written on large cards with a picture denoting the meaning on the back. Students must read the word. Then they can check the meaning by looking at the picture on the back.

- Use sheets of matching exercises consisting of traffic and street signs and their corresponding meanings.

- For survival reading comprehension practice, use a selection of actual or adapted classified advertisements, numbered by difficulty, with multiple-choice questions for each ad.

- Use a selection of short stories, numbered by difficulty, with a set of comprehension questions for each story.

Writing

- For vocabulary and sentence writing practice, use single words written on index cards divided into meaning-related sets of five. Encourage students to write a sentence with each word.

- For preliteracy skills practice, use a set of alphabet cards. Encourage non-literate students to copy the letters.

- For functional communication practice, use a set of one-sided dialogues. Students can write the missing parts.

- Use a folder of picture sequences (e.g., cartoons). Students choose one sequence and write a description of what is happening.

Most literacy educators now believe that such skills-based activities should always be integrated into larger themes that focus on communication and meaning. Only after groups have worked together on holistic, real-life literacy task should they be encouraged to work on specific skills.

The dangers in emphasizing individualized instruction

Some programs feel that the best way to deal with multilevel literacy students is to individualize instruction. Teachers design worksheets (and in some cases use computer programs) geared toward the individual level of each student. Thus non-literate students might draw circles and lines or spend their time identifying letters that are different from the rest such as marking the "d" in a row of "b"s. Beginning literacy students might read short passages and answer comprehension or write sentences that contain prespecified words.

Such individualized instruction may have common sense appeal, but it is not an effective way to help language minority adults develop literacy. Since true literacy development is a cognitive process that develops in response to a social need, literacy students learn best in groups. Group interactions allow learners to explore ideas through talking and reading, get feedback on their written ideas, and respond to the ideas of others. Such group interactions can also provide a supportive environment for adults who have not been successful in traditional school settings. ESL learners should not be deprived of the benefit that literacy groups provide.

Individualized instruction serves to isolate literacy learners from those who could help and support them, marginalizing them in the school system. By focusing on pencil and paper tasks (or simulations of such tasks on computer), individualized instruction deprives literacy learners from demonstrating their strengths of real word knowledge and everyday problem solving. We now know that individualized instruction has not been effective in teaching students how to communicate in a second language. Similarly, individualized instruction in reading and writing is not an effective means of fostering literacy.

Promising practices

The following are examples of promising practices used in innovative programs to build a community of learners among those who are just "awakening to literacy" and those who are well on their way to becoming independent readers and writers. These examples come from experienced teachers whom we have talked to or read about. These promising practices are meant to illustrate what has worked for some teachers and may serve to inspire other teachers of multilevel classes to create their own.

◘ Informal assessment at the beginning of each class

More than anything else, teachers learn from observing and listening to learners as they read and write. Innovative teachers often open each class with an activity that brings the class together and allows the teacher to see who is making progress and who needs special help. One example of an opening activity is "social chat," a dialogue between teacher and students before class.[8] For the beginning student, this social chat may consist mainly of listening, but the intermediate and advanced students may decide to both listen and speak. The teacher takes mental notes on who speaks up and who needs further encouragement and then designs appropriate activities for each group.

At the Lao Family Literacy program in St. Paul, for example, the teacher often asks learners about the previous night. As learners talk, she finds out about the aunt who had to go to the hospital, the children who had fallen ill, and the young men who played soccer in the park. She responds to each learner in either English or Hmong (or both) and asks follow-up questions. In this way, she not only finds out who is getting better at English and who still prefers the native language, she also gets a good sense of the accomplishments as well as the worries and concerns of the group. This teacher has also developed a daily log for her group in which she documents the "anecdotal evidence" gleaned from these talks. Documenting accomplishments and concerns allows her to adapt her lessons to the needs of the different groups in her class.

◼ Pictures do the talking

Pictures and other visuals work very well in multilevel classes because they have two important benefits.

1.   Pictures present an important avenue to reading and writing for those who may still struggle with literacy.

2.   Pictures offer a challenge for those who can read and write a little.

Strip stories, for example, in which a series of pictures tell a story, give learners the idea of a narrative before print is introduced. Those who are new to English and literacy may talk about the story in their mother tongue before offering ideas in English. Once texts are introduced, the accompanying pictures allow beginning readers to look ahead and predict what the text might say while stronger readers can focus on the printed page.[9]

Asking students to comment on a Freirean "code"[10] or problem represented in pictures, movies, collages, or songs, works in a similar manner. The code can be discussed in small groups in the mother tongue and ideas can then be shared in English. Learners for whom English is still difficult can give one word answers while those more fluent can provide greater details. The challenge for the teacher then becomes to respond to either group in authentic ways such as commenting on meaning, responding to affect, and encouraging learners to link the code to their own lives. (See also the curriculum module by Maria Malagamba-Roddy.)

◼ Storytelling

Storytelling and associated approaches such as language experience allow learners to use the language that they know, controlling the vocabulary and structures that they use. Storytelling also gives beginning learners the opportunity to present themselves as individuals who have ideas, charm, and a sense of humor, who will not be judged solely as being "limited" in their skills. Storytelling may include sharing folk stories, myths, personal experiences, or thoughts of what might be happening in a picture. It can also include simulations that involve role plays, such as "your teenage daughter wants to stay out past midnight with her friends, what do you tell her?"

Storytelling can also close the culture gap as learners from one culture come to see commonalities with students from cultures that appear vastly different. The Refugee Women's Alliance program in Seattle, for example, gives refugee women from around the world the opportunity to share personal experiences as well as folk tales through a storytelling curriculum. A facilitator or teacher encourages the women to explore cultural events (weddings, births, funerals) and then helps them to discover common themes among accounts from different cultures.[11]

◻ Skill sharing through peer teaching

Pair activities that match learners with different types of knowledge can be used as opportunities for skills sharing. Activities in which learners can showcase their strengths and effectively teach each other have two significant advantages: they help learners to share what they know and allow them to benefit from someone else's experience. In the multilevel classroom, such activities can link the sharing of a non-linguistic skill (e.g., administering home first aid) with literacy activities. Working in pairs, one student may talk about a particular procedure, while another writes down each step. The roles can be reversed as well, so that non-literate students act as interviewers using a tape recorder, illustrations, or their own system for remembering information to report information back to the class.

There are many variations of this approach. Workplace literacy programs often ask workers to share their knowledge about tools. In an ESL literacy program in San Diego, learners who have been in the class longest act as a "welcoming committee" for new students, orienting them to classroom routines. (See the curriculum module by Nancy Hampson.)

Pair activities that encourage learners to share skills, knowledge, and information are also effective in multilevel classes with learners from different countries. In one activity, one learner acts as the interviewer and scribe for an important event, such as the first day of school. The other learner acts as the "cultural informant," describing the event. At REEP in Arlington, Virginia, skills sharing sometimes takes place in front of the computer where a learner with keyboarding skills inputs a story for a non-literate student.

◼ Learners generate their own materials

Stories written by other students can bring learners together around the shared opportunities of reading, talking, and writing about personal experiences. While the stories are read aloud, non-readers can listen, new readers can follow along, and proficient readers can volunteer and take turns giving a voice to the author. In the discussions that follow, non-writers can contribute ideas and share their own hopes, sorrows, and dreams. Learner-generated stories often have the ring of authenticity and the strong sense of voice that "textbook stories" lack.[12] Using learner-generated themes as a basis for discussion and literacy development also helps beginners to see that their ideas count as much as the ideas of those who are more proficient.

◼ Learners make their own decisions

Group or pair activities that allow learners to decide who should carry out what tasks help them decide for themselves the roles they want to play. At El Barrio Popular Education Program in New York, learners take pictures in the community and label what they see. As students strike out in pairs, they decide who should be the picture taker and who should be the recorder, changing roles as appropriate.[13]

At REEP, for example, learners are asked to interview someone in the class to find out more about their preferences in foods, movies, weekend activities, etc. Interviewer roles are not assigned. As the activity gets under way, the "bolder" students naturally take the lead, moving across the room and engaging others in conversation. Many times, the "initiators" of the interview then coach their partners on how to ask questions and help them record their answers. Workplace programs often use interview grids to find out more about the range of jobs that people have had in the past or the various skills required in their present jobs. Family literacy programs often have parents interview each other about their children and use the information to find out more about their experiences with schools.[14]

Interview strategies can also be used in "contact assignments" that ask learners to interview family members or acquaintances. Since the interview is private, learners may choose the language they prefer and take down notes in any mode they like (mentally or in their own code). Since no one will see their notes, learners need not be embarrassed about using invented spelling or incomplete sentences. As the semester progresses, these interview notes can turn into biographies where learners can express their knowledge of the person through a variety of media, including drawings, photographs, songs, poems, or stories.

◖ Reading and writing for an audience

Setting up a message board can also help all learners get involved in the social aspect of literacy. The teacher can start by leaving a message for one or two people in the group, and individual learners can leave messages for each other. They must recognize that in order to get a message, they may need to leave a message first. Messages can be in any form and can include secret notes, announcements, birthday greetings, or "for sale" signs. Like dialogue journals, message centers show learners that language and literacy exchanges are ongoing and that reading leads to writing, which may in turn lead to action.

REEP has set up a "gallery" in the hallway where student work is displayed. These include photographs captioned by students, proverbs from different cultures, poems, and collages produced by students. The gallery also includes a large sheet with a message or a question to which passing students are encouraged to write a response. Other students, in turn, either respond to the original message or to what previous students have written.

◖ Bilingual communication helps understanding

In programs where the teacher speaks the language of the students, learners sometimes switch between using English and the mother tongue. Not being constrained by their limited English, students can freely express their ideas and opinions while learning English.   David Spener tells of an activity called "inquietudes" in which students ask (in Spanish) about English expressions or words they did not understand.[15]   The teacher or the group then provides explanations in English or Spanish. In some programs, learners spend part of class discussing ideas or problems in their mother tongue and then select a spokesperson to report the results to the larger group in English.

◖ Computers facilitate writing

Learners who have a difficult time with the mechanics of literacy can be greatly helped by computers. Stories that they have dictated or painstakingly written can be word processed and printed out, resulting in a "professional look" that can compete with papers written by more proficient students. Stories can be printed in large type for students who have difficulty with small print. In addition, learners can suggest changes to their stories that can be easily made on the computer, saving hours of time rewriting. Templates of different kinds of notes or letters can be stored on the computer, serving as examples for students who would like to see what "professionals" have written under similar circumstances.

El Barrio has examples of letters written to authorities in a computer file. Learners can call up these letters on the computer and get a sense of what an official greeting or closing might look like. The Lao Family Literacy program in St. Paul has examples of notes from parents to teachers on the computer. These notes have blank spaces that the parent then fills in by hand with the name of the teacher and the child.

Summary

Teaching literacy in a multilevel classroom is a challenging task. It requires a good sense of learners' abilities and strengths, clearly defined tasks (possibly developed by the learners themselves), and some form of grouping and evaluation. Setting up centers, designing projects, organizing the class into groups, and developing opportunities for pair work may initially take a great deal of effort and patience. Encouraging students to contribute ideas for shared tasks and making it possible for them to develop ownership of their projects may be one way to face the challenge and share the burden of the multilevel classroom.

Here is a summary of effective strategies:

- Be sensitive to differences in learners' backgrounds, attitudes, and perceptions when setting up groups.

- Use ongoing assessment to get a good sense of learner needs.

- Evaluate the success of each activity as you go along.

- Involve learners in making group decisions about interesting topics, relevant materials, and effective groupings.

- Provide a wide range of experiences so that different kinds of learner needs are met at different occasions and use different kinds of activities around a common theme with the goal of pleasing all your students some of the time.

- Give learners the opportunity to self-direct their learning through group work, pair activities, and joint projects.

- Use literacy centers as resource and information centers, not only as skill labs.

- Avoid the dangers of individualized instruction.

Reflections: Learning students' needs

The following questions are designed to help teachers get to know the students in their ESL literacy classrooms so that they can develop activities that meet the varying needs of all students.

Learner characteristics

1. What characteristics do learners in your group share?

2. What personal differences exist among the group? Consider the following:

   - personal backgrounds, including age, gender, employment status, and family relationships

   - home culture and society

   - previous experience with schooling

   - present interests, needs, and goals

   - proficiency in oral English

   - literacy level in the native language and in English

   - literacy practices in their respective communities and in their daily lives.

3. Given these differences and similarities, which type of group is most appropriate, heterogeneous or homogenous?

Perceptions and attitudes

1. Do your students differ in the way they look at the world, each other, and/or U.S. society? How?

2. How do they conceptualize learning and literacy?

3. Do you see any real or potential conflicts that deserve attention when grouping students? Consider the following differences in:

    *   ethnic groups or groups from different political systems

    *   age, social status, and gender

    *   learning styles (traditional and current)

    *   conceptions of literacy (reading means reciting a passage without making mistakes; writing is copying from the blackboard).

4. What strategies suggest themselves for dealing with differences in learner perceptions and attitudes?

5. What strategies have teachers you know found successful?

Continuous assessment

1. What have you done in the past to find out more about the different kinds of ESL literacy students in your program?

2. Which assessment strategies have been successful? Which need to be modified?

3. Which of the following types of assessment are missing from your assessment efforts?

    *   general assessment of community needs, concerns, and goals with a special emphasis on ESL literacy

    *   intake interviews to get a broad description of the learner's background, interests, needs, and goals

- initial assessment to provide enough information on language and literacy for effective placement and curriculum development

- classroom observations to flesh out profiles developed at intake and during initial assessment

- self-reflection and learner feedback to find out which activities are successful and which need to be modified

- classroom-based assessment to see who is progressing and who may need additional support.

Literacy activities

1. Given your learners, your teachers, and your resources, which multilevel activities show the greatest promise? Why?

2. Which of the following activities might not be feasible for your program?

   - project work and other shared tasks

   - activities built around themes

   - literacy centers.

Promising practices

1. Every program has teachers who have developed promising practices in dealing with a multilevel class. What promising practices exist in your program?

2. What strategies or tips might help new teachers?

Endnotes

1. See Center for Applied Linguistics, 1983.

2. See Bell, 1988, p. 3-4.

3.   See Bell, 1988.

4.   See Center for Applied Linguistics, 1983, p. 108.

5.   Bell (1988) suggests a variation on the health theme in which students learn to read different labels on medicine bottles. While more advanced students learn to read directions, lower level students can match poison symbols with words or work with a clock face to show what time the medicine needs to be taken. Another option would be an environmental print activity in which lower level students sort all the packages that say "Acetaminophen" from those that say "Aspirin."

6.   See also Bell, 1988 and Spener, 1990.

7.   See Center for Applied Linguistics, 1983.

8.   See also Bell, 1988 and Spener, 1990.

9.   This strategy has been adapted from Wallace, 1988.

10.   Codes (or "codification" in Freire's terms) are concrete expressions of a problem or theme; besides having visual representations, themes can also be encoded in written dialogues or stories. For a full discussion on how to use codes (and how to implement a Freirean approach in the classroom), see *The Teaching Approach of Paulo Freire* by Nina Wallerstein, 1983, or *Making Meaning, Making Change* by Auerbach, 1990.

11.   For a discussion of this curriculum, see the site report on the Refugee Women's Alliance in Seattle in *Adult ESL Literacy Programs and Practices: A Report on a National Research Study*, by Gloria J. A. Guth and Heide Spruck Wrigley, Aguirre International, San Mateo, CA (Guth & Wrigley, 1992).

12.   For examples of learner-generated stories, see Voices Magazine; *Stories to Tell Our Children* by Gail Weinstein-Shr, 1992; and *Our Lives: Authentic Student Stories for Developing Reading and Writing Skills*, by Myron Berkman, 1990. To help learners generate their own stories, see also *Personal Stories* by Koch et al., 1985.

13.   For details, see the site report on El Barrio Popular Education Program in *Adult ESL Literacy Programs and Practices: A Report on a National Research Study*, by Gloria J. A. Guth and Heide Spruck Wrigley, Aguirre International, San Mateo, CA (Guth & Wrigley, 1992).

14.   See also Madeline Rhun's unit on family literacy, "Everything Happens for the Best" in *Talking Shop* by Nash, et al., 1989.

15.   See Spener, 1990.

References

Auerbach, E. R. (1990). *Making meaning, making change: A guide to participatory curriculum development for adult ESL and family literacy.* Boston: University of Massachusetts [in press (1992), Regents Prentice Hall/Center for Applied Linguistics].

Bell, J. (1988). *Teaching multilevel classes in ESL.* San Diego, CA: Dormac.

Berkman, M. (1990). *Our lives: Authentic student stories for developing reading and writing skills.* Palatine, IL: Linmore Publishing.

Center for Applied Linguistics. (1983). *From the classroom to the workplace: Teaching ESL to adults.* Washington, DC: Author.

Guth, G. J. A., & Wrigley, H. S. (1992). *Adult ESL literacy programs and practices: A report on a national research study.* San Mateo, CA: Aguirre International. (Available from the U.S. Department of Education, Clearinghouse on Adult Education and Literacy).

Koch, K. D., Mrowicki, L., & Ruttenberg, A. (1985). *Personal stories: A book for adults who are beginning to read. Books 1 and 2.* Palatine, IL: Linmore Publishing.

Nash, A., Cason, A., Rhum, M., McGrail, L., & Gomez-Sanford, R. (1989). *Talking shop: A curriculum sourcebook for participatory adult ESL.* Boston: University of Massachusetts, English Family Literacy Project [in press (1992), Regents Prentice Hall/Center for Applied Linguistics].

Spener, D. (1990). *Suggested structure for meetings of home-based ESL classes for native speakers of Spanish.* Unpublished manuscript. Washington, DC: Spanish Education Development Center.

Voices. Surrey, B.C.: Lower Mainland Society for Literacy and Employment.

Wallace, C. (1988). *Learning to read in a multicultural society: The social context of second language literacy.* New York: Prentice Hall.

Weinstein-Shr, G. (1992). *Stories to tell our children.* Boston: Heinle & Heinle.

Chapter 4

Using Computer and Video Technology in Adult ESL Literacy

Today's computer and video technologies are more powerful and versatile than ever before. Although not always affordable to small adult ESL literacy programs, these technologies are becoming more widely available. Yet the use of high technology in language and literacy teaching remains controversial. On one hand, such technology holds the promise of making language and literacy learning easier and more exciting for teachers and learners. On the other hand, poorly designed software threatens to reduce literacy to its simplest terms and to counteract good teaching practice. The field now faces the challenge of examining the role that technology can play in supporting the language and literacy development of ESL adult learners without compromising the integrity of meaning-based literacy education. This chapter provides information that will help programs meet that challenge.

This chapter examines the role of technology, in particular computers and video, in teaching ESL literacy. It is divided into three sections: "Background: Technology pros and cons," "Practice: Using Technology in the Classroom" and "Reflections: Linking Technology and Program Focus." The "Background" section explores the advantages and disadvantages of using technology with ESL literacy learners as well as the issues raised by introducing technology into the curriculum. The "Practice" section presents (1) cases in point to illustrate how programs are using technology to teach ESL literacy and (2) promising practices in using technology. The "Reflections" section provides questions to help teachers decide whether using technology would be appropriate for their program.

Background: Technology pros and cons

Decisions about the use of video and computers in adult ESL literacy programs require an understanding of the circumstances in which these technologies are to be used. To be effective in its technology applications, a program needs to be aware that teachers and learners may differ in their attitudes toward technology. This section discusses the pros and cons of using computer and video technology in teaching ESL literacy from the viewpoints of teachers and learners.

ESL literacy teachers and attitudes toward technology

Teachers are often ambivalent about computer and video technologies. While they may not be convinced that technology can play a significant role in the language and literacy development of their students, they don't want to be left behind as new technologies with potential benefit for learners develop. While some teachers see technology as a new horizon, others feel strongly that available teaching software has failed to fulfill its promise of providing adult second language learners with access to meaning-based literacy.

Teachers differ in their interests and talents regarding technology. While some are true "techies" that take to technological innovations easily, others have difficulty grasping basic concepts and thus may be slow to warm to the idea of using technology with their students. Sometimes these teachers can be won over by access to technologies that simplify their own labor intensive tasks, such as word processors that allow teachers to prepare resumes for their next jobs or spreadsheets that calculate grades.

Teachers who are not ready to use technology in their own teaching might be open to sending their students to computer labs. These labs can help teachers by offering software programs that support their efforts to teach English and literacy. For example, a lab might offer software that creates crossword puzzles or other games out of a word list that students have developed in class. Or it might offer software that generates cloze tests, comprehension questions, or skimming and scanning activities, based on reading passages that the teacher has chosen. Coordinating efforts with the computer lab offers benefits for both teachers and students: both groups are oriented to the technology, without anyone having to be a computer expert.

Adult ESL literacy learners and attitudes toward technology

ESL literacy learners also differ in their attitudes vis a vis technology. Many are curious about computers, often more so than their teachers. These learners often see access to technology as a means to educational and occupational advancement. Others, particularly older learners, may feel overwhelmed by the requirements of technology or may not be quite ready for its use. In particular, they may feel overwhelmed and frustrated by the software programs available in self-access labs since much of the present educational software requires a higher level of proficiency in English and in literacy than most literacy learners possess. As a coordinator for a Hmong literacy in Minnesota remarked "A pencil is high tech as far as our students are concerned."[1]

What attracts many ESL literacy learners to technology? A good number are highly motivated to learn how to use computers since such knowledge may make them more competitive in their search for better paying jobs. Many parents see computer knowledge as a way of helping their children in school, while others enjoy the different modes of learning that technology can offer. Research has shown that, while these adults may not necessarily learn more or learn better from a machine than from a teacher, many learners show more positive attitudes when the information is presented on the screen. The extent to which motivation and positive attitudes are due to novelty has not been established. Increased self-esteem may also be a benefit as adults learn to master new technologies and become comfortable using computers and VCRs. In many cases, adults enjoy the privacy that using the computer affords and appreciate being able to move through activities at their own speed.

Technology for adult ESL literacy learners

Special characteristics of adults need to be considered when selecting appropriate technologies. As a rule, adult ESL literacy learners have a great deal of knowledge about the "real world," posses tremendous coping skills, have established effective social networks, and are capable of thoughtful reflection.

To be successful in introducing technology to this group, programs need to select materials that take advantage of and maximize these strengths. Materials such as software and videotapes that treat adult learners like children or assume that they are empty vessels to be filled with bits and pieces of language and literacy trivia will be counterproductive.

ESL literacy learners who are non-readers or very new readers have special needs that must be taken into account when technology is introduced. For example, literacy learners may have difficulty with software programs that use written instructions, use low-frequency vocabulary, and are difficult to get in and out of. When selecting appropriate technologies for these learners, one thing should be kept in mind: "new readers are not new thinkers."[2] Deficit-oriented software, such as programs that begin teaching the alphabet without reference to context, can actually hinder literacy development by making adults feel less competent than they are. In the view of many educators, any technology that asks adults to complete only low level tasks has only limited value in helping adults achieve full literacy.

Practice: Using technology in the classroom

Many programs have come to realize that literacy and technology can be linked in five fundamentally different ways. There is the possibility of using computers to teach ESL literacy directly, a promise that in many ways has yet to be fulfilled. Another possibility involves using the problem solving capabilities of the learners to help them access technology so they can take advantage of the opportunities that technology offers. Once such access is available, ESL literacy learners can use technology to help them with tasks that require literacy. Video technologies can be effective in providing a visual context for teaching language and literacy. Finally, technology can be used as a tool to promote social interaction and communication in the literacy classroom.

Using computer technology to teach literacy

This approach holds some promise for learners who are motivated to use technology on their own and eager to work with computers. Existing technologies include large self-contained learning systems or courseware focusing on reading skills, grammar knowledge, and vocabulary building; individual skill and drill software programs; "authoring" or "authorable" programs, where teachers can take existing software and customize it for their class; and interactive videos. For teachers who want to combine classroom teaching with computer support, software programs are available to design quizzes, cloze tests, or vocabulary games. In some cases, teachers can adapt available programs so that they include vocabulary or reading passages generated by learners in the class.

Many educators caution against using available computer technology as the sole means to teach literacy. Most software on the market is based on a very narrow skill-based definition of literacy that ignores the social aspects of learning and reduces literacy to a series of discrete chunks to be mastered before any kind of natural reading and writing can take place. For the most part, existing software denies learners the opportunity to look at literacy holistically. In addition, the very features that make technology attractive to some (privacy, independent learning) may be counterproductive to the development of initial literacy since it may cut beginning learners off from the social support they need to gain confidence in their ability to understand and use real-life literacy.

A special concern for adult ESL literacy is the fact that most computers programs cannot recognize non-native writing, including the approximations of English that many ESL learners use. In most cases, the computer cannot tell the difference between a nonsense sentence and a meaningful sentence that contains grammatical errors. For example, many programs will accept sentences such as "yesterday, I ate the house" while disallowing sentences such as "Yesterday, my brother, he die."

Given these shortcomings, the label "learner-centered," as used by many manufacturers of literacy courseware, is misleading. Existing courseware is generally not designed to let learners generate ideas; nor does it respond to what was written in any genuine way or allow experimenting with language. As the term is used in marketing, "learner-centered" often means that students are given a pre-test that determines where in the package they should start instruction. Once instruction has started, learners are marched through the program in a lock-step approach which, at best, allows them to skip some sections before a unit is completed.

In response to the inflexibility of such software, some technology experts are now demanding that manufacturers develop programs that respond to ideas generated by the learners. These experts call for software that is "learner-driven", not just learner-centered, and emphasize the need for manufacturers to listen to the ideas of literacy educators. However, they also point out that the software companies don't appear responsive when teachers explain what they need.[3]

Helping learners to access computers

Although many teachers have found the educational software designed for ESL and/or literacy quite disappointing, they still see the need to help their students access and use computers. They want their students to become comfortable with computers, gain familiarity with the keyboard or with a mouse, and learn how to use various types of software. These teachers find that, when they put the emphasis on access to technology and computer awareness, the literacy orientation represented by the software becomes less of an issue. The primary concern of most of these teachers lies in finding software that is interesting, easy to understand, and fun to use while allowing literacy learners to get in and out of the program without difficulty.

Such an approach might be a good starting point for programs that are not happy with the materials presently on the market and do not have the resources to develop their own computer-based materials. By seeing a value in students' using technology for its own sake, not just for the learning of language and literacy, teachers can concentrate on finding software that is easy to learn and that students enjoy working with. With concerns about technology "out of the way," teachers can focus on developing rich literacy activities using more conventional means.

Using technology to facilitate literacy tasks

Many ESL literacy teachers use computers to demonstrate how technology can make complex literacy tasks easier. They may show beginning students how to use "clip art" to illustrate their writing or how to use graphics software to create flyers, posters, or announcements. Many programs use computer software to create and publish learner-generated materials such as language experience stories, yearbooks, or biographies, and some teach learners how to use a simple database so they can build their own bilingual dictionary. Workplace programs sometimes use spreadsheets to help learners design a budget for a class party or to calculate the money they make working overtime. Some literacy programs use word processors to create templates for resumes, letters of inquiry, or notes to teachers.

Many educators think that application software (e.g., word processing packages, databases, spreadsheets) shows much greater promise for literacy teaching than available educational software. Without teaching literacy per se, application software can support various forms of literacy, including prose, quantitative, graphic, and document literacy. There is an additional benefit: seeing their efforts printed by a computer gives even literacy learners a sense of being "real writers." In using these applications, some teachers ask students with keyboarding skills to act as a scribe for someone else's language experience story.

Using technology to provide a visual context

Many ESL teachers use video technology to provide a visual context for their literacy teaching. They may present videotapes of the evening news as a spring board for discussing social and political issues or present taped conversations and role plays as a starting point in examining the way language is used in various social situations. Some teachers also show learners how to record their own videos: learners may tape their own role plays and then analyze the language, non-verbal behavior, or tone that might be most effective in a given situation.

When used with ESL literacy learners, video technology can be a powerful tool in developing both listening comprehension and language awareness. Through case studies shown on tape, videos can provide insights into the socio-cultural dimensions of literacy and provide opportunities for problem solving. When the stories presented on tape touch on personal problems or social issues, they can act as a starting point for problem-posing.

Using technology to promote collaborations and social interaction

Many teachers ask learners to work together in pairs or groups and make decisions about how best to use the technology available to them. Some teachers encourage learners to work with a partner to discover the answers to grammar, vocabulary, or pronunciation exercises that appear on the computer. Such activities allow learners to debate about correct and incorrect responses and in this way develop language awareness. Other teachers set up collaborations that make it possible for learners to use computers in designing projects, creating texts, or interpreting a story that appears on the screen. Some family literacy programs have set up intergenerational projects that encourage parents and teachers to use computers for family math or storytelling. In other programs, learners from different sites take part in cultural exchanges through telecommunication.

Cooperative learning of this kind shows great promise in supporting literacy development for ESL adults. This use of technology supports the social dimensions of literacy as students learn to construct knowledge for themselves. Collaborations also promote the interpersonal dimensions of literacy since they allow learners to take advantage of each other's talents and skills.

Integrating technology into the literacy curriculum: a sample unit

The following chart shows how computers and videos (both interactive and conventional) can be used to put sound literacy teaching into practice. The chart illustrates a unit based on the theme of "disasters" such as earthquakes, fires, floods, and tornados. Since many students have had first-hand experience with one or more of these disasters, the theme can be used to link personal experience to common events. If used in an open-ended fashion, this theme can help learners explore their own concerns and examine community issues as well (e.g., methods of fire prevention or disaster relief efforts).

As illustrated in the chart, the unit contains two parts. Part one demonstrates how technology can be used to introduce ideas, encourage discussions, and provide jumping off points for various literacy events. Part two shows how computers can facilitate skill enhancement by allowing learners to focus on particular aspects of reading and writing. The chart also contains three columns. Column one outlines the instructional aims that a teacher might be trying to achieve. Column two explains how technology could be used to achieve these aims while column three lists the types of technologies that are used.

The unit demonstrated in the chart does not represent an actual lesson that has been taught using the technologies mentioned. Rather it is a synthesis of ideas meant to illustrate how technology can be part of a meaning-based curriculum. While all the technologies described are available in one form or another, the software may not be available for ESL literacy.

Sample Unit: ESL Literacy and Other Natural Disasters

Part I. Making Meaning: Oral Communication and Interactive Reading and Writing

Instructional Aims	Activity	Type of Technology
1. Connecting background knowledge with new information; building a frame of reference for language and literacy activities.	Students watch video clips or slides and look at posters or emergency symbols related to fires, earthquakes, volcanoes, and tornados, and then discuss what they see.	video; film; slides; photographs
2. Connecting learner experience to reading and writing; linking oral language with written language; negotiating meaning as part of a group process.	In small groups students discuss recent experience with disaster and as a group generate a story; story is transcribed and put on computer by a scribe; students read, discuss, and revise stories and work on skills enhancement.	computer; word processing program
3. Building comprehension strategies (predicting from context; confirming; revising) while building listening comprehension.	Students watch video or short film clips of a particular disaster; sound is turned off and in small groups students try to predict vocabulary and language used; predictions are discussed and recorded (movie can be shown again with closed captioning); predictions are discussed.	video (closed-captioning if available)

4. Developing effective reading strategies.	Students are introduced to a disaster story written by a student; they start by seeing only the title and pictures; the computer suggests some words and structures that might be in the story; students pick words from the list and then go on to read the story as it appears on the screen. As they read the story, the computer shows the results of their predictions by highlighting the words that they have picked.	computer; simple authoring software
5a. Strengthening communication skills and interaction strategies.	a. Students watch video of police or relief worker interviewing a victim; students discuss the questions that were asked; students watch for non-verbal clues.	a. video
5b. Linking everyday events with problem solving and with literacy.	b. Students role play then fill out relevant forms (e.g., police report, hospital admissions forms, damage reports). Sample (simplified) forms are on the computer.	b. computer

6. Using learner experience as a basis for developing graphic literacy.	Students interview each other; ask about country of origin and year of entry in the U.S., find out who has lived through big storms, earthquakes, droughts, fires, etc.; someone inputs data into the computer; students choose options to generate graphs showing time-lines and distributions.	computer, graphics software, database software
7a. Linking problem solving and communication skills.	a. Students watch critical incident on video and decide how the problem could be handled, choosing options. They role play the interaction and then watch various scenarios on interactive videodisc.	a. interactive video, computer, word processing program
7b. Creating meaning through writing and role plays.	b. Students tell of similar incidents in their own lives and create language experience stories.

c. Students create their own videos around extended role plays such as different ways of getting the landlord to fix plumbing damage after an earthquake. Students study, discuss, and critique their own video performance. | c. video |

8. Providing bilingual support.	a. Teacher provides preview/review activities in the native language before and after showing a film or video; sound is closed captioned in the native language.	a. video with closed captioning capability
	b. Instructions for a computer program are spoken in the native language; a bilingual dictionary is included.	b. computer, software with dictionary and sound capability
9. Building background knowledge.	Guest speaker comes to a class and discussion is taped and closed captioned for beginning students; tape is discussed and becomes basis for language lessons.	video; computer

Sample Unit (ctd): ESL Literacy and Other Natural Disasters

Part II. Getting it Right: Skills Enhancement

Instructional Principle	Activity	Type of Technology
1. Develop concepts and vocabulary.	As students move through materials, they create their own word banks and their own bilingual dictionaries; entries include sample sentences.	computer; simple authoring software
2. Building cognitive skills and strengthening problem solving activities; creating language awareness.	Students develop categories for the concepts and terms they have developed; sentences such as "The house burned to the ground" can be listed under FIRE; students either move text around or type in their own examples.	computer; word processing
3. Supporting the reading process.	Students work with a text on the computer, answering pre-reading questions; practice skimming and scanning and answering comprehension questions; the software controls the reading speed and highlights key terms, generates questions, analyzes answers, and offers help; computer generates cloze activities and language games.	computer; reading program that allows authoring

		computers, word processing with grammar, spelling, and dictionary support
4. Supporting students in the writing process.	LEA stories or essays are generated by the students and printed; students decide whether they want to add, delete, or change anything; changes are made on the computer; final editing takes place when students are ready - spelling, mechanics, and formatting; final essays are published as class news, newsletters, or yearbooks (other publishing efforts can involve flyers, recipes, birthday cards, etc.)	
5. Strengthening awareness of sound/symbol relationship.	Students learn to do "tricks with print": as they work with texts and vocabulary items, students highlight patterns such as consonant clusters (earthquake/birth date) or syllable similarities (quake/shake); then work on phonics programs that teach similar sounds; students listen and repeat sounds.	computer; sound capability

Two models of technology use

In adult ESL literacy programs, two models for technology use are common, the self-access model and the class-based model. The following pages briefly describe these models while Cases in Point illustrate how programs in the field have implemented each approach.

Self-access model

Self-access technology allows individual learners to use technology in their own time and at their own speed. Self-access is most often presented as part of a learning lab, where a facilitator gets learners started and answers questions. Self-access permits learners to select software that interests them and allows them to work at their own speed on the specific skills they want to develop.

◆ Case in point: a self-access learning center

The Adult Learning Center at REEP offers state of the art computer and video technology to enhance ESL and literacy learning.[4] The center offers computers of different types, as well as other equipment such as the Franklin Spanish-English electronic dictionary, Language Masters, cassette recorders, videos, and print materials. The learning center is staffed by a team of 15 trained ESL teachers who also teach in the general ESL and/or the workplace literacy program. Staff work with learners to develop individual learning plans which include an assessment of the learner's language skills, learning goals, and the selection of appropriate materials. The REEP Center is used two ways: (1) learners can drop in and work with the available technology on a self-access basis and (2) learners visit the lab as part of their regular class under the guidance of a teacher. This teacher may suggest learning activities such as writing stories collaboratively or working in pairs on software designed for grammar or pronunciation practice. REEP recommends that those ESL learners with very little experience in reading only use the lab with the help of a literacy teacher.

Class-based model

The class-based model requires that the teacher moderate how technology is used and integrate technology into the existing language and literacy curriculum. This model holds promise in supporting the principles of meaning-based literacy education since it allows for group decision making around the computer and links literacy activities developed in the classroom with computer use.

◆ *Case in point*

The Bronx Educational Service (BES), a community-based literacy program, has integrated computers into its curriculum and is using them in the classroom on a daily basis.[5] BES uses small group work (6-10 students) in most of its classes.

A typical BES class may evolve as follows. The teacher prepares a unit on crime that includes plans for a videotape, problem posing, learner-generated writing, and various skill enhancement activities that have been designed on the computer. Before the tape is shown, learners discuss the topic and list examples of criminal activities that they are familiar with. The list is used to discover similarities in word forms. A discussion ensues about crime-related issues. A list of concepts is generated from the discussion and the video is shown and discussed. The teacher asks learners to write about crime as part of their homework.

When the class reconvenes, learners work together independently of the teacher. They discuss their writing, compare word lists, input what they have written into a computer, or work on one of the skills programs the teacher has created on the computer (cloze, missing letters, spelling drills). After half an hour, the teacher will hand out the list of crime vocabulary words from the previous class and ask learners (who are still working in groups) to work on this and pick five to ten words that especially interest and challenge them. Two students then enter the words that were selected on the computer. The students choose a software program that will create a game or exercise with these words. These computer activities can then be used at any point by other students. The rest of the class divides into new groups. While some students may choose to enter the crime paragraphs they have written, others may discuss, edit, or rewrite their stories using pen and paper.

For BES, the ongoing success of the class-based technology model rests on a firm methodological principle: it is important that students always use pen and pencil in conjunction with the computer. All words, sentences, and paragraphs created on the computer are also written down and are read to the teacher or shared with the class. Reading aloud and rewriting what appears on the screen reinforces learning and ensures that learners understand what is on the computer screen.

Discussion

Class-based technology holds a great deal of promise for ESL literacy learners. Successful implementation, however, requires extensive staff development. BES has spent hundreds of hours training its staff over the first two years of the program, sending staff to conferences and receiving substantial training from experts. This training was supplemented by formal in-house meetings every week, and staff discuss the program on a regular basis over lunch. The BES example suggests that, to be effective with ESL adult literacy learners, class-based technology requires a strong commitment from all concerned.

Promising practices

◻ Closed-captioned television

In closed-captioned television, the audio portion of a program is converted into written words that appear on the bottom of the TV screen, like untranslated subtitles in a foreign movie. A number of ESL programs have bought TV sets that are equipped with the decoders that make these subtitles visible. These programs have found that understanding and comprehension improve as learners watch TV and look at the writing on the screen. Close-captioned TV supports the theory that learning is improved when learners are exposed to information that occurs simultaneously in three forms: they see a visual image, hear the dialogue or narration, and read the text of what they hear.[6]

◻ Interactive videodisc

REEP is currently working on creating interactive videodisc materials to help train students in housekeeping and other areas of the hotel/motel industry.[7] The interactive videodisc lessons allow ESL learners to practice the language needed at the workplace by watching video scenes that show interactions between employees and guests and between employees and their supervisors. The initial videodisc materials are based on training materials originally developed by the hotel/motel industry for native speakers of English. The REEP staff has repurposed these materials to make them interactive and has developed lessons that focus on the language needed to succeed at the job. Video lessons are available for two levels of literacy, beginning and intermediate, with the intermediate level containing more onscreen text and more difficult structures and vocabulary.

◘   Videotape in the workplace

El Paso Community College, in partnership with Levi Strauss, has developed a set of videotapes that form the basis for a workplace curriculum.[8] The videotapes present narrated footage that was shot in a garment manufacturing plan. Each video segment involves a theme of interest to learners (e.g., worker safety, the impact of new technology). Interspersed throughout this footage are cuts of interviews with actual garment workers who respond extemporaneously to questions related to a given theme. The video is shown to the class to provide learners with both a visual context for the theme and with comprehensible oral language input. After watching the videotape, learners read a short piece and discuss the topic from their own perspectives. Learners then move on to writing a passage about their personal experience with the topic. The final activity involves an outside task in which learners either explore ideas further, pursue learning on their own (e.g., reading a newspaper or listening to the radio), or do additional writing.

◘   Telecommunications

A number of programs now use computers as a medium of communication between various sites. One project of interest to ESL literacy and native language literacy programs is the de Orilla a Orilla (from shore to shore) project that links teachers and learners from the United States with sister classes in Puerto Rico, Argentina, English- and French-speaking Canada, and Mexico.[9] Teachers use teleconferencing to plan joint projects with other teachers, and learners use computers to plan projects and send messages across the borders using computers and modems. Classes also trade monthly cultural packages containing photos, maps, letters, school projects, and local memorabilia, as well as some older technologies such as audiotapes or slides. Although this project is designed for secondary schools, similar collaborations could be established between adult ESL and native language literacy programs as well.

The Haitian Multi-Cultural Service Center provides access to online bulletin board services and interactive communication opportunities for literacy students.[10] The literacy student can (with or without the help of a scribe) type her/his text into the computer and then send it electronically to a student at another program. Students tend to send Language Experience stories and comment on each other's ideas. Learners also "talk" to each other about topics such as things to do in Boston.

◘ Multimedia for new readers

Interactive videodisc programs using computers with CD ROM have started to appear. These systems combine video, still photographs, and audio. Interactive activities allow adults with little reading ability to understand text and compose stories. In a project developed in Europe, learners are introduced to video scenes, titles, and sentences that can be used to create stories on the computer.[11] A man and a woman, whose faces appear in a window on the screen, act as video guides to show learners how to use the mouse and guide them through the program.

The program offers learners photos and scenes and lets them choose titles or headlines that might match these scenes. The audio component of the program reads the various titles to the learner who then selects her choice. The selected title appears next to the photograph and the learner is now ready to listen to and read a number of sentences that are related to the topic. By selecting sentences and moving them around on the screen, learners can create stories to accompany the picture.

Photographs and sentences are built around themes that were identified as high interest topics for adults by the Adult Literacy and Basic Skills Unit in Great Britain. Topics include the impact of divorce on children and difficulties in finding low-cost housing. The program also contains skill enhancement activities such as cloze tests and skimming activities that ask learners to find their own names or the name of their street from a list. The "video guides" also give learners helpful hints on how to use what they already know to help them with their reading.

◘ Collaborations around computer and video technologies

Many programs encourage learners to work together on the computer. REEP pairs learners from different language backgrounds so that they can jointly create a story. These students use English as their common language to "negotiate meaning" and decide what to write. At other programs, parents and children work together in intergenerational activities, creating family biographies, playing math games, or making birthday cards. In some programs, learners work together to create flyers and announcements for upcoming events.

In some programs, learners videotape class role-plays (e.g., returning an item to the store) and then discuss various ways of becoming consumer advocates. In others, learners develop interview guides and then videotape "the man on the street" to get opinions. Videos are shown in class and the content becomes the basis for further literacy work.

◻ Self-publishing through computers

In many programs, students publish magazines, yearbooks, or newsletters on the computer and use graphics software to add designs and clip art to illustrate their publications. At El Barrio Popular Education Program, a group of learners developed a photo-novela that dealt with the concern that parents have about their children not receiving quality schooling.[12] Originated by a student, the story was developed by the class and then produced by the students with the help of computers. The student group then talked about the process and presented their work at an Adult Basic Education Conference.

Software is also available for learners to create signs, that can be posted around the school or produce posters that contain favorite messages or announce events. These programs can also be used to help learners create notices for bulletin boards or to write notes for teachers and neighbors. Learners who still have difficulties writing fluidly can take pride in producing "professional work," especially if the results can be posted around the school. Computer-savvy learners can help others create these products.

◻ Using timelines and charts

Software is available that lets learners create timelines that chronicle important family milestones or historical events. These timelines can either illustrate writings or become the basis for texts. Programs that create charts and graphs may be especially helpful in workplace programs where statistical process control is used. Such programs allow learners to graph events such as the weather, the ups and downs of their checkbooks, or provide charts on data that learners have collected about each other: average height or age, average number of years out of school, average pounds of rice consumed per month, etc.

Implications for staff development

Many educators have pointed out that the effectiveness of technology in the literacy classroom is largely dependent on the ability of the teacher to choose, adapt, and use various technologies effectively. When working with literacy learners especially, how the technology is used may be as important if not more important than the quality of the software and hardware itself.[13] Above all, technology should never be used to interfere with sound literacy teaching.[14]

Technology changes the role of the teacher. Once computers or interactive video programs are introduced, literacy activities tend to become much more student-focused. As a result, the teacher acts more like a resource person or a facilitator than the knowledge expert, and teaching is decentralized. Many teachers will need strategies for becoming comfortable in that new role. As technology takes hold, staff development will have to confront the difficult problem of showing teachers how to create learning environments that are fundamentally different from the ones that they themselves have experienced.

In order to maximize the use of technology in a program, the fears as well as the strengths of the staff must be recognized. Programs must find ways to utilize the special talents of the "techies" while shielding the "technophobes" from unnecessary technical details that may overwhelm them. For the latter group, programs may need to choose simple, "user friendly" computer software that reduces technological barriers. To meet the different needs of teachers, interest groups can be set up that allow teachers to share information and jointly develop ideas.

To meet the needs of all teachers, literacy programs that are fully committed to technology might best be served by hiring a technology coordinator who is excited about technology, understands its role, and can train others. Such a coordinator can help ensure that the technology used supports teachers by enhancing their existing teaching skills and helping them to build new skills.

Conclusion

Technology decisions are value decisions. Every time administrators and teachers choose a certain type of software or configure a learning lab, they make a statement about their beliefs about the nature of language, literacy, and learning. These choices reflect a program's view of learner needs and program goals and the role of teaching. When it comes to technology, the end result is often determined neither by the learners nor by the teachers, but rather by what is available in the marketplace. Experience has shown that some technology oriented adult education programs are in danger of allowing hardware and software vendors to define literacy for them.[15] To counteract this trend, many innovative ESL literacy programs have taken a proactive stand. They have examined the uses and functions of technology in light of their own needs and adapted available technologies accordingly.

As new technologies become available, programs face the difficult challenge of finding and successfully implementing software that

- respects the background, interests, and needs of the adult ESL literacy learners

- fits within the literacy framework a program has established

- motivates learners and takes advantage of the strengths that immigrant adults have

- promotes active learning and full engagement with literacy

- presents literacy in its many dimensions

- reflects the principles of adult learning, second language acquisition, and literacy development

- is consistent with sound teaching practice

- supports teachers by enhancing their existing skills and helping them build new skills

Reflections: Linking technology and program focus

This section contains two activities to help programs make informed decisions about the use of technology in the ESL literacy classroom. The first part consists of key questions that need to be answered before technology can effectively be used with ESL literacy learners. The second part is a chart designed to help teachers match up learner needs with available types of computer software.

Administrators and teachers should ask themselves the following questions before making technology part of their ESL literacy curriculum:

1. How can we get information about what technology is available and what technologies might be best, given our goals and our program focus?

2. Do our ESL literacy learners want and need access to technology and how is such access best provided?

3. Is available technology the best medium for teaching and learning, given the approach to ESL literacy we support?

4. Is technology available to support the dimensions of literacy our program focuses on?   How should such technology be used?

5. Does the available technology promote the kind of engagement with learning that full literacy development requires?

6. How do we find experts to help us build our own capacity to understand and use technology effectively?

7. How can we acquire the resources necessary to maintain the technology path we have chosen?

Choosing Appropriate Computer Software:
Linking Learner Needs with Software Features

Learner Needs	Software Feature to Look For
1. My students have little literacy but would like to work with computers.	The software allows students to "play with the computer" without requiring reading or keyboarding skills (familiarity with the alphabet may need to be developed).
2. My students prefer to work independently, practicing language (and making mistakes) in private; they enjoy being able to develop literacy skills at their own speed.	The software is primarily designed for individual student use.
3. My students like to work in pairs or in groups so they can help each other with literacy questions and computer problems.	The software lends itself to group problem solving, project work, and cooperative learning activities.
4. My students want software that allows them to play with ideas and texts (reading traffic signs, recognizing symbols and logos, reading simple stories and poems, creating simple cards and announcements).	The software focuses on teaching initial literacy through real-life contexts, using environmental print, or other whole language activities.
5. My students enjoy activities that involve the learning of subskill (recognizing capital and small letters, practicing letter formation, phonics, spelling, see/say word lists).	The software focuses mostly on skill and drill activities (phonics, grammar, spelling, pronunciation, choosing correct sentences).

6. My students are interested in software that requires problem solving and focuses on teaching the skills needed for literacy in pre-academic and pre-vocational setting.	The software focuses on language strategies (predicting and confirming, using context clues, test taking, interpreting pictures and developing graphs, analyzing data, developing concepts, and building content vocabulary).
7. My students enjoy playing games with language and respond enthusiastically to software programs that are fun to use.	The software teaches language through games; it contains bells and whistles such as sound, graphics, or animation.
8. My students like to receive native language support and/or are interested in biliteracy and translation.	The software has a bilingual dictionary and offers translation assistance.
9. My students learn better when computer work is tied to the themes we are discussing and to the activities we do in class.	The software can be adapted to include classroom activities; content information and vocabulary can be added.
10. My students and I are interested in keeping score and want to get feedback on the language and literacy development of the class.	The software has a record keeping function that allows teachers to store data on learner progress (grades, types of books read types of texts written); software allows teachers to design and use progress charts such as reading and writing inventories and learner profiles; software program is simple enough for learners to chart their own progress.

Endnotes

1. See Lao program site report in Guth & Wrigley, 1992 It must be noted that the program, nevertheless, has instituted the use of computers.

2. M. Good, personal communication, April 18, 1981.

3. See Gueble, 1990a.

4. See the REEP site report in Guth & Wrigley, 1992.

5. See Deveaux, 1987.

6. See also Gueble, 1990b.

7. See the REEP site report in Guth & Wrigley, 1992.

8. See the El Paso Community College site report in Guth & Wrigley, 1992.

9. See Cummins & Sayers, 1990.

10. See the site report on Haitian Multi-Service Center in Guth & Wrigley, 1992.

11. See Good, 1991.

12. Personal communication with Klaudia Rivera, May 21, 1992.

13. See Huss et al., 1990.

14. See also the policy paper of The Computers in Literacy Committee of the Metro Toronto Movement for literacy which contains the phrase, "The bottom line, finally, is that for some practitioners and learners, the best use of computers may be none at all" (cited in Poulton et al., 1990).

15. See Turner, 1990.

References

Cummins, J., & Sayers, D. (1990). Education 2001: Learning networks and educational reform. In C. J. Faltis, & R. A. DeVillar (Ed.), *Language Minority Students and Computers* (pp. 1-29). New York: The Haworth Press.

Deveaux, J. P. (1987). Effective practice: From the computer lab into the classroom. *Focus on Basics*, *1*(2), 2-4.

Good, M. (1991). The reading disc: The application of technology to learning. In Outreach and Technical Assistance Network (OTAN) (Ed.), *Proceedings of the Fifth Annual Adult Literacy and Technology Conference* (26-26.2). La Puente, CA: OTAN.

Gueble, E. (1990a). Learner-centered instruction in the workplace. *Adult Literacy & Technology*, *4*(3), 1, 10-14.

Gueble, E. (1990b). Closed-captioned TV and ESL instruction. *Adult Literacy & Technology*, *4*(3), 1, 15-16.

Guth, G. J. A., & Wrigley, H. S. (1992). *Adult ESL literacy programs and practices: A report on a national research study.* San Mateo, CA: Aguirre International. (Available from the U.S. Department of Education, Clearinghouse on Adult Education and Literacy).

Hanson-Smith, E. (1991). *How to set up a computer lab: Advice for the beginner.* La Jolla, CA: Athelstan.

Huss, S., Lane, M., & Willetts, K. (1990, November). *Using computers with adult ESL literacy learners. ERIC Digest.* Washington, DC: Center for Applied Linguistics, National Clearinghouse on Literacy Education.

McCurry, N., & McCurry, A. (1992). Writing assessment for the 21st century. *The Computing Teacher*, *19*(7), 35-37.

Poulton, B., Garber, N., & MacMillan, C. (1990). Sharing ideas in Canada. *Adult Literacy & Technology Newsletter*, *4*(3), 8.

Schipper, D. (1991). Practical ideas: Literature, computers, and students with special needs. *The Computing Teacher*, *19*(2), 33-37.

Sheingold, K. (1991, September). Restructuring for learning with technology: The potential for synergy. *Phi Delta Kappa*, pp. 17-27.

Stone, A. (1987). Beyond "return": Expanding the use of computers for literacy learning. *Focus on Basics, 1*(2), 1, 4-5.

Turner, T. C. (1990). You are what you speak: Language, teaching and technology. *Adult Literacy & Technology Newsletter, 3*(4), 1, 10.

Chapter 5

Native Language Literacy

Teaching literacy in the native language/mother tongue of the learners is one of the best options for programs serving non-literate learners who share a common language. Learning to read and write in a language they understand, instead of in a language they are trying to acquire, affords students a measure of power and control that is not easily matched in an adult ESL literacy class. While native language literacy classes may be offered in any language (classes exist in Hmong and Haitian Creole for example), Spanish is by far the most dominant, a fact that is not surprising given the large number of Spanish speakers in the United States.

Programs that offer mother tongue literacy differ in their aims. Some have full biliteracy and bilingualism as their goal. They see the mother tongue as inextricably bound to ethnic and cultural identity and seek to maintain the cultural and linguistic roots of the community through literacy.[1] Others see literacy acquisition in the native language primarily as a stepping stone to English literacy. They recognize that knowledge of the writing system of one's first language is an important tool in acquiring literacy in a second (or additional) language. Yet, no matter what their aims, these programs have found literacy in the native tongue to be highly effective in introducing reading and writing to adults who are new to literacy.

This chapter examines the various uses of the learners' native languages in ESL literacy teaching. The chapter is divided into three parts: "Background: The Case for Using the Native Language," "Practice: Using the Native Language in ESL Literacy Teaching," and "Reflections: Understanding Literacy Contexts." The "Background" section discusses research findings on the use of the native language in teaching and examines the special issues raised by using the native language of the learners in teaching. The "Practice" section presents (1) cases in point that illustrate how programs use native language in teaching ESL literacy and (2) promising practices that teachers could incorporate into their teaching. The final section, "Reflections," lists questions to help teachers gain a better understanding of the contexts in which their programs operate so that they can make decisions about how the native language might be used with the learners.

Background: The case for using the native language

While there are no large scale research studies that show the exact relationship between native language literacy and English literacy in adults, there are some indications that first language literacy skills result in greater competency in the second language.[2] Although more research is needed to determine the degree to which literacy skills in one language aid or impede the learning of literacy in the other, it is now generally acknowledged that it is easier to learn to read and write in a language one fully understands. Because reading is based on oral language, learners who are still struggling with English will learn to read more quickly in their native language.

Relationship between first and second language literacy

Research conducted with children provides strong support for the hypothesis that literacy in the native language is strongly related to literacy in an additional language.[3] There is also considerable evidence that,even when the language in question uses a different writing system, readers are able to apply the visual, linguistic, and cognitive strategies they use in first language reading to reading in the second language.[4]

Perhaps the most exhaustive discussion of the interrelationship among first language literacy, second language acquisition, and the development of cognitive skills is provided by Cummins.[5] His interdependence hypothesis holds that literacy skills learned in the first language transfer to the second language, thus establishing one common underlying language proficiency. Cummins holds that strong literacy in the first language will facilitate not only literacy in English, but will form the foundation for acquiring the cognitive skills needed for academic success. While Cummin's theories have formed the basis of many mother tongue literacy classes, further research may be needed to determine to what extent such transfers are aided or inhibited by social, cultural, and psychological factors.[6] Hornberger, for example, suggests that the contexts for biliteracy need to be examined before the full benefits of literacy in the native language teaching can be understood.

When to teach literacy in the native language

Should literacy always be introduced in the native language of the learners? Research suggests that the answer depends on a variety of factors. The program context, attitudes of learners and teachers toward learning native language literacy, and the status of both languages in the wider community may all play a role.[7] In her framework for biliteracy, Hornberger suggests that the success of native language literacy programs depends on

- which languages are promoted by the community or by the society at large

- how much either language is valued in the home, the schools, and the community

- to what extent the speakers depend on oral versus written communication.[8]

In the experience of many adult literacy programs, the size of the language group and the educational background of the learners are also key factors in determining whether literacy should be introduced in the mother tongue or in English. There now is general agreement that adults with few years of schooling in their home countries, who have not acquired literacy on their own, can greatly benefit from a native language literacy program. Such programs can either be offered in conjunction with a class focusing on oral communication in English or in sequence with an English literacy class.

Language diversity: a resource or a problem

One of the factors that influences program success deals with societal and individual attitudes toward biliteracy. Research has shown that the degree to which native language literacy is recognized and valued in the U.S. varies widely.[9] Three common viewpoints are frequently voiced regarding language diversity. As Ruiz points out, language diversity can be seen as either a "resource" or a "problem." The resource orientation sees both economic and personal benefit in multilingualism, regarding the language skills of immigrants as a resource that should be conserved and developed, particularly in schools and the workplace. This orientation sees mother tongue literacy as an important economic asset that can help workers reap the economic benefits of the skills they already have.

The language diversity as "problem" orientation, however, views cultural diversity as a weakness to be overcome rather than one of the country's greatest strengths. Advocates of this view often see English mono-lingualism as the only acceptable social condition.

A third orientation chooses to ignore non-English literacy, considering English literacy as the "only literacy that counts."[10] When this orientation shapes policy, several negative outcomes may result: (1) important knowledge and skills are ignored, (2) literacy surveys present a skewed picture of the true levels of reading and writing of the population, (3) program decisions are made on false premises, and (4) learners arc defined by what they don't know (English), rather than what they do know (their mother tongue).

There now is agreement in the field that positive language attitudes promote self-esteem and that increased self-esteem is an important corollary to literacy development. In light of these views, many innovative programs support a native-language-as-a-resource orientation to literacy.

Responding to learner expectations

Learner attitudes and expectations can also influence the success of both native language and ESL literacy. Adults in ESL literacy programs often want to learn English as fast as possible and sometimes see learning to read and write in the native language as a roundabout way of achieving their goal. Innovative programs have found four strategies helpful in introducing the idea of native language literacy to their students:

1. Respond to the concerns of learners. Some learners express a desire only to learn literacy in English and not in their native language. With these learners, it is best to acknowledge their concern that literacy in the native language might hold them back or impede their progress in learning English.

2. Discuss the nature of literacy development and show that literacy develops fastest if it is linked to a language the learner already speaks.

3. Give examples that show how adults with literacy in their native language acquire literacy in English more easily.

4. Present various opportunities that allow learners to experiment with literacy in English and in the native language and offer a choice of classes. Ask learners with only a few years of schooling to give native language literacy a chance for a few weeks and then let them decide which class to pursue.[11]

Curriculum materials

One problem in teaching literacy in a language other than English to language minority adults is the lack of appropriate curriculum materials. Beginning Spanish language materials are available from Latin America but may not be appropriate for many programs. According to Arango, many of these materials are designed for peasant groups and are not as relevant in an urban context. Some contain local-specific vocabulary which is not widely used or understood. Others are designed for political purposes such as "civic-military campaigns." These books can contain aggressive ideological content which may offend some learners.[12] Appropriate materials for other languages are equally difficult to find.

Many innovative programs have found that the extensive use of textbooks can inhibit an approach based on student experience. Not only are the themes in such materials predetermined but, many times, they have little to do with the current circumstances of the students.[13] Since it is difficult to find materials that are responsive to the diverse cultural and language background of the learners and allow for original contributions by students, many teachers prefer teacher-assembled kits or learner-generated materials rather than commercially published textbooks.[14]

Learner assessment, placement, and program evaluation

Adequate methods of testing adults in their native language are not widely available. Since few standardized tests have been designed, most programs have developed their own forms of assessing their students. Peggy Dean describes how assessment in adult Spanish literacy programs can be achieved using alternative assessments.

> Individual files were kept of examples of student work sheets, and math tests along with classroom observations. Progress, needs and performance levels were kept to aid teachers in best directing the students ... [T]his material was used to demonstrate to an individual that they had mastered the material and should reach out into more challenging areas.[15]

In many programs, the latter outcome — students learning that they "can" and "do" learn — is one of the most significant results for those adults who, for whatever reasons, can only stay with a program for a short time.

Program evaluations often rely on learner input. For example, in addition to using retention and class attendance as indicators of program success, Young and

Padilla measured the impact of their Spanish literacy program at the individual level by documenting what students accomplished once they had graduated. Some examples of these accomplishments include the publication of two poems in a book by one graduate and an award won by another student for helping to maintain bilingual programs in the school district.[16]

Program models for teaching literacy in the native language

When used in ESL literacy programs, mother tongue literacy classes essentially follow one of three models:

1. In the bilingual model, literacy in the native language is taught alongside English language development. This model has the advantage of allowing learners to acquire literacy and English simultaneously, an option that is attractive to many learners who want to learn both as soon as possible. The bilingual model requires a teacher who is both bilingual and knowledgeable about literacy development and second language acquisition.[17]

2. In the coordinate model, learners participate both in a native language literacy class and an ESL class. In this model, class time can either be split between a literacy and an ESL component, or the classes can be offered one after the other during the same teaching cycle. This model does not require bilingual teachers. However, it does require that one teacher share the language of the learners and understand literacy issues and that a second teacher be experienced in ESL teaching.

3. In the sequential model, non-literate learners start by taking a native language literacy class. Once they have acquired a certain threshold level of literacy, they transition to an ESL class. This model has the same staffing requirements as the coordinate model, but carries with it the danger that some learners become impatient about not learning English soon enough.

Practice: Using the native language in teaching

Native language literacy programs are offered in a variety of settings, including community-based organizations, adult schools, and community colleges. Given this diversity, it is not surprising to find different perspectives on literacy teaching. Some programs support the socio-cultural dimensions of literacy and put a strong emphasis on social issues and community concerns. Others stress the personal dimension and emphasize the needs of the individual learner over the concerns of the community.

Approaches

Many native language literacy programs, particularly those offering Spanish literacy, offer a variation on the participatory approach. (See "Participatory Approach" in chapter 2 and the curriculum modules by Peggy Dean, Maria Malagamba-Roddy, Deidre Freeman, and Celestino Medina in chapter 9.) Some programs use a participatory approach throughout the program, inviting learners to participate strongly in all aspects of the program (either individually or as part of a committee). Others use certain aspects of the Freirean pedagogy only in the classroom, where they set up problem posing activities or use key words to increase literacy skills. Other literacy approaches, such as "whole language" and "language experience," originally developed for native speakers of English, have also been used successfully in native language literacy programs (see chapter 2).

Using community themes as part of the participatory approach

A participatory approach to teaching literacy meets many of the requirements of sound literacy teaching.   It

- builds on oral language

- takes advantage of background knowledge

- focuses on themes that are of interest to adults

- helps learners examine the circumstances of their lives

- enables them to overcome barriers by focusing on action along with knowledge.

Participatory teaching often starts with "community themes" that have been identified through an ethnographic process of investigation in the community. To be effective, these themes should be "loaded" with the concerns of the group and represent issues of importance to the learners.[18] These issues are then captured in the form of "codes."[19] These codes can take many artistic forms: pictures, drawings, models, slides, songs, skits, or language experience stories. The code serves as a vehicle for dialogue within the group. In "A Freirean Approach to Peacemaking,"[20] Moriarty shows how such a dialogue can be developed through a progression of questions. In this example, the code is represented by a picture. Moriarty suggests the following sequence:

1. **Perception: looking at the picture**

   What do you see? What is happening in this picture? What can you "read between the lines"? How does that make you feel? How do you think the people in this picture feel?

2. **Personal experiences: listening to each other**

   Can you see yourself in this situation? Where are you in the picture? Can you see people you care about? Tell us what is going on in your situation.

3. **Group experience: choosing a focus for common work**

   Many people have mentioned _____ (propose a common theme). What do you already know about _____ from your own life? How are your experiences the same or different?

4. **Social analysis: building a broader picture of the problem**

   We are posing the problem of _____. In what ways does this picture reflect _____ in real-life? In what ways do you find this picture distorted or misleading? How would you change this picture to make it more realistic? If this is a problem for so many people, why does it continue? In what ways is it perpetuated or institutionalized? Who benefits from this problem continuing to exist? Where does this problem come from? What are its historical roots? What are its cultural, social, and economic causes? What are the consequences of this problem for you? For others that you know? What other problems arise from this _____? What information are we missing? What do we need to know to change this situation? How can we find that information? Whom might we work with?

5. **Action: finding a way to work on the problem together**

   If you had all the power in the world, what would you do to change this problem situation? If you didn't have to be afraid of anything, what would you like to do? What limitations do we have to take seriously at this time? What particular possibilities do we have at this time? What would be appropriate and feasible for this particular group to do about this problem? What is one concrete thing that we might try to help us take hold of this problem?[21]

6. Evaluation: being realistic about our expectations

What do we hope will happen as the result of our actions/work? What probably will not happen right now? How will we know if this particular action has been successful? When will we meet again to evaluate our work?

Using the native language in teaching ESL literacy

Native language literacy classes are not the only place where the mother tongue language of the learners is used. Many ESL literacy programs incorporate the native language into their ESL teaching. They have found that using the learners' language saves time and helps students to learn more quickly and understand more fully. These programs feel that when the native language is used at appropriate times, ideas can be discussed, and concepts do not have to be watered down because of lack of understanding in English.

Some ESL literacy programs disagree with this perspective. They hold the view that opportunities for using English need to be maximized in the classroom and any time given to the native language detracts from English literacy development. Many learners share this view, seeing use of the native language as a waste of time that could be used for practicing English.

To be sure, there are a number of challenges that must be faced if a bilingual or multilingual approach is used in ESL literacy classes: (1) some learners may resent use of the native language while others may welcome it; (2) the teacher may share a common language with some of the students, but not with others, which may cause feelings of jealousy; (3) it may be difficult to balance time spent on English versus time spent in the mother tongue; (4) well-meaning teachers may underestimate their students' ability to deal with issues in English.[22]

How do adult ESL literacy programs cope with these challenges? Many have found the following strategies helpful:

- Ask learners to report on language use and literacy practices outside of the classroom; when do they use English and for what purposes? When do they use the native language? When is it helpful to be bilingual? When is it important to know English?

- Explore language attitudes and ask both teachers and learners to share their perceptions of the advantages and disadvantages of bilingual classrooms; acknowledge concerns.

- Discuss the role that both English and the native language can play in helping learners to acquire English and develop literacy; provide examples.

- Provide opportunities to "try out" different ways of using language in the classroom (English only, native language only, concurrent translation, or bilingual support); let teachers and learners decide what they like.

- Discuss results or "share the experience."

- As a group, establish preliminary ground rules for using English and the native language in the classroom; try them out.

- Revisit the issue a few weeks later to see if attitudes have changed and if the group wants to modify its rules.

Benefits of a dual language approach to literacy

In many ways, the aims of ESL literacy classes and native language literacy classes are the same, to enable adults whose mother tongue is not English to live with confidence in an English speaking country, to make choices, to use their skills and to be themselves. To that end, using the mother tongue of the learners, whether in native language literacy classes or in ESL literacy classes, offers a number of advantages:

- Learners can discuss their needs, goals, and concerns without having to confront a language barrier; barriers to learning are more easily explored.

- Rich dialogue and authentic communication are made possible; ideas and opinions can more easily be expressed, examined, and challenged.

- Connections between culture, oral language, and literacy are strong, a key factor in literacy success.

- Social context, personal experiences, culture, and literacy form a natural connection; the identity of the learner is validated.

- Second language literacy is more easily achieved since a person must learn to read "just once;" writing processes are easier the second time around.

- Many of the cognitive and metacognitive skills attained through first language literacy can be transferred to second language learning.

- Shared control and joint decision making are more easily accomplished if language is not a barrier.

- Classroom participation is facilitated, increasing motivation and self confidence; connections between learners and teachers are enhanced through a shared language.

- Community members are more likely to participate in needs assessment activities if they can express their opinions in their native language.

- Staff are likely to come from the community of the learners, or similar communities, and can help establish stronger links with the community than otherwise possible.

Cases in point: literacy dimensions in native language literacy programs

Although most successful literacy programs try to combine literacy in the classroom with life beyond the school, they differ in how much attention they pay to the personal, social, cultural, and political issues that are part of learners' lives. To varying degrees, native language classes may try to respond to one or more of the following dimensions of literacy: personal, socio-cultural, or socio-political.

Personal dimension

When focusing on personal contexts, programs may ask learners to discuss when and where they use language in day-to-day communication and which language they use. Discussions may examine the personal goals of the learners regarding biliteracy and learners' perceptions of what literacy means to them. Activities are designed to build the basic literacy skills needed for the achievement of individual goals. Some programs may emphasize both an individual and an interpersonal dimension by giving learners the opportunity to tell stories and share common experiences (family life, birthdays, holidays) with others in the group.

◆ *Case in point*

In a literacy program in Illinois, the teacher sometimes links literacy with familiar Spanish song lyrics, such as the popular Mexican song "La Bamba." (See *Breaking the Literacy Barrier with a Song* in chapter 9.) Learners listen to the song, discuss what the song means, and then complete various literacy activities based on the key words they have identified in the lyrics. Literacy activities may include identifying letters and syllables, writing down selected words and phrases, or doing cloze exercises. In addition, learners may write a language experience story that talks about the ideas that the song brings to mind.

Socio-cultural dimension

In programs that focus on the socio-cultural dimensions of literacy, learners examine letters, stories, poems, or newspapers from different cultures and discuss how the format and language of these materials differs. They then go on to write a story in a style they like. Learners may discuss the differences and similarities in schools between the home culture and mainstream U.S. culture or talk about the difficulties of raising children in the U.S. They then develop grids and charts that show these differences.

Community issues may be explored as part of this dimension as well. The class may interview family and neighbors in order to investigate the history of various languages in the community or look at the role that immigrants have played in the survival and economic development of the neighborhood. To illustrate these histories, learners may draw timelines and make photo-collages.

In workplace programs, the group may explore differences in culturally determined notions, such as being on time or responding to authority, and read a dialogue or a case study that shows cross-cultural misunderstanding.

◆ *Case in point*

The Lao Family Community of Minnesota tries to link the home culture of the Hmong it serves with adaptation to the mainstream community. In the family literacy component, both Hmong and English are used in the beginning classes in an effort to strengthen the role of the Hmong parents and increase their understanding of the local school system. The program uses both materials from Hmong culture (folk tales) and from the schools that the children attend (notes, permission slips, report cards) to build literacy in the two languages. Translation is frequently used to move from Hmong to English and vice versa.

One of the goals of the program is to build background knowledge in U.S. laws and conventions in a way that is culturally congruent with Hmong values and traditions. To that end, speakers from community agencies, such as public health and law enforcement, work together with the staff of Lao Family to develop presentations dealing with sensitive subjects. Topics have included child immunizations (many Hmong fear inoculations will hurt their children), state marriage laws (traditionally Hmong girls have married very young), and hunting laws (the Hmong are not used to needing a license to hunt). Topics are evaluated in an annual questionnaire that asks teachers to indicate which subjects interested their students most, which they liked the least, and in which areas their students need more information.

Socio-political dimension

Programs that focus on the socio-political dimensions of literacy often emphasize "critical literacy" as one of their goals. In these programs, learners sometimes discuss issues, such as discrimination and prejudice, or social problems, such as crime, and discuss how communities can address these issues. Sometimes gender issues, such as domestic violence and sexual harassment, are discussed. At other times, health issues may be a concern (job related stress for example). In some union programs, learners discuss employment opportunities in the community and the changes that are necessary so that immigrant workers can get better paying jobs.

The relationship between literacy and class may also be explored. Learners may examine the roles played by those who are literate (or fully English proficient) and compare them to the roles played by individuals who are labeled "illiterate" or "limited English proficient." Some programs discuss the changes in power that occur as one member in the family becomes biliterate and bilingual and others do not. Learners may write about their own experiences or read about the lives of others who have faced similar challenges. Some programs may discuss language rights issues, including the right to an interpreter in court or the right to speak English during breaks at work.

◆ *Case in point*

El Barrio Popular Education Program, a community-based organization in the East Harlem Section of New York, involves its students in research in the community where they discover and document issues that affect their lives. For example, when learners became interested in housing issues, they counted the number of abandoned and occupied buildings in their neighborhood and interviewed community leaders about the housing crisis. The learners, most of whom are women with children in public schools, then developed graphs and charts showing a pattern of neglect. As a group, they then discussed strategies for influencing housing policies. (See *Co-constructing the Foundations, A Bilingual Curriculum on Housing* by Celestino Cotto Medina and Deidre Freeman in Chapter 9.)

In one class, the women in the program read about a sexual harassment incident based on a simple story of a former student who had been "bothered" by a supervisor on her first day at work. In working with the story, they followed a process that is often used in participatory programs. They

- listened to the teacher read the story

- discussed what happened and tried to "get the facts straight"

- read the story as a group as well as individually

- listed the options that were open to the woman who had been harassed (rejecting the teacher's suggestion as naive)

- wrote down their comments or told their own story

- shared their writings with others.

Native language literacy practice: summary

Teaching literacy in the native language is a successful approach that is culturally responsive and linguistically appropriate for learners who are non-literate. The native language programs that we visited have learned how to capitalize on the social, cultural, and linguistic background of their students, many of whom had not previously been successful in ESL classes. These programs in particular have been able to provide a classroom atmosphere that is both reassuring and stimulating, with teachers who validate what learners know and challenge them to grow further. As do all good schools, these programs offer learners ongoing opportunities to interact with each other, to experiment with literacy, and to extend their own cultural knowledge and experience.

The next section presents promising practices in using the learners' native language to enhance ESL literacy teaching.

Promising practices

Teaching and learning in two languages do not take place only in native language literacy classes. Many ESL classrooms use the language of the learners as well. The following practices illustrate how some programs use the learners' languages to facilitate comprehension, strengthen communication, and build cross-cultural and intergenerational understanding.

◘ Learners compare languages

Using what learners know about their mother tongue can be an effective tool for understanding English. Some programs have learners compare the cultural values that underlie different proverbs ("the quacking duck gets shot" versus "the squeaky wheel gets the grease"), while others may compare grammar structures ("English spoken here" versus "se habla español"). Others use cognates or words that sound similar (e.g., construir = to construct) to build a strong vocabulary base.

◘ Staff learn another language

Many ESL programs that teach only English literacy, nevertheless, try to help staff develop an understanding of what it is like to struggle with literacy in a language one does not fully understand. Many tutorial programs, for example, use a made-up or a foreign language to give their volunteer staff a sense of the challenges their students face in trying to interpret print in English. Other programs provide incentives for teachers to study the language of the learners. One program in Philadelphia uses tutors from the University who study Khmer (Cambodian) and pairs them with Cambodian learners who need English literacy. By exchanging English and Khmer lessons, learners gain a chance to be both students and teachers, thus leveling traditional power relationships between those who teach and those who learn.

◘ The community supports the program

Programs that, for whatever reason, cannot offer a native language literacy course often involve members from the learners' community in various aspects of program planning, implementation, and evaluation. Community members who have backgrounds similar to those of the students can understand the anxiety of the learners and give confidence to those who have lost confidence in their ability to acquire literacy as adults. Used as counselors or teachers, they can become confidants for students who feel the need to share family and other problems. Community members who are part of an advisory board can provide valuable insights into economic, cultural, and political issues that affect literacy education. Those who come to class to give presentations can serve as role models and interpreters for the mainstream culture. In many instances, interactions with professionals from the community provide learners with the opportunity to discuss literacy issues at a deeper level and gain access to information about community services.

Many times people who share the same ethnic or linguistic background of the learners may help ESL teachers in and out of the classroom as translators, tutors of individuals and small groups, and sources of cultural information that teachers can incorporate into literacy lessons.[23] In other cases, bilingual assistants help teachers develop cases studies, generate themes for problem posing, or prepare photos and slides that depict life in the community.

◘ Bilingual communication solves classroom problems

Bilingual teachers in ESL literacy classes often use the native language of the learners to "set the stage" or help learners understand difficult concepts. Some may use only a few key words to introduce a topic, while others preview and review the content of the lesson to maximize comprehension. In some cases, bilingual teachers use the native language to explain linguistic or cultural differences and, in others, to clarify concepts and give instructions.

◘ Literacy maintains cultural legacies

In many communities, the native language is the medium through which cultural traditions are passed. The language gives the individual the identity which ties her to the group and sets her apart from other groups. Many programs feel that it is important to strengthen that identity by encouraging cultural transmission activities, such as documenting life stories from the native culture or writing letters to family members left behind.[24] Some programs ask learners to develop their autobiographies over the course of the class and then publish these accounts at the end of each cycle. The books are shared with family and friends.

Basic principles

Educationally sound native language literacy programs follow some of the same principles as good ESL literacy programs. They provide a meaningful context for literacy development, base reading and writing activities on the interests and experiences of the learners, link what happens in the classroom to the lives of the learners outside of school, and provide opportunities for learners to participate in decision making.

Reflections: Understanding contexts for biliteracy

Successful literacy teaching is based on an awareness of the contexts in which learners use literacy in English and the mother tongue. The following questions can help you, the teacher, find out more about these contexts. They can also form the basis for subsequent "literacy awareness" activities to be used by both learners and staff.

1.   Where do your students use English and where do they use the mother tongue? Which language is dominant in a particular context and why?

    •   home/family

    •   immediate neighborhood/larger community/society

    •   your class/school-related

    •   work/employment-related.

2.   What kind of reading and writing do learners do in various contexts? What materials and texts do they use? Which texts include "quantitative literacy" (math)? Which include "graphic literacy" (charts, etc.)? Which could be classified as "prose literacy" and which as "document literacy"?

    •   bills and pay stubs

    •   signs, labels, prices, prescriptions, notices, bumper stickers, etc.

- letters, postcards, personal notes, and informal notes from teachers

- official correspondence (permission slips or releases) and church announcements

- lists (to do lists, grocery lists)

- books, stories (including photo novellas), newspapers, and magazines

- schedules (bus, work, and children's school schedules)

- outlines (TV listings, menus, store directories)

- forms

- directions (repair manuals, recipes).

3. Where do your students feel the strongest? Where would they like support? What intrigues them and what do they care about the most? Beyond functional tasks, what kind of reading and writing would your students like to do?

4. What social networks do your students have? With whom do they associate with and what languages do they use?

5. How do learners manage to "negotiate print" (i.e., figure out what an official document says or get information and ideas on paper)? What practices work well for them? If they don't understand something, do they

- guess at the meaning?

- avoid or ignore the difficult part?

- use family, friends, or co-workers to interpret?

- use assistance provided by community agencies?

- pay professionals to read or write (transcribe) for them?

6. What issues concern your students (in their personal life, in the community, in society, and world-wide)? What would they like to hear about, read about, and write about? What topics are they tired of?

7. What activities could you develop to find out more about your students' "literacy lives?" How can you help your students develop an awareness of the role that language and literacy plays in their own lives?

8. How would you and your colleagues answer these questions about yourselves?

Endnotes

1. As Hornberger points out, in many cases, both prevalent language policies and community contexts mitigate against the development of full biliteracy and the maintenance of the native language (Hornberger, 1992).

2. See Penfield, 1986, p. 50 citing the work of Robson & Burtoff.

3. See Swain, et al., 1989.

4. See Ovando & Collier, 1985.

5. See Cummins, 1979.

6. See McGroarty, 1988.

7. See Ogbu, 1990; Skutnabb-Kangas & Cummins, 1988; Hornberger, 1989; Reder, 1987.

8. See Hornberger, 1989.

9. See Macias, 1990; Ruiz, 1988; Leibowitz, 1969.

10. For a more extensive discussion of these issues, see Macias, 1990; Macias, in press; and Wiley, 1991.

11. These examples are based in part on discussions with two native language literacy programs, El Barrio Popular Education Program in New York and the Haitian Multi-Service Center in Dorchester, Massachusetts. See site reports in Guth & Wrigley, 1992 for details.

12. See Arango, 1989.

13. See Arango, 1989.

14. See also approaches chapter, particularly the materials checklist.

15. See Dean, 1989, p. 8.

16. See Young & Padilla, 1990.

17. See Rivera, 1990.

18. P. Moriarty, personal communication, May 14, 1992. See also Moriarty, 1989.

19. See also Wallerstein, 1983 and Auerbach, 1990a.

20. See Moriarty, 1989. See also Moriarty, 1980; Wallerstein, 1983; and Wallerstein, 1987.

21. Moriarty also suggests several criteria to be used in choosing a particular course of action. These include: We can do it, we can do it together, we can evaluate our work next time we meet, we will learn something, we will have an impact, we will coordinate with similar efforts, and we are prepared to deal with the consequences of our actions.

22. See also Hopkins, 1989.

23. See Rivera, 1990.

24. We first heard Gail Weinstein-Shr use the concept of literacy as cultural legacy. The examples presented here also include ideas gleaned from Skutnabb-Kangas and Klaudia Rivera.

References

Arango, A. (1989). Cartillas de alfabetización. *El Español en Marcha, 2*(2), 2-4.

Auerbach, E. R. (1990). *Making meaning, making change: A guide to participatory curriculum development for adult ESL and family literacy.* Boston: University of Massachusetts [in press (1992), Regents Prentice Hall/Center for Applied Linguistics].

Cummins, J. (1979). Linguistics interdependence and the educational development of bilingual children. *Bilingual education paper series, 3*(2), Los Angeles: California State University, Evaluation, Dissemination and Assessment Center.

Dean, M. (1989). *Scope and sequence key competencies.* Des Plaines, IL: Northwest Educational Cooperative.

Guth, G. J. A., & Wrigley, H. S. (1992). *Adult ESL literacy: Programs and practices.* San Mateo, CA: Aguirre International. (Available from the U.S. Department of Education, Clearinghouse on Adult Education and Literacy).

Hopkins, S. M. (1989). Use of mother tongue in the teaching of English as a second language. *Language Issues, 2*(2), 18-24.

Hornberger, N. H. (1989). Continua of Biliteracy. *Review of Educational Research, 59*(3), 271-297.

Hornberger, N. H. (1992). Biliteracy contexts, continua, and contrasts: Policy and curriculum for Cambodian and Puerto Rican students in Philadelphia. *Education and Urban Society, 24*(2), 196-211.

Leibowitz, A. H. (1969). English literacy: Legal sanction for discrimination. *Notre Dame Lawyer, 45*(7), 8-67.

Macias, R. (1990). [Response to "Teacher supply and demand"]. In C. Simich-Dudgeon (Ed.), *Proceedings of the first research symposium on limited English proficient students' issues* (pp. 406-412). Washington, DC: U.S. Department of Education, Office of Bilingual Education and Minority Languages Affairs.

Macias, R. F. (in press). Inheriting sins while seeking absolution: English literacy, biliteracy, language diversity and national statistical data sets. In D. Spener (Ed.), *Adult biliteracy in the U.S.* Englewood Cliffs, NJ: Prentice-Hall Regents.

McGroarty, M. (1988). Second language acquisition theory related to language minority adults: Cummins, Krashen and Schumann. In S. L. McKay & S. C. Wong (Eds.), *Language diversity: Problem or resource?* (pp. 295-337). New York: Newbury House.

Moriarty, P. (1980). By teaching we can learn: Freire process for teachers. *California Journal of Teacher Education, 7*(1).

Moriarty, P. (1989). A Freirean approach to peacemaking. *Convergence, 22*(1).

Obgu, J. U. (1990). Minority status and literacy in comparative perspective. *Daedalus, 119*(2), 141-168.

Ovando, C., & Collier, V. (1985). *Bilingual and ESL classrooms.* New York: McGraw-Hill.

Penfield, J. (1986). ESL Literacy and the new refugees: Priorities and considerations. *Adult Literacy and Basic Education, 10*(1), 47-57.

Ramirez, J. D., Yuen, S. D., Ramey, D. R., Pasta, D. J., & Billings, D. K. (1991, February). *Final report: Longitudinal study of structured English immersion strategy, early-exit and late-exit transitional bilingual education program for language-minority children. Executive summary.* San Mateo, CA: Aguirre International.

Reder, S. M. (1987). Comparative aspects of functional literacy development: Three ethnic American communities. In D. A. Wagner (Ed.), *The future of literacy in a changing world* (pp. 250-270). New York: Pergamon Press.

Rivera, K. M. (1990). *Developing native language literacy in language minority adult learners. ERIC Digest.* Washington, DC: Center for Applied Linguistics, National Clearinghouse on Literacy Education.

Ruiz, R. (1988). Orientations in language planning. In S. L. McKay & S. C. Wong (Eds.), *Language diversity: Problem or resource?* (pp. 3-25). New York: Newbury House.

Skutnabb-Kangas, T., & Cummins, J. (1988). Concluding remarks: Language for empowerment. In T. Skutnabb-Kangas, & J. Cummins (Eds.), *Minority education: From shame to struggle* (pp. 391-395). Clevedon, England: Multilingual Matters.

Spener, D. (1990). *Setting an agenda for study in home-based ESL classes with native speakers of Spanish.* Unpublished manuscript.

Swain, M., Lapkin, S., Norman, R., & Hart, D. (1989, March). *The role of mother tongue literacy in third language learning.* Paper presented at the Convention of the American Educational Research Association, San Francisco.

Wallerstein, N. (1983). The teaching approach of Paulo Freire. In J. W. Oller, & P. A. Richard-Amato (Eds.), *Methods that work: A smorgasbord of ideas for language teachers* (pp. 190-213). Rowley, MA: Newbury House.

Wallerstein, N. (1987). Problem-posing education: Freire's method for transformation. In I. Shor (Ed.), *Freire for the classroom: A sourcebook for liberatory teaching* (pp. 33-44). Portsmouth, NH: Boynton/Cook/Heinemann.

Wiley, T. (1991). *National measures of literacy: What we need to consider. ERIC Digest.* Washington, DC: Center for Applied Linguistics, National Clearinghouse on Literacy Education.

Young, E., & Padilla, M. (1990). Mujeres Unidas en Acción: A popular education process. *Harvard Educational Review, 60*(1).

Chapter 6

Learner Assessment

You can't send that to Springfield.

> — Massachusetts funder responding to a teacher who says she can feel that her students are making progress.[1]

WYTIWYG: What you test is what you get[2]

Learner assessment and program evaluation are two of the most troublesome issues in English as a second language (ESL) literacy. On the one hand, there are demands for tests that are valid and reliable and that can be used for program comparison. On the other hand, there are strong calls to keep assessment program-based and learner-centered. Disillusioned with many of the standardized tests, yet concerned about ongoing demands for accountability, literacy educators are searching for assessments that are fair to learners, informative to teachers, acceptable to funders, and comprehensible to those outside of the program. Implementing or developing sound assessments for ESL literacy has become a big challenge — a task made even more difficult because a common framework for assessing the various dimensions of ESL literacy does not yet exist.

This chapter compares standardized and program-based assessments and provides strategies for developing an assessment framework. It is divided into three sections: "Background: Options in Assessment," "Practice: Linking Assessment and Approach," and "Reflections: Selecting Alternative Assessments." The "Background" section discusses the advantages and disadvantages of different approaches to literacy assessment. The "Practice" section contains three parts: (1) cases in point that illustrate how adult ESL literacy programs are assessing learners, (2) promising practices in alternative assessment, and (3) five steps for developing an assessment framework. The "Reflections" section presents an assessment selection chart and lists questions to ask to make sure that a particular assessment meets the needs of the program.

Background: Options in assessment

Learner assessment is complex because it cannot be discussed apart from other program issues. Since curriculum and assessment are linked, a program's choice and implementation of assessments reflect its view of language, literacy, and learning, whether these ideas are consciously articulated or not.[3] Which assessments are chosen and how the assessment process is carried out not only illustrates what "counts as success" but also reveals something about the roles that learners and teachers play in the program. In essence, assessment decisions are based on pedagogical (and in some cases political) concerns that reflect the philosophies, theories, and approaches that a program supports. If assessment is to be an effective part of an ESL literacy program, it must fit into the overall framework the program has chosen for itself. (See the literacy framework in chapter 2.)

Approaches to literacy assessment

Given the many perspectives on the roles, functions, and uses of literacy, it is not surprising that approaches to literacy assessment vary widely. Some programs focus on evaluating overall communicative competence through integrated tests, while others focus on one or more particular areas, such as reading, writing, speaking, and listening.

While most literacy assessments focus on knowledge and performance, as measured by choosing the right answer on multiple choice tests, there now is increasing support for assessments that try to capture the reading and writing process through interviews, surveys of literacy behaviors and practices, and the use of portfolios.

A major summary of evaluation in adult literacy[4] divides assessment into four areas:

- standardized testing, which may be either norm referenced (students are compared to each other, most often across programs) or criterion referenced (student achievement is compared to an externally derived standard)

- materials-based assessment, in which assessment is based on a particular set of teaching materials, often commercially packaged and sold

- competency-based assessment, in which learner performance is compared to pre-established competencies that need to be achieved

- participatory assessment, in which learners play a significant role in deciding both the content and process of assessment.

For program purposes, we can combine these four assessments areas into two broad categories:

- general assessments, such as standardized tests, that are designed to measure achievement, knowledge, and skills of large groups of students across programs and are said to have content validity

- program-based assessments, that reflect the educational approach and literacy curriculum of a particular program and thus have both content validity and curriculum validity.

In other words, while some tests may be appropriate because they do indeed measure what they say they measure and thus have content validity, other assessments may be even more appropriate because they also measure what the program teaches and thus have curriculum validity.

Standardized testing

When it comes to systematic assessment across programs in the general assessments category, standardized tests dominate adult education. This is true for second language learning, adult literacy, and ESL literacy. One reason for the popularity of standardized assessments may lie in the history of testing in the United States, which has emphasized the need for program accountability above the need for quality teaching.[5]

Federal and state requirements

Contrary to popular belief, the U.S. Department of Education does not select or approve standardized tests for states to use in their adult education programs. Nor does the federal government demand that all students be tested. Adult education programs that receive federal funding are merely required by law to provide standardized test data as one indicator of program effectiveness, and a state need not have standardized test data for every student. The states, themselves, do indeed have the flexibility to determine which criteria to use in measuring effectiveness within the federal framework for reviews and evaluations.[6]

The responses from the field to these requirements vary. On the one hand, there are states that express serious concerns about any requirement for standardized testing, suggesting that these demands be dropped or made optional. On the other hand, there are states that would like to see the federal government indicate which tests should be used for assessment purposes and thus lighten the states' burden of decision making.

Types of standardized tests used in literacy programs

Most larger adult literacy programs use some form of commercially available standardized test to report student data to their funding source. The most common tests are group-administered adult basic skills tests such as the *Tests of Adult Basic Education* (TABE), the *Adult Basic Learning Examination* (ABLE), or selected portions of the *Comprehensive Adult Student Assessment System* (CASAS).

While some literacy programs use the TABE or the ABLE for both their native English speakers and their second language learners, others use tests specifically designed for ESL students. These include the *Basic English Skills Test* (BEST), which includes an oral interview section, and the Basic Inventory of Natural Language (BINL), which provides for a grammatical analysis of spoken language samples. Another individually administered test is the *Reading Evaluation Adult Diagnosis* (READ), used by the Literacy Volunteers of America.[7]

Advantages of standardized tests

Standardized tests are popular because they offer certain advantages: (1) their construct validity and scoring reliability have been tested; (2) they are cost-effective and don't require a great deal of training to administer; (3) funding sources accept them as part of the documentation of program accountability; (4) they allow for comparisons of learner progress across programs; and (5) they give learners a sense of where they stand compared to students in other programs.[8]

Disadvantages of standardized tests

In spite of these apparent advantages, standardized tests have a number of disadvantages. According to many literacy educators, standardized tests

- fail to distinguish between language, literacy, and culture. In other words, they don't tell us whether a learner has trouble with an item because (1) he or she is unfamiliar with the cultural notion underlying the task, (2) lacks the requisite knowledge of English vocabulary or sentence structure, or (3) does not have enough experience with reading and writing to complete the task

- reduce the complexity of language and literacy learning to a set of skills

- don't reflect what has been taught or capture all the learning that has taken place

- don't capture changes in language use and literacy practices beyond the classroom and don't provide data on the socio-linguistic and affective dimensions of language and literacy

- don't discriminate well at the lower end of literacy achievement, failing to capture experience with environmental print or provide information on the different levels of "initial literacy," such as being able to write the names of one's children but not those of strangers

- focus on pencil and paper tasks, the very things that literacy students have trouble with

- don't provide opportunities for literacy students to show what they can do in "real-life"

- fail to show how learners deal with literacy in the mother tongue, treating English literacy as "the only literacy that counts"[9]

- may be used for "gatekeeping purposes" (a particular danger in workplace literacy programs) without clear evidence that the test results justify the decisions made.

Standardized tests and ESL literacy students

While these shortcomings hold true for any standardized language or literacy test, there are additional concerns if these instruments are used to assess ESL literacy students.

ESL literacy students may not be familiar with the cultural conventions underlying these tests. For example, one ESL test asks students to read a label on a piece of pre-packaged meat, listing weight, price per pound, and total price. Students who are not used to buying their meat pre-packaged may have difficulty understanding the underlying concept, even though they might be able to read the individual words.[10] Standardized tests, in an effort to be "fair" to all, either discount the unique background knowledge that learners bring to school or assume that cultural conventions are shared across countries.

Standardized tests often fail to distinguish between language problems, in which the learner is unfamiliar with the language or concepts of the test item, and literacy problems, in which the learner lacks the requisite reading and writing skills but could easily respond to similar items presented as part of a conversation.

Standardized tests treat language and literacy as isolated from the social context of the learner. Students are assessed individually and no help may be given or received. ESL literacy students, as a rule, work together to help each other solve problems that require English or reading and writing and often develop strong coping skills and social networks that allow them to deal with problems that require literacy. By disallowing access to resources, peer assistance, or group work are "cheating," standardized tests fail to measure the very strengths that literacy students bring to class.[11]

Most standardized tests fail to take into account the wide range of literacy practices in which learners engage in their mother tongues. By disregarding the biliteracy aspect of ESL literacy, they give the impression that literacy in English is the only literacy that counts and deprive programs of valuable information about learners' past experiences with literacy.[12]

We will now turn to a discussion of the program-based alternative assessment movement and examine program efforts to address these issues.

Program-based and other alternative assessments

In an effort to make assessment more responsive to the concerns of learners and teachers, many programs are developing alternatives to standardized tests. While some of these tests are commercially available, others are program-based or "home grown."

Commercially available tests used in adult ESL literacy programs include the following:

- the *Henderson/Moriarty ESL Placement Test*, designed to assess literacy and oral skills of both literate and non-literate adults

- the *English Language Skills Assessment* (ELSA, now available as CELSA), a test that measures reading comprehension and grammatical proficiency

- the *California Adult Learner Progress Evaluation Process* (CALPEP), a reading and writing inventory that seeks to identify reading and writing habits, learner goals with respect to literacy, and estimated proficiency levels in reading and writing

- the *English as a Second Language Oral Assessment* (ESLOA), a test designed to help tutors measure a learner's ability to speak and understand English.

Examples of commonly used program-based assessments include the following:

- checklists that provide a record of the skills and competencies a learner has attained

- true/false or multiple choice tests that allow programs to assess the knowledge that students have gained or the skills that they have developed while in the program

- anecdotal evidence that serves as examples of success; such evidence is often culled from discussions with other adults who interact with the literacy learners (e.g., employers or supervisors in workplace programs, children's teachers in family literacy programs, or counselors in general programs)

- daily or weekly charts that list learner accomplishments or document significant literacy events that have taken place (e.g., a supervisor notices that an immigrant worker has started to speak up in meetings).

Integrated assessments that provide evidence of the overall proficiency of a second language learner are also common. In this category, we find holistic writing assessments, as well as cloze tests and dictations. However, most of the programs we studied had not yet fully incorporated these program-based assessments into an overall framework.

Advantages of program-based assessments

Many ESL literacy programs use a combination of assessments, including standardized and other commercially available tests, for placement and program-based assessments to measure learner progress. Many, if not most, innovative programs see great promise in alternative assessments that are program-based. In the eyes of many ESL literacy educators, program-based assessments offer the following advantages. Program-based assessments

- reflect the local curriculum and provide information that is helpful to the program

- are developed by the individual program, sometimes with the help of evaluators or other researchers, and thus are responsive to the program context

- focus on learning processes, not just outcomes, allowing for trial and error instead of giving learners just one chance to answer each question; they do not insist on a "cold start" response[13]

- actively involve learners by giving them the opportunity to (1) discuss their goals and interests in literacy, (2) choose the kind of reading and writing they want to be evaluated on, and (3) talk about what they have learned. In other words, they are part of a process in which assessment is done with adults, not to them.

Most importantly, perhaps, alternative assessments go beyond conventional skills-based notions of language and literacy. When carried out as part of an initial intake process and repeated at regular intervals during the teaching cycle, they can provide information that can be used for curriculum development.

Increasingly, alternative assessments also focus on non-linguistic factors, such as learners' changing perceptions of what it means to be literate, how to help one's children to enjoy literacy, increased confidence in one's ability to deal with tasks that require literacy, and a stronger voice in presenting one's own ideas.

What should be assessed?

The difficult decision about what should be assessed, along with a determination of how to handle mandated tests, remains with the individual program. For each program, determining which aspects of language and literacy should be assessed depends on which elements of English and literacy the program wants to emphasize. But after decisions about philosophy, curriculum, and teaching have been made, the key question that will drive the assessment remains "what counts as success?"[14] Given the complexity of language and literacy development, there are a number of indicators for literacy success that programs might focus on. These include two categories of evidence: progress related to language and literacy development and evidence of program success in non-linguistic domains.

Evidence of success in language and literacy development include the following:

- increases in English proficiency, including gains in strategic, socio-linguistic, grammatical, and rhetorical competence

- progress in reading, including increased use of reading and writing strategies; systematic use of verbal and non-verbal clues to access print, predict meaning, and confirm predictions; broader range of reading materials selected and read; and more sustained reading

- progress in literacy development, including greater ability to express thoughts, ideas, and feelings in print; developing a sense of voice; and demonstrating style and creativity

- greater ability to use literacy in efforts to link personal experience with the experience of others and with writings from the larger community, society, and the world

- greater approximation to standard English writing conventions; increased ability to self-edit

- greater sense of "critical literacy," using language to connect personal and collective experience and to examine the circumstances of one's life

- a broader range of literacy practices in the classroom, at home, in the community, and at work

- a broader view of the role that literacy can play in one's life and in the life of the community.

Evidence of success in non-linguistic domains include the following:

- increased participation in a language and literacy program

- greater confidence in one's ability to handle challenges, a feeling of greater independence, and pride in one's accomplishments

- increased opportunities for job placement or advancement, admission to vocational or training programs, and transition to mainstream ESL or academic classes

- greater involvement in community activities or in school activities, such as plays or parent-teacher conferences

- significant gains in the affective domain, including greater confidence in one's ability to learn and to use literacy as a means of accessing information and services.

Who cares about assessment results?

There is now a growing recognition that both the format and content of assessment needs to be linked to the information needs of the audience, be they learners, teachers, program administrators, or funders. Assessments should be responsive to the needs of

- students who want to know how they are progressing or where they stand vis-a-vis other students in the program

- teachers who are interested in the results of their teaching and want to explore the relationship between instructional methods and learner achievement

- program staff who need to make decisions about placement, course offerings, and curriculum

- funders who may require evidence that their money has not been wasted and request information that allows them to compare learner achievement across programs

- stakeholders from the learner's community, family, or workplace who want to know what impact the literacy program is having on areas beyond the school.

It would be very difficult for any one assessment to fulfill all of these functions and satisfy all of these needs, an insight that has led to a call for multiple assessments, or assessment clusters, made up of components that focus on different aspects of learner proficiency, progress, and performance.[15] The difficulty of finding or developing appropriate assessments is further complicated by the various functions that assessments serve and the many uses they fulfill.

Assessment at different stages of a program

Assessments have multiple functions and multiple uses. They (1) provide information on the context in which literacy occurs (workplace, family, school, community); (2) serve as initial assessments of the strengths that learners bring to the program and of the challenges they face; (3) indicate the levels of proficiency learners have attained in language and literacy; (4) help document the needs, goals, and interests of the learners; (5) document the progress learners are making and the changes that occur in their lives; and (6) provide evidence of program success and show where a learner may need additional development or support.

Different forms of assessments serve different functions, and different types of assessments are used at various stages of a program. These types include community needs assessments, intake assessments, initial assessments, progress assessments, and performance reviews.

Community needs assessments

Community needs assessments are designed to identify the needs and goals of potential participants. Information may include demographic data, and information on employment patterns in the community, and the availability of childcare or transportation services. Needs assessment information is often used to decide on scheduling, class sites, and the kinds of ancillary services will be provided. At the worksite, the needs assessment often takes the form of a "situational analysis," which describes the context in which the workplace literacy program takes place.

Intake assessments

Intake assessments are designed to elicit information regarding learners' needs, goals, and prior educational backgrounds, including previous experience with both schooling and literacy, whether in English or in the mother tongue. Intake increasingly includes information on how, where, and why learners are using English and literacy in their daily lives, such as at home, in the community, at work, or in their interactions with the school system. Some intake assessments also try to probe the perceptions of literacy that learners bring to class and the expectations that learners bring to the program.

Initial assessments

Initial assessments are designed to gauge how proficient a learner is in English and may also measure what levels of biliteracy he or she possesses. Used as diagnostic tests for placement, for development of a learning plan, or as a baseline against which progress can be measured, initial assessments now frequently include learner self-assessment, and, in some cases, peer assessment.

Progress assessments

Progress assessments are designed to show changes in the ways students are interpreting print and using literacy. While these assessments have traditionally been dependent on how well students can do pencil and paper tests, we now increasingly find assessments that look beyond the test and seek information on how learners use literacy to explore and express ideas, solve problems, or effect changes in their lives. Progress assessments are often used in formative evaluations designed to provide feedback to learners and teachers and improve program services and literacy classes.

Performance reviews

Performance reviews or summative evaluations are carried out during the end of a project and include information on learner assessment. To meet the needs of the outside evaluator, the monitoring agency, or the funders, summative evaluations may need to contain assessment data that has been aggregated across components, summarized, and made comprehensible to an audience external to the program.

Need for greater teacher involvement

In most ESL literacy programs classroom teachers are somewhat removed from the assessment process although, they may be called upon to administer the test.[16] There is now a growing recognition in the field that teachers' opinions count, since their insights into the students, their own teaching, and the effectiveness of the program overall cannot be obtained by any other means.[17] As Rigg points out,

Just as only the adult students can see from the student's perspective, only the teachers have their perspective. Only the teacher has repeated observations of both students and students' academic efforts; usually only the teacher has collected samples of work over time, created under varying circumstances.[18]

In some programs, the line between teaching and testing is being blurred. We now see a trend toward continuous monitoring and ongoing progress evaluation through a process that not only integrates assessment into classroom teaching but involves students along with teachers in making judgments about the progress that is being made. Unlike the conventional model in which administrators take charge of needs assessment, initial diagnostic tests, and placements, alternative models seek teacher input on all phases of the assessment process.

Challenges for the field

Given both the prevalence and shortcomings of current standardized tests, the field faces a formidable challenge. To do the job that assessments are meant to do, programs need support in selecting or developing literacy assessments that

- respond to the information needs of different audiences

- reflect the program focus and answer the questions that learners and teachers have regarding the success of the program

- inform teaching, capture the richness of literacy learning, and provide evidence of learner progress and program success

- allow for learner participation and collaboration among staff

- are valid and reliable

Practice: Linking assessment and approach

How do programs negotiate between taking advantage of standardized tests that are readily available and easy to use and developing their own assessments through a process that is time-consuming and often cumbersome? Many ESL programs seek to reach a compromise, choosing the best of the available assessments (or using whatever standardized test is mandated) and supplementing these tests with home grown assessments.

Trying to address concerns about validity and reliability, a number of programs are involved in systematic efforts to define those aspects of literacy they find important and to train teachers in the use of the relevant assessment tools.

As mentioned before, the content and process of assessment will depend on a program's philosophy, its focus, and its approach to language and literacy. The following cases in point illustrate how six quite different programs are developing assessment frameworks that are appropriate to their context.

Matching assessment to learner needs

The following case in point illustrates how one adult ESL literacy program in Rhode Island developed an alternative framework for documenting learner progress.

◆ *Case in point: the learner evaluation grid*

Keenly aware of the need to measure student progress and feeling the pressure toward accountability, the staff of the literacy/ESL program at the International Institute of Rhode Island developed a process for documenting the changes that occurred as learners participated in the program. As a starting point, the program examined existing tests and found them to be either too difficult or too simplistic for their students. They also explored how other countries, particularly England, grappled with thorny assessment issues.

Moving back and forth between evaluation theory and their own classroom practice, they followed an action research model that involved four phases: planning, action, observation, and reflection. Through a process that was cyclical and recursive, they documented the issues they thought about, the interactions they witnessed, the activities they implemented, and the results they observed.

As they analyzed their observations, the categories that emerged were represented in the form of a grid — refined over a couple of years with input from practitioners and researchers. The final grid (next page) serves as an alternative assessment framework. The grid shows the progress of one student who had come to the Institute, not ready to read and write, but very much concerned about alphabet issues. After he had left the Institute and worked with a tutor for awhile, the student returned ready for literacy.[19]

Evaluation grid

	Intake Interview Feb. 29/88	6 Month Evaluation	1 Year Evaluation	Recommendation re ongoing placement Oct 2/89
Oral Fluency	can make himself understood; been in country since 1966	absent from Jul. - Nov. Little change		Called in August. Was out of country from Feb. 89 - June 89
Aural Comprehension	can understand most English spoken in observable context	as before/ fossilization	as before	will be placed in same class if he returns
Interactive Behavior	seems to like people; likes sharing his ideas and opinions	As R came to know people, he would respond to them very warmly. If he didn't feel close to people, he'd ignore them/not learn their names.		
Cognitive Skills	no sound/symbol recognition; very little retention of words he's been shown	seemed to make little visible progress during this period	returned with firm grasp of alphabet in English; has begun retaining some sight works and volunteering for writing tasks; beginning to share and derive meaning from print	
Meta-cognitive Awareness	knows he wants to learn to read/write; on third day asked for work with alphabet	always heads notebook page with title "Writing"; asks for certain kinds of assistance	heads pages with "Writing" + date + alphabet in English; has begun retaining some sight works and volunteering for writing tasks; beginning to share and derive meaning from print	
Literacy Goals	unclear		to read: says "reading is very important to read bills"	
Employment Goals	unclear; vision and other problems might preclude serious employment goals	never explicitly mentioned: seems that R can't really work		
Health	see above	vision problems continue; no longer able to drive; could not come to school; given home tutoring		

Reprinted with permission from Collignon, Isserlis, Smith, 1991

Involving learners through participatory assessment

In addition to the thrust toward more learner-centered assessments, there is a movement to share control of the evaluation process with the adults who participate in the program. Some literacy educator point towards the need to redefine the role of the learners so that they can become involved in identifying their own goals and purposes for literacy. For example, Wolfe suggests having learners choose materials to be read during an assessment, select the writings they want to have reviewed, and provide self-reports of progress through journals and peer interviews. She further suggests that assessments should be done "with" adults, rather than "to" them.[20]

Some programs are beginning to think about assessment as a "service provided to the participants and teachers in the program, rather than a vehicle for funding sources to monitor success according to abstract, generalized standards."[21] Lytle and others report on the difficulties inherent in sharing control and in setting up a mechanism that involve students assessing each other. They make it clear that changing the process of evaluation and assessment calls into questions many of the underlying assumptions and perceptions held by teachers, administrators, students, and staff. This questioning requires reconceptualizing and reassessing literacy definitions, purposes, interests, and roles.[22] As Fingeret points out in discussing participatory programs, participatory assessment "should be viewed as a process of cross-cultural communication, negotiation, and mutual learning."[23]

There are now a number of programs that involve learners in documenting their own language and literacy success. The assessment model developed by the University of Massachusetts Family Literacy Program illustrates a participatory assessment model.

♦ *Case in point: Learners evaluate their own progress*

In *Making Meaning, Making Change*, Auerbach describes an assessment model that is part of a participatory framework.[24] This model, implemented as part of the University of Massachusetts Family English Literacy Program, looks at the process of designing and implementing an assessment framework and lays out the tools that can be used in participatory assessment. Based in part on the work of Lytle and Wolfe, the program suggests strategies for involving students in the assessment process during various stages of the program: during initial intake, as the class moves along, and toward the end of the cycle. The program suggests the following strategies for end of cycle assessments:[25]

- peer interviews in which students ask each other questions that they have generated individually or collectively. Questions can deal with topics such as "what have you learned in the class?," "what can you do now that you couldn't do before?" or "what should change about the class?"

- student-teacher conferences in which questions asked at intake might be reviewed. Answers to these questions can show that learners (1) have made changes in literacy practices (when, where, and how they read), (2) have increased the range of literacy materials they use (movie guides, newspapers, letters), or (3) made changes in the support systems they use or the support they provide to others (spouses, kids, neighbors), or the type of literacy interaction around literacy in the family (listen to kids read to them, writing notes to the teacher, taking kids to cultural events)

- student self-evaluations in which learners use charts, checklists, or narrative writing to show changes that may have occurred in their goals, interests, and needs for language and literacy

- class evaluations in which groups of learners anonymously provide feedback on the class, discussing what they disliked or what they would change

- program evaluations in which students from various classes come together to discuss programmatic issues like class structure, curriculum content, use of the native language, child care scheduling, class size, grouping, and funding concerns.

Developing assessment models in competency-based programs

Some workplace literacy programs link assessment and competencies. Both the Arlington Education and Employment Program (REEP) in Virginia and the Workplace Literacy Partners in Cook County, Illinois offer examples of this approach. They teach ESL and literacy within an employment context, using a functional context approach that links language learning with job improvement. What components do they seek to evaluate and what language and literacy competencies are assessed?

◆ *Case in point: Assessing competencies*

REEP seeks to assess individual learner progress, course effectiveness, and impact on the workplace, using a variety of instruments with structured input from learners, teachers, and supervisors. Five general areas of work performance are assessed: (1) initiative at work, (2) understanding English, (3) productivity at work, (4) speaking English, and (5) quality of work.[26] These areas are categorized into three areas of literacy education:

1. specific communication skills and behaviors that relate to job performance, such as "understanding oral instructions" or "being able to communicate without translation"

2. general communication behaviors such as "getting along and working well with co-workers" or "reporting problems, repairs, and changes"

3. work performance categories, such as "following safety rules and safe practices" and "taking the initiative."

The assessment instruments that REEP uses include (1) competency checklists that document skills and behaviors related to job performance, (2) learner self-evaluations, and (3) checklists used by supervisors to rate the improvement in work performance of employees who have participated in the program.

◆ *Case in point*

The Workplace Literacy Partners in Cook County divide their assessment and evaluation into three areas: (1) individual participants' learning; (2) course effectiveness; and (3) impact on the workplace.

The program has designed a Competency Master List that forms the basis for the needs assessment, curriculum development, progress documentation, and final evaluation. Examples of competencies are "describe job duties," "describe tools and machines used on the job," or "read safety signs." At the end of each cycle, students are tested on the core competencies identified for their job and their literacy level. Competencies are assessed through both pencil and paper tests and performance-based evaluations. The program stresses that end of cycle assessments are delivered by someone other than the students' classroom teacher to ensure greater reliability.

Developing assessment in whole language programs

Some programs develop assessments that are congruent with a whole language approach. The Small Group Instruction, offered as part of "Literacy Education Action" at El Paso Community College in Texas, and the Tech Prep Academy, offered at a UAW-Chrysler plant in Michigan, are developing assessment frameworks that are closely linked to the whole language philosophy both programs support.

◆ *Case in point: Whole language-based assessment*

The Small Group Instruction Project at El Paso Community College uses a curriculum that is based on generative themes important to the students. The El Paso program is developing a framework that assesses the various areas of language and literacy that learners, teachers and coordinators find significant. In trying to evaluate learner progress, the program is developing an assessment framework that includes the following three assessment tools:

1. a literacy behavior profile that identifies classroom interactions and includes questions such as does this student "attend regularly," "participate verbally in class," "use English in class," and "display critical thinking"

2. a reading inventory that includes a description of readings the student has mastered, along with a checklist for indicating evidence that the student has understood the materials, checklist categories include "oral response to affective questions in Spanish (or English)," creative writing response, informal discussion with friends and classmates, and "use of knowledge gained from readings outside of classroom"

3. A student writing evaluation that includes:

    •   strengths and limitations in writing behaviors; descriptors may include phrases such as "writes independently but asks for constant assistance from tutor," "asks tutor for spelling of individual words," and "asks tutor for spelling of entire sentences"

    •   mechanical/kinetic skills, such as "writes on lines," "leaves spaces between words," and "forms letters of uniform size"

    •   sentence structure skills such as "the student uses adjectives/adverbs/pronouns correctly" and "the students uses complete sentences"

- affective dimensions of writing. Here categories include "student writes from personal experience," "expresses emotions in writing," "shows pride in work," and "will read aloud to tutor (classmate)"

- links between classroom work and outside literacy. Teachers are asked to provide examples to items, such as "Has this student approached you to initiate literacy use? Describe" or "Has the student given you an indication that s/he is using the literacy skills used in your group outside of class? Describe."

The information gathered on these questionnaires about behaviors, skills, and strategies is rated on a 1 to 3 scale (never, sometimes, often) and recorded during the second week of class, at mid-cycle, and at the end of a cycle. During that time, teachers also collect three writing samples to evaluate. In addition to marking quantitative information on the assessment form, teachers also write a short paragraph outlining the progress that a particular student has made during the cycle. The assessment process is continuously examined and refined to reflect new insights.

♦ *Case in point: Assessing writing holistically*

The Tech Prep Academy model, implemented through a collaboration between UAW-Chrysler and Eastern Michigan University in Trenton, supports a similar approach to writing assessment. As part of its whole language portfolio approach, the Academy supports an assessment scheme that has been adapted from the Writing Project at Ann Arbor High School.[27] Although the categories were originally developed for native speakers of English, they can easily be adapted for ESL literacy programs, especially those that have learners create language experience stories. In fact, there is an additional benefit for ESL learners: the scheme can also be used to assess retellings of stories that have been dictated to a teacher or a tutor.

[See Writing Assessment Table, next page]

Writing assessment

A. Authenticity/voice/ engagement of the reader	4 = Expression strongly reflects the writer's emotional and or intellectual involvement in the topic. Strongly engages the attention of the reader.
	3 = The writer is engaged in the topic and engages the reader.
	2 = Uninteresting; not engaging; perfunctory.
	1 = Writing seems to be a mechanical exercise. Marked by cliches, hazy generalization, meaningless expressions.
B. Focus/organization/development	4 = Focuses on one main idea. Has clear beginning, middle and end. Well-organized and well-developed through examples.
	3 = Focused and organized but may have a flaw in coherence or incomplete closure. incomplete development. Explanation is strongly implicit.
	2 = Lack of clear focus, organization, or development. Narrative but not explanation.
	1 = Disorganized; undeveloped; unconnected generalizations.
C. Sentence mechanics/language	4 = Few mechanical, usage, or sentence errors. Language used with fluency and variety.
	3 = Some minor mechanical usage or sentence errors. Language used competently to express ideas.
	2 = Enough usage errors to attract attention away from the content. Sentences understandable, but unconventional.
	1 = Language and mechanical errors impair meaning.

Common features of cases in point

Assessment models of the kind developed at REEP, Workplace Literacy Partners at Cook County, the Tech-Prep Academy, and Literacy Education Action include two significant components:

- they provide descriptors of behaviors, skills, and processes

- they allow for numerical scores that can be aggregated across assessments and used in final evaluations.

Promising practices

Innovative programs know that in order for such scoring to be reliable, each language and literacy profile needs to be judged by several raters independently. In many cases, raters need a great many opportunities to discuss their judgements and come to a consensus of what constitutes literacy success.   If alternative assessments are to compete with standardized tests to provide accountability to audiences outside the program, focused staff development efforts are necessary.

Alternative assessments in adult ESL literacy are relatively new. The field is borrowing ideas from evaluations and assessments designed for ESL programs in the public schools and from literacy programs designed for English speaking non-readers.   The following practices show promise for adult ESL literacy.

◻ Student-teacher interviews and conferences

Student-teacher interviews and conferences involve discussions between teachers and individual learners. Such conferences may focus on particular pieces of reading and writing that learners are working on, or they may try to document changes that are occurring over time. Some conferences focus on whether learners (1) have made changes in literacy practices (when, where, and how they read); (2) increased the range of literacy materials they use (movie guides, newspapers, letters); (3) made changes in the support systems they use or the support they provide to others (spouses, kids, neighbors);   (4) changed the way they use literacy in their family (listening to children's stories, writing notes to the teacher, taking kids to cultural events).

◘ Reading and writing profiles

Profiles not only assess language and literacy skills that learners have, but also focus on the strategies they use. Skills may include competencies, such as "following directions as they appear on street signs" or "addressing an envelope," while strategies may focus on "using context to predict meaning" (e.g., through environmental print activities). Quite often these profiles include data on affective factors as well (e.g., "volunteers information" or "expresses emotions in writing").[28]

◘ Reading files and free reading logs

Reading files and logs record what learners have read and their reaction to it. In some cases, these files include checklists on what learners can read, do read, and would like to read (e.g, the Bible, newspapers, letters from home, TV guides, bills, advertisements, recipes, children's report cards, paychecks). Other programs might use a box in which students place cards that indicate what they read, when they read it, and how much they liked it.

◘ Portfolios

Portfolios contain samples of learner progress along with comments on the work done. In many cases, learners choose the work they want to see included, such as pieces of other people's writing they have enjoyed reading, their favorite language experience stories, or samples of their "best" handwriting. As a rule, teachers help students organize the information and, in collaboration with other teachers, decide on procedures for analyzing and interpreting the data.[29]

◘ Learner profiles

Learner profiles contain teachers' comments on students' general language development in ESL and their progress in reading and writing in their primary language and in English. To help teachers manage classroom observation and allow for comparisons across classrooms, these records often contain forms, charts, and scales that show how students are becoming more fluent and independent in their reading and writing. In some programs, these profiles include information from student files, such as data on attendance and assignments completed, as well as biographical information.[30]

◼ Questionnaires and surveys

These assessments probe the reactions of stakeholders, such as employers, representatives from the learners' community, or family members. These may seek data such as levels of satisfaction with the program, observed changes at the workplace, perceived increases in skill levels or attitudes, growing interest in school related communication, job placement or advancement, and other changes attributable to participation in the program.[31]

◼ Role plays, case studies, and simulations

Through role plays that surround a literacy event (e.g., an official looking letter arrives in the mail and the group must respond), teachers can assess the coping skills that students use to deal with everyday literacy materials. These coping skills may include guessing meaning from context, looking up key words, checking letterhead, logos, and/or the address of the sender. Asking students what they might do in a particular situations (such as being given a traffic ticket or receiving an eviction notice) can help teachers to identify the level of background knowledge that learners have. Similarly, having someone "play" a mother who has been asked to conference with the child's teacher about a report card will provide information about the learner's experience and expectations of such literacy events. Repeated several times throughout the semester, reports of role plays can help document learner progress in oral language and literacy as well as in understanding of common socio-cultural events.

Developing a framework for alternative assessment

Alternative assessments are often program-based and learner-centered. Programs interested in developing such assessments may want to set up an evaluation committee or assessment group that involves teachers, learners, and curriculum coordinators. The group can then be charged with developing an evaluation process that meets the needs of the program.

Here are some steps that programs can use to develop their own alternative assessment framework.

Step one: examine your program

Come to a common understanding of what program features should be reflected in the assessment framework. Consider

- program goals, curriculum orientation, and program focus (oriented toward general, workplace, family, or community literacy)

- overall curriculum and approach to teaching language and literacy, including stance toward biliteracy

- learner characteristics, including goals, interests, and proficiency levels, as well as readiness to participate in self-assessment

- teachers' views and preferences regarding testing and assessment

- functions that the assessment should serve

- audiences that care about assessment results

- programs constraints such as limited time and resources to develop alternative assessments, a mandated curriculum, or required tests.

Step two: decide what you want to assess

Determine what areas to emphasize and choose two or three significant elements to focus on initially. Areas to assess may include:

- learner needs and goals (what learners want to be able to do with literacy)

- literacy practices (how learners use literacy in their every day lives, inside and outside of the classroom, and how literacy is used in the community or at the workplace)

- reading and writing strategies (how learners go about making sense of print)

- performance (what learners can do with literacy)

- conventions (how close learners come to using the norms established for standard English, such as legible hand writing or standard spelling)

- perceptions (what literacy means to learners; how learners judge their own capabilities and their own progress)

- voice (how learners use literacy to express their own ideas, feelings and opinions)

- interactions (how learners support each other in interpreting and creating literacy; how they interact with others beyond the classroom)

- knowledge (how much learners know about the topics they read and write about)

- understanding (what learners have grasped about the way language and literacy work and the way learning develops)

- life changes (what changes learners have made in their lives since participation in the literacy program).

Make sure all the areas that learners list in their goal statements are included. Decide what might be considered progress or "success" in the areas you have chosen. Include teacher, learner, and "outside" perspectives in your definitions of success.

Step three: choose an appropriate assessment

Based on the results in steps two and three, decide what kind of assessment makes most sense for each area. Consider standardized as well as alternative assessments, and general as well as program-based ESL literacy assessments.

Choose the forms of assessment that are likely to give you the results you want: teacher/learner conferences, classroom observations, one-on-one interviews, surveys, group discussions, writing samples, reading inventories, learner profiles. Decide who should be involved, (teachers, learners, employers, counselors). Balance "expert" evaluation (teachers, supervisors) with peer and self-evaluations.

Discuss the assessment tools that allow you to collect the information you need: interview protocols with room for comments, checklists, observation charts and grids, scales or rating sheets, open-ended comment forms, and anecdotal records.

Decide what balance you want between (1) information that is reported in an open-ended descriptive format and (2) information that is reported in the form of numbers and graphs. Develop several assessment instruments to try out (see examples under cases in point in this chapter). Make sure your instruments include some open-ended sections that capture unintended outcomes. Include room to write down comments that teachers and learners may have.

Step four: conduct a trial run

Ask teachers and learners to try out the instruments. Discuss reactions and results and make changes where appropriate. Refine and expand instruments as the program progresses. Choose additional areas to assess.

Step five: implement program-wide

Discuss how the trial assessments can be instituted program-wide and what adjustments need to be made so that the forest does not get lost for the trees. Decide what level of detail is necessary for different audiences: (1) individual learners and teachers, (2) program staff, (3) outside stakeholders, and (4) funders. Decide how results can be aggregated so that you can show success on a program-wide basis and report results to stakeholders outside the program.

Making decisions about assessment

Assessing literacy in its many forms is difficult, especially if the audiences differ in their information needs. The assessment selection chart (next page) is designed to help programs select appropriate assessment tools.

Assessment selection chart

Category	What are our purposes in choosing an assessment?	If yes, then...
Funding/ Accountability to outside agency	• to document the success of the program to an outside source (such as a funder)	check requirements/regulations and select assessment that will meet them
	• to comply with federal, state, or local requirements	find out if required test can be replaced or supplemented by alternative assessment
Program Design	• to determine the need for classes especially designed for literacy students	choose a needs assessment that identifies learners characteristics
	• to diagnose student levels of proficiency so they can be placed in the appropriate class	select an assessment that provides sufficient information on beginning levels of English and native language literacy
Instruction	• to document student literacy achievement	select performance based assessments that showcase learners' strengths
	• to identify the practices and strategies that students display as they interact with print in the classroom and beyond	look for process oriented assessment that can show progress over time
	• to provide feedback to students and teachers	select an interactive format that includes opportunities for self-assessment
	• to keep the curriculum responsive to student and teacher needs	select assessments that have curriculum validity

Summary

It is now generally accepted wisdom in education that no single measure should serve as the basis for assessing and evaluating all aspects of student ability and learner growth. Programs that are mandated to use certain standardized tests might consider advocating for better and more relevant tests while, at the same time, instituting alternative assessments that are more learner-centered. As the need for program-based evaluation of literacy education continues, staff development efforts need to focus on helping teachers develop assessments that document the gains that students are making in acquiring greater literacy. Finally, the field should work towards procedures and processes that document progress in literacy in ways that are acceptable and comprehensible to those outside of the teaching community.

As programs are developing their own program-based assessments, and, as they are involving learners in curriculum and evaluation processes, different kinds of instruments will need to be developed. Such instruments may include observation and interview guides, focus group protocols, portfolio assessments, learner profiles, and evaluation grids. The next step will be to use and field test these instruments so that they can become a reliable means of measuring progress. The data gained from such instruments can then be aggregated into chart form and, where appropriate, quantified, so that the information can also be used to compare groups of students in the same program and classes across programs. In many adult ESL literacy projects, alternative assessments which are program-based and learner-centered already have a great deal more validity than most standardized language tests. Individual projects now face the challenge of defining their vision of success and developing instruments that capture the changes that take place as language minority adults gain access to literacy.

Reflections: Selecting alternative assessments

When selecting an assessment, a program might consider the following questions:

1. Is the assessment clearly designed to assess both ESL and literacy?

2. Is there a clear relationship between literacy assessment, the needs of the students, and the goal of the program? If not, what steps are being taken to align assessment efforts with the program focus?

3. Does the assessment adequately differentiate on the lower levels of the literacy continuum? If not, what other measures need to be developed to identify various levels of print awareness and beginning literacy?

4. Is there more than one source of assessment, such as self-evaluation, interview, and pencil and paper assessment?

5. Does the assessment focus on literacy practices and literacy use (i.e., what students can do with literacy) or does it merely identify letter and word recognition skills?

6. Does the assessment identify students' strengths? Is the assessment likely to confuse or frustrate students or make them feel stupid? How can this situation be remedied?

7. Does the assessment satisfy the funding source but provide little information to teachers, students, and curriculum developers? How can the situation be improved?

8. Is the assessment working well for all levels of the program (administration, curriculum, classroom) but not acceptable to the funding source? How can the program work towards acceptance of its alternative assessment efforts?

9. Is there a quick turn-around between the time the assessment is given and the time students and teachers see the results? Are the results interpreted in a way that makes sense to teachers and students?

10. Is there a clear relationship between the assessment and the curriculum? Is there a feedback loop between the curriculum and the assessment so that a change in one is reflected in the other?

11. Does the assessment allow for teacher and student input and participation?

12. Does the assessment differentiate between various literacies, such as functional literacy (completing everyday literacy tasks), prose literacy (understanding text commonly found in newspapers or textbooks), and document literacy (figuring out what a certain form might be all about or recognizing official notices that require a response)?

13. Does the assessment evaluate both reading comprehension and writing skills?

Endnotes

1. See Balliro, 1989.

2. See California State Department of Education, 1990.

3. This is true even in programs, or perhaps especially in programs, where a particular test is mandated, since any program has the option of talking to teachers and students about testing issues and/or supplementing required tests with other assessments.

4. See Lytle & Wolfe, 1989.

5. See Resnick & Resnick, 1985.

6. See Sticht, 1990.

7. See Sticht, 1990 and Jackson, 1990.

8. See also Brindley, 1989.

9. See Macias, 1990.

10. See Weinstein-Shr, 1990.

11. See Wolf et al., 1991.

12. See Macias, 1990 and Wiley, in press.

13. See Wolf et al., 1991.

14. See Auerbach, 1989.

15. For a discussion of assessment clusters and multiple ways of evaluating progress, see Auerbach, 1990; Collignon et al., 1991; Edelsky & Harman, 1988; Lytle & Wolfe, 1989; Resnick & Resnick, 1985; Heald-Taylor, 1989; Wolf et al., 1991.

16. See Balliro, 1989.

17. See Rigg, 1991.

18. See Rigg, 1991, p.7.

19. For a full discussion of the process, see *A handbook for practitioners,* by Collignon et al., 1991.

20. See Wolfe, 1988, p. 4.

21. See Sterling, 1989, p. 52.

22. See Lytle et al., 1989.

23.   See Fingeret, 1989, p. 14.

24.   See Auerbach, 1990.

25.   See Auerbach, 1990, p. 228.

26.   See Peterson, 1990.

27.   Adapted by Soifer and others from Ann Arbor High School Teachers, 1984; for details on the Academy Model, see *The complete theory-to-practice handbook of adult literacy* by Soifer et al., 1990.

28.   See Wrigley, forthcoming.

29.   See Tierney et al., 1991.

30.   See Barrs, 1990.

31.   See Rigg, 1991.

References

Amnesty education program review: An integration of program leadership and instructional improvement. (1990). Sacramento, CA: California State Department of Education, Amnesty Education Office.

Auerbach, E. R. (1989). Toward a social-contextual approach to family literacy. *Harvard Educational Review, 59*(2), 165-181.

Auerbach, E. R. (1990). *Making meaning, making change: A guide to participatory curriculum development for adult ESL and family literacy.* Boston: University of Massachusetts [in press (1992), Regents Prentice Hall/Center for Applied Linguistics].

Balliro, L. (1989). *Reassessing assessment in adult ESL/literacy.* Unpublished manuscript. Boston: Roxbury Community College.

Barrs, M. (1990). The primary language record: Reflection of issues in evaluation. *Language Arts, 67*(3), 244-253.

Brindley, G. (1989). *Assessing achievement in the learner-centered curriculum.* Sydney, Australia: Macquarie University, National Centre for English Language Teaching and Research.

Collignon, F. F., Isserlis, J., & Smith, S. (1991). *A handbook for practitioners: ESL/literacy for adult non-native speakers of English.* Providence, RI: International Institute of Rhode Island, Literacy/ESL Program.

Edelsky, C., & Harman, S. (1988). One more critique of reading tests - with two differences. *English Education, 20*(3), 157-171.

Fingeret, A. (1989). The social and historical context of participatory literacy education. In A. Fingeret, & P. Jurmo (Eds.), *Participatory literacy education* (pp. 5-16). San Francisco: Jossey-Bass.

Heald-Taylor, G. (1989). *The administrator's guide to whole language.* Katonah, New York: Richard C. Owen Publishers.

Jackson, G. B. (1988). *Measures for adult literacy programs.* Washington, DC: American Institutes for Research, ERIC Clearinghouse on Tests, Measurement, and Evaluation and The Association for Community Based Education.

Lytle, S. L., Belzer, A., Schultz, K., & Vannozzi, M. (1989). Learner-centered literacy assessment: An evolving process. In A. Fingeret, & P. Jurmo (Ed.), *Participatory literacy education* (pp. 53-64). San Francisco: Jossey-Bass.

Lytle, S. L., & Wolfe, M. (1989). *Adult literacy education: Program evaluation and learner assessment.* Information series no. 338. Columbus, OH: ERIC Clearinghouse on Adult, Career, and Vocational Education.

Macias, R. (1990). [Response to "Teacher supply and demand"]. In C. Simich-Dudgeon (Ed.), *Proceedings of the first research symposium on limited English proficient students' issues* (pp. 406-412). Washington, DC: U.S. Department of Education, Office of Bilingual Education and Minority Languages Affairs.

Peterson, M. (1990). *Evaluation report: REEP/Hotel Workplace Literacy Project. 1988-1990 grant period.* Arlington, VA: Arlington Education and Employment Program.

Resnick, D. P., & Resnick, L. B. (1985, April). Standards, curriculum, and performance: A historical and comparative perspective. *Educational Researcher*, pp. 5-20.

Rigg, P. (1991). Theory in evaluation. *TESOL Adult Education Newsletter*, *XVIII*(2), 7-8.

Soifer, R., Irwin, M. E., Crumrine, B. M., Honzaki, E., Simmons, B. K., & Young, D. L. (1990). *The complete theory-to-practice handbook of adult literacy: Curriculum design and teaching approaches.* New York: Teachers College Press.

Sterling, R. (1989). Literacy skills measurement and program evaluation. Toward a model of alternative assessment. *Literacy and the marketplace: Improving the literacy of low-income single mothers. A report on a meeting of practitioners, policymakers, researchers, and funders* (pp. 50-55). New York: Rockefeller Foundation.

Sticht, T. G. (1990). Measuring adult literacy: A response. In R. L. Venezky, D. A. Wagner, & B. S. Ciliberti (Eds.), *Toward defining literacy* (pp. 48-53). Newark, DE: International Reading Association.

Texas Education Agency. (1990). *Assessment of adult limited English proficient students: A guide to available instruments.* Austin, TX: Author.

Tierney, R. J., Carter, M. A., & Desai, L. E. (1991). *Portfolio assessment in the reading-writing classroom*. Norwood, MA: Christopher-Gordon Publishers.

Weinstein-Shr, G. (Preparer). (1990). *NCLE Q & A: Family and intergenerational literacy in multilingual families*. Washington, DC: Center for Applied Linguistics, National Clearinghouse on Literacy Education.

Wiley, T. G. (in press). Disembedding Chicano literacy: The need for group-specific approaches to adult literacy. *Stanislaus, Journal of the School of Education*, Long Beach: California State University.

Wolf, D., Bixby, J., Glenn III, J., & Gardner, H. (1991). To use their minds well: Investigating new forms of students assessment. In G. Grant (Ed.), *Review of research in education*. Washington, DC: American Educational Research Association.

Wolfe, M. (1988). Effective practice: A progress report from New York. *Focus on Basics*, 2(1), 5-7. Boston, MA: World Education.

Wrigley, H. S. (forthcoming). *Green card English: Curriculum making as politics*. Unpublished doctoral dissertation, University of Southern California.

Chapter 7

Curriculum

Curriculum is to be tested by students and teachers, not students and teachers by curriculum.

— Stenhouse, 1975[1]

The common sense definition of curriculum as "a course of study" is a designation that implies that curriculum is static, relatively neutral, and value-free, the result of purely technical decisions. However, this definition ignores the social, political, and economic contexts that influence the goals and content of the literacy program. These contexts help determine who is to benefit from what kind of knowledge, under what circumstances, and to what end. As a result of inquiries into the social nature of learning, curriculum discussions are starting to address issues related to gender, race, and social status, with women's issues sometimes receiving special consideration.

There is now a growing realization that curriculum decisions are value decisions that reflect the educational orientations a program supports and the social goals it seeks to attain. In many ways, this awareness parallels the shift in literacy definitions wherein literacy, previously defined as a set of skills divorced from social context, is now increasingly viewed as a set of social practices that are culturally determined.

Perceptions of curriculum development are changing as well. In the conventional view curriculum development is a linear, sequential process that is completed before teaching begins. Since this view does not reflect program practice, some educators are starting to research the complex ways in which actual programs make curriculum decisions. As a result of these inquiries, curriculum development is now often perceived as a dynamic process in which literacy goals, curriculum content, classroom practice, learner assessment, and staff development are interrelated and negotiated through a continuous process that involves staff, teachers, and learners.

This chapter addresses two significant components of curriculum: (1) the overall educational goals that a program is trying to achieve through its curriculum and (2) the processes that are used to develop the curriculum. The "Background: Curriculum Orientations" section of this chapter examines six curriculum orientations, each geared toward a different educational goal. The "Practice: Curriculum Development" section presents two models of curriculum development illustrated by examples from the field. The "Reflections: Making Curriculum Decisions" section offers programs questions to consider before making decisions about their own curriculum.

Background: Curriculum orientations

Curricula in ESL literacy programs vary greatly from site to site, yet each curriculum reflects a certain view of language, literacy, and learning. While a few programs show a clear one-to-one relationship between a specific philosophy and the literacy education they provide, most draw, either explicitly or implicitly, from several orientations.[2]

Basic orientations to the literacy curriculum

There are a great many philosophies of education, each leading to a different kind of curriculum. As a background for ESL literacy programs, these philosophies can be grouped into six basic orientations. Each reflects a distinctive view of the role that literacy education should play in the learner's lives and in the society at large. Each of these orientations has a definite focus and gives rise to a particular literacy curriculum. These orientations are defined by the goals they seek to attain. The orientations are

- common educational core
- social and economic adaptation
- development of cognitive processes
- personal relevance
- social change
- technological management of education

As programs seek to define their own perspectives on literacy, examining these orientations can shed light on the assumptions, theories, and values that shape language and literacy education.

Common educational core

The common educational core orientation is based in large part on "academic rationalism," one of the oldest and most basic orientations to the curriculum. It is grounded in the tradition of eighteenth century liberal education that was designed to offer the best for the best, a goal supported by modern day writers on cultural literacy such as Bloom and Hirsch. This orientation is designed to provide for all students a common set of educational experiences, including the development of basic literacy skills, a command of standard English, and an understanding of common cultural knowledge. The knowledge and skills thus transmitted are seen as the shared intellectual base that is necessary for advancement through the academic ranks and entry into the mainstream.

ESL literacy programs that emphasize this orientation often take a "basic skills" approach. These programs tend to emphasize the established standards in reading and writing that should be acquired by all (e.g., a sound basis in phonics, proper spelling and punctuation, and correct interpretation of a reading passage). Reading sections in basic skills texts tend to shy away from controversial subjects, such as AIDS, domestic violence, or workers' rights, focusing instead on discussions of American values and shared traditions.

Advocates of a common core perspective believe that immigrant and minority students must be taught the values of the mainstream society along with the language skills needed to succeed academically and professionally. In this view, learners must be made aware of the standards by which their literacy efforts will be measured at various gate-keeping points, such as the GED test or entry into Job Training Partnership Act (JTPA) programs. To do less, these advocates maintain, might preclude language minority students from access to better jobs and higher education.

The critics of the common core orientation regard this perspective as elitist and accuse its advocates of "crippling ethnocentrism" and contempt for the language, literacies, and social interactions of those "outside the circle of power." They charge that this orientation tends to promote a deficit model of literacy in which language minority adults and their families are seen as culturally inferior, educationally deprived, and linguistically impoverished.[3]

Social and economic adaptation

This orientation sees the functions of school as helping to meet the critical economic needs of the learners, the community, and the society at large. It is designed to help adults acquire the skills and knowledge needed to be self-sufficient, to function effectively in society, to access services, and to integrate into the mainstream culture.

Social and economic adaptation is rooted in the social efficiency education movement of the early 1900s. The goal is to design a curriculum that will contribute to a smoothly running, efficient society by preparing students for the adult roles they are to occupy later in life. It focuses on "scientific" curriculum-making, diagnostic assessment, achievement testing, and a course of study based on needs assessment.

In the United States, this orientation gained prominence in the 1970s. Based on the Applied Performance Level Study, competency-based approaches to ESL and to literacy were developed and took hold in the field.[4] In refugee education, both in the United States and in oversees refugee camps, the social and economic adaptation perspective is represented by a curriculum that is geared towards self-sufficiency and employment. The theory is to help students acquire the life skills needed to find work, maintain jobs, and function proficiently in the new society.[5]

Many ESL literacy programs emphasize social and economic adaptation. In their curricula, the skills and knowledge needed for successful participation in the society are outlined in the form of competencies[6] and tested through standardized assessments that focus on mastery. This orientation is particularly strong in ESL literacy programs that focus on life skills or on "functional context skills" in the workplace. The social adaptation perspective also underlies the functional ESL curriculum first developed in England and popularized through the Council of Europe.[7]

Social and economic adaptation has powerful critics. While most acknowledge that newcomers need to know the language associated with finding jobs, housing, and healthcare, they question the underlying assumptions of the functional curriculum as it is taught in ESL programs. These critics point toward the "hidden curriculum" of life skills teaching, which appears to train refugees and immigrants to be obedient and not make waves and accept their role on the social order.[8] These hidden curricula often imply that a lack of economic success on the part of language minorities is due to their inadequate English or their failure to follow social rules (such as dressing appropriately for a job interview). These critics also claim that the approaches commonly used in life skills programs seldom allow immigrants to discuss the pressing social problems that they face (e.g., lack of affordable health care, lack of employment beyond menial work, inadequate housing). From the critic's perspective, an orientation geared toward social and economic adaptation serves to reproduce the social and economic inequalities between the U.S. mainstream and language minorities.[9]

To some critics, social and economic adaptation is dominated by a "factory model" in which the notions of critical thinking and the interrelationship between culture and power may disappear under the imperatives of the economy and the demands of the labor process.[10] In discussing literacy for employment, a number of educators are pointing out that workers often do not need the competencies outlined in a conventional workplace literacy program.[11] Workers often either already have the requisite skills (otherwise they would not have been able to obtain those jobs) or the jobs themselves require very little literacy and offer no upward mobility. In addition, in many workplace literacy programs, the learners' own stake in becoming literate is too often lost in the search for ways to make workers more productive.

Development of cognitive processes

This orientation focuses on the development of cognitive and linguistic processes, emphasizing "learning how to learn" as its goal. It stresses process over content, strategies over skills, and understanding over memorization. In encouraging adults to make their own meaning by interacting with each other as well as with the text, it recognizes both the social context and the social construction of knowledge. Originally influenced by the early work of John Dewey and the scientific approach of developmentalists like Piaget, this perspective now relies on the works of cognitive psychologists and psycholinguists, such as de Beaugrande, Neisser, Rumelhart, and Smith.[12] In ESL literacy, the cognitive processes orientation is reflected in the "interactive reading" approach, reading for academic purposes, and some aspects of the whole language curriculum.

ESL literacy programs that emphasize this orientation tend to use approaches that focus on the development of cognitive and linguistic strategies. These may include predicting meaning from context, confirming predictions, using one's knowledge of the world to express ideas in writing, and learning to identify word patterns and recognize letters.[13] Literacy programs that stress meta-cognition (learning how to learn), problem solving, and language awareness also fall into this category.

Some educational writers criticize this orientation as part of an ideology that sees meaning as primarily psychological and person-centered. They charge that the content presented and the experiences provided through this approach ignore the conflicts of the wider society and thus divorce learning from social action. Critics further suggest that this orientation has shown little concern for the class, race, and gender-related history of different groups of students. In Giroux's view, for example, the emphasis on individual "meaning-making" ignores the fact that the language practices used in school carry political, economic, and cultural significance.

Personal relevance

The personal relevance orientation emphasizes the primacy of personal meaning and the school's responsibility to develop literacy programs that make such meaning possible. Its major focus is on the educational development of the individual and the psychological freedom that results from experiencing a personally relevant curriculum within a non-coercive environment.

Grounded in the humanism of Carl Rogers[14] and Abraham Maslow[15] this orientation supports learner initiatives and self-directed learning. It maintains that adults are able to assess their own learning needs and goals and, if given the right tools, are capable of evaluating appropriate learning strategies and assessing their own progress.[16]

In ESL literacy, programs that focus on social relevance support approaches that emphasize the affective dimensions of the reading and writing process. They see personal growth and self-actualization through literacy as principal goals. An ESL literacy curriculum that focuses largely on autobiographies and personal accounts (e.g., language experience) is also representative of this orientation.

For some critics, the personal relevance and the cognitive processes orientations share the common view that knowledge is a subjective construct arrived at through interactions between speakers or between a reader and a text.[17] These critics maintain that neither orientation explicitly addresses the broader economic and political issues related to the social distribution of knowledge and thus fail to link personal experience to a larger socio-cultural context. Other educators point out that defining literacy solely in terms of helping students to achieve their personal goals does not "address the public's need to measure literacy attainment in quantifiable form."[18] As Lytle points out, "A student might count a gain in feelings of self-worth as more important than a gain in reading and writing skills, per se, but such growth is not possible to capture in numbers, nor is it asked for by public funding agencies."[19] Diekhof also finds changes in personal life style suspect as a measurement of literacy progress.[20]

Social change

Issues of culture and power lie at the heart of the social change, social reconstruction, or liberationist orientation. Radical theorists like Apple and Giroux see the schools not only as cultural agencies but as political sites as well.[21] This perspective seeks an examination of the hidden curriculum thought to underlie some competency-based programs and challenges educators to examine a school system in which certain forms of literacy and language are legitimated while others are devalued.[22] This orientation sees illiteracy not as a cause of poverty or underemployment, but rather as a result of inequitable social conditions. Adherents of this orientation also stress that, while literacy can be used as one of the tools of empowerment, reading and writing or speaking English in themselves do not confer power and control. The social change orientation finds its strongest implementation in "participatory" program designs.

ESL literacy programs that emphasize this orientation tend to address the issues of power and control on both the classroom level and at the program level. In an effort to equalize the power differential that exists between teachers and students, liberationist programs attempt to set up educational opportunities that put adults in charge of their own learning. Teachers see themselves not so much as experts from whom all knowledge emanates, but rather as facilitators and co-learners with different kinds of experiences and different resources at their disposal. Increasingly, these programs go beyond sharing power in the classroom towards sharing control of the entire program — making it possible for participants to become active in designing, implementing, and evaluating educational offerings.

The social change perspective has given rise to many participatory, Freirean-inspired literacy curricula. Citing Freire, these programs maintain that traditional literacy approaches ignore the culture, language, and social issues that both inform and dignify the everyday life of the poor. In this view, traditional teaching is not only repressive and alienating, but it also reinforces the dominant view of language minority adults as inferior and responsible for their location in the power structure. Freire proposes an approach that recognizes the "cultural capital" of the oppressed in order to dignify their voices, experiences, and modes of interaction. His approach encourages them to produce class "texts" that reflect the social and political issues important to their lives.[23]

The social change orientation itself is sometimes critiqued by mainstream scholars as a paternalistic approach that works under the assumption that all language minority students feel oppressed and want to work towards changing the society. Using their own classroom experience as a basis, many teachers maintain that their students want to develop the language, knowledge, and skills that will help them to move beyond the gate-keeping points that society has set up so that they can gain access to the mainstream society.

The participatory, dialogical model common to Freirean pedagogy has also been critiqued as one in which the teacher, by becoming a co-learner, abdicates the role of the expert that students come to expect. As Delpit points out, in the context of using a process model of teaching literacy, this approach may give the impression to students "that there are secrets being kept, that time is being wasted, that the teacher is abdicating his or her duty to teach."[24]

Technological management of education

The orientation that seeks technological management of education has its roots in the social efficiency movement. This model claims to be useful and adaptable to any educational undertaking, be it literacy for academic preparation, for daily life, or for the workplace. Many of the curriculum technologists have built their materials on the curriculum model championed by Tyler,[25] stressing pre-determined objectives, purposeful activities, scope and sequence, and standardized evaluation instruments. The technology orientation employs models and language borrowed from industry, using terms such as diagnostic testing, literacy audits, behavioral objectives, training modules, teacher training, and learning outcomes.[26] It is often linked to "individualized instruction" in which students are pretested, given assignments to complete, and then assessed to determine whether they have mastered the required concepts.

ESL literacy programs that emphasize this orientation use commercially developed literacy packages that teach basic literacy, focusing primarily on alphabet and phonics skills and word and sound recognition. Literacy curricula based on this orientation often include computerized program management components that assess students, move them through an instructional sequence, and track their progress. For example, in some technology-based curricula, the computer program generates information about each lesson that the student has attempted and reports on several aspects of student achievement and effort (or lack thereof). Students who move too fast through an instructional set and, in the process, get all the answers wrong may get reported as "not trying hard enough." Similarly, if students take too much time between answers (talking to their friends or daydreaming, perhaps), the computer will report that insufficient time was spent "on task."[27]

The technology-managed orientation has many critics. Some object to what they see as the ahistorical, apolitical, unethical, and atheoretical stance of curriculum making in the "scientific" mode. Others see the behavioral objectives and standardized assessment procedures used in these packages as a form of social control that makes it easy to manipulate teachers and students alike. Still others argue that individualization as applied to ESL literacy ignores the cultural background of many immigrant students because it runs counter to their preferred cultural learning mode and may deprive the learners of opportunities to draw on the strength of their collectivity with other students. [28]

Teacher educators have voiced additional concerns. Many find that, at a time when many teachers involved in the education of language minority students are concerned with their lack of status and professionalism, a technologically designed curriculum, pre-packaged for education management, will only further contribute to what has been called the "de-skilling" of teachers. They feel that curriculum orientations that stifle the creativity and enthusiasm of teachers will in turn stifle the creativity of students, making literacy education an experience to be endured rather than appreciated and enjoyed.

Combining orientations

While a number of ESL literacy programs fall squarely into one orientation or another, others are not so easily categorized. For example, most social change education programs don't focus exclusively on consciousness raising and political emancipation, nor does a competency-based program necessarily preclude the discussion of socio-political issues.[29]

Experience in the field has shown that while some programs are becoming more effective by moving towards a well-articulated model, others may be innovative precisely because they resist categorization. Instead of trying to adhere to only one orientation and forsaking all others, a number of programs are developing their own orientation, seeking to find a conceptual framework that allows them to deal effectively with the tensions that characterize literacy education for adults. We are now seeing programs that want to show their students how to effectively operate in this culture and society, while at the same time, teaching them to challenge authority and stand up for their rights. Similarly, we are finding programs that combine a cognitive skills orientation with a focus on personal relevance in an effort to prepare students for the challenges of mainstream academic or vocational programs. Additionally, teachers are exploring ways of linking learner-generated stories based on personal experience with the larger social, cultural, and political issues of the community.

Thus, we find that the field is moving away from dichotomous thinking in which ESL literacy education is viewed in terms of good or bad, black or white, and mainstream or alternative.[30] Instead, we find "curriculum configurations," in which aspects of various orientations are intermixed to yield maximum usefulness for a given context. As contexts change, so does the emphasis on a particular orientation. At any given time in a program, there may be greater emphasis on social change and less on social adaptation and more of a focus on cognitive development and less on academic rationalism. The value of such a curriculum can no longer be judged solely in terms of its "political correctness." It must now be evaluated in terms of its responsiveness to program goals, learner needs, and teacher preferences.

In spite of this apparent synthesis, strong distinctions remain, and most successful programs are not in danger of succumbing to mindless eclecticism. Thus we find a number of programs that give primary emphasis to one orientation while integrating some aspects of others. A workplace program, for example, might be strong in its emphasis on social adaptation, less forceful in its focus on personal relevance, fair in the areas of cognitive development, and rather weak in its social change orientation. To what extent the implementations of a particular orientation results in differences in learner outcomes has yet to be determined.

Practice: Curriculum development

All adult ESL literacy programs must decide what to teach since language is complex and it's many dimensions cannot all be taught at the same time. In looking at the many possibilities of language and literacy teaching, educators must determine what might be developmentally appropriate for any given group at any given time. To help make these determinations, curriculum development becomes necessary.

Curriculum framework

For curriculum development to be effective, a curriculum framework needs to be designed that links the following components:

- articulation of program aims, including support of various orientations

- identification of learner needs and goals (linguistic as well as non-linguistic/social)

- curriculum content and organization

- ways of teaching (approaches and methods)

- teaching resources (materials, technologies, texts)

- assessment measures

- linkages between these areas

A series of questions might help programs make decisions about curriculum development. The literature suggests the following questions to be used as guides:[31]

Key questions for curriculum development

There are four basic questions that must be answered as the curriculum takes shape:

1. What educational purposes should the program seek to attain?

2. How can learning experiences which are likely to be useful in attaining these aims be selected?

3. How can learning experiences be effectively organized?

4. How can the success of learning experiences be evaluated?

Successful programs make curriculum decisions with the help of a conceptual framework that links program goals and learner needs with instructional content, classroom teaching, and progress assessment. Yet curriculum development is much more difficult than it might appear. Many programs struggle for months, if not years, to develop a curriculum that brings learners, teachers, and administrators together in a common vision of what is worthwhile and what is feasible.

The process does not end when a framework is developed. On the contrary, the hard work may lie ahead. Successful programs know that in order to remain responsive to changing situations, curriculum development must be an ongoing, dynamic process that demands energy and commitment from all participants — administrators, teachers, and learners. To be effective, a curriculum framework in adult ESL literacy also requires the understanding and support of policy-makers and funders.

Curriculum development models: conventional and alternative

Although there are different ways of developing a curriculum, there are two major approaches that have influenced curriculum making in adult ESL literacy. Each reflects a distinctive view of the nature of language, literacy, and learning, and the role that teachers and learners should play in that process. Curriculum development models can be grouped into two broad categories, conventional and alternative.

The conventional model specifies objectives, content, scope, sequence, and testing measures before instruction begins. Used extensively in the United States and in Europe, it emphasizes outcomes and skill mastery and reflects a management model that stresses teaching by objective. The underlying premise of the conventional approach is that teaching is a skill that can be achieved by learning and mastering specific techniques.

The alternative model allows most curriculum content to emerge from classroom interactions as the course progresses. There is no pre-established sequence, topics appear and reappear as necessary, and the focus remains on the process of learning and teaching. This model reflects ethnographic and participatory approaches and works under the assumption that teaching is an art that thrives on experimentation.

Both approaches have strong advocates in the field and, while they are not necessarily mutually exclusive, most programs emphasize one approach over the other.

Cases in point

Decisions about curriculum content and curriculum processes are not always made freely. Some ESL literacy programs have a prescribed curriculum with topics and skill areas that need to be "covered" in some way. Others, while they may have greater flexibility overall, must still respond to funding mandates that demand at least a certain amount of pre-specified content. Other programs, however, have been free to shape their curriculum according to their own philosophy.

Conventional model: teaching with competencies

In adult education programs that have a systematic way of developing curriculum (many do not), the conventional approach is most often implemented along the lines of the Competency-Based Education (CBE) model. In ESL literacy, CBE curriculum development is perhaps best exemplified by the Mainstream English Training Language (MELT) project,[32] a well-articulated framework that links needs assessment, student performance levels, objectives, instructional content, and testing in one coherent package. Used extensively in refugee programs teaching life skills and employment skills, the model presented at the time of its development a significant advance over curricula whose scope and sequence was defined by grammatical categories.

The cornerstone of the CBE approach are competencies, defined as a "performance-based process leading to demonstrated mastery of basic and life skills necessary for the individual to function proficiently in society."[33] In an ESL literacy context, this means performing tasks that involve actual language use, such as following directions on a machine (e.g., "deposit money here") or writing one's name on a form. Various tests are then used to determine whether a particular competency has been mastered.[34]

While the CBE curricula differ from program to program, most offer a combination of the following:

- life skill domains, such as employment, housing, transportation, and schooling

- life skill competencies, such as reading a bus schedule or filling out an employment application

- cross-topics, such as functions (asking for clarification) or notions (time, money) that cut across the life skill domains

- basic literacy skills, sometimes called enabling skills, that are necessary before a competency can be achieved (e.g., being able to write numbers before writing a check)

- grammatical structures and vocabulary, that are required for a particular life skill such as understanding command forms as background for following instructions or familiarity with models such as "could I" or "would you" for polite requests.[35]

◆ *Case in point: Project Workplace*

Project Workplace in Illinois offers a competency-based workplace literacy curriculum which provides the framework for job-specific syllabuses used at particular sites.[36] The process works as follows:

Content

The project provides its full time staff with a core curriculum listing seven domains deemed critical for workplace communication.

1. Job performance
2. Clarification/verification
3. Work schedule/time sheet/paychecks
4. Safety
5. General work related strategies and procedures
6. Social language
7. General company communication

These job domains appear on a master list, together with representative competencies, situations, vocabulary, and grammar structures for each. (See chart, next page.)

Process

At each job site, staff conducts a literacy audit and then prepares a list of competencies that could be taught. The list goes to company managers and supervisors who select those items they find essential by marking "critical," "important," or "not important." At some sites, union representatives also give input. For example, a competency at the beginning level ESL literacy class for a sewing machine operator may be "reading the production ticket specifying ticket number, pieces to be sewn, and number of minutes the task should take."

Based on the responses to the survey rating the competencies and the literacy audit, a specific curriculum is developed for each job site. Vocabulary items and structures are adapted for various proficiency levels, and learners are given opportunities for input during the first week of class and as the course progresses. Assessments are designed to gauge to what extent learners have achieved the competencies that were taught.

Competency	Basic Skills	Language Skills: Vocabulary	Language Skills: Grammatical Structures	Activities	Resources Materials
Identify job titles, department and department functions		Job Titles: Departments Manufacturing processes Machines Tools Products	Imperative verbs Simple present Expressions of time Modal verbs	Information gathering at worksite Guided discussion Information gap Written task Sight word reading	Worksheets
Identify products company manufactures.	Reading: Recognize common words and meanings Use table of contents, index, and glossary to locate information within a text	Products: (categories) Small wares Transport Food warning	Simple present	Sight word reading Information gathering at worksite Written exercises	Company catalogue

A curriculum framework of this kind, which links job performance with competencies and competencies with assessment provides clear accountability data to teachers, students, employers, and funders. This may be one reason why the CBE model has become the dominant model in workplace literacy.

Alternative model: The whole language curriculum

A number of ESL literacy programs are finding pre-specified objectives both too restrictive and too unrealistic for their classes. In discussing participatory curriculum development, Auerbach sums up this point of view by saying

> Curriculum content ... can't be developed before the educator ever comes in contact with the class, but rather has to be built on the particular conditions, concerns and contributions of specific groups of participants at a particular point in time.[37]

For many educators, this means setting a curriculum framework that contains broad goals and explores hypotheses. "If we do X in the classroom, Y might happen. Let's find out." Literacy educators who support broad aims over narrow objectives often cite research that shows that teachers do not teach by objectives, nor do students learn through them.[38] Instead, they believe literacy develops through continuous engagement with a wide variety of written language forms.

Curricula emphasizing broad aims are given a number of names: "participatory" (since teachers and learners work together to create a curriculum), "emergent" (since content and processes come out of the experience of the learner), "dynamic" (to show the continuous interplay between needs, content, and assessment), "whole language" (since language is not split into discrete objectives), or "negotiated" (to show that there may be a tension between what a program is able to teach and what learners may want).

How do programs develop an alternative curriculum? Many start with an existing framework that includes potential themes along with language and literacy activities that have worked in the past. The term "retroactive curriculum" describes the reality of programs' moving toward an alternative curriculum. Teachers start with a broad idea of what they might teach. Then, through experimentation, student input, observation, and reflection, a new curriculum framework emerges that can be used as a guide to subsequent classes.[39]

◆ *Case in point: Literacy Education Action*

The literacy program at El Paso Community College serves as a good example of broad-based, ongoing curriculum development.[40] Embracing a holistic/Freirean based approach, project staff uses broad-based goals, program-generated themes, and literacy activities as a framework for a curriculum that combines culture, content, and communication.

Content

Themes may focus on social issues (discrimination, gang violence), personal concerns (building self-confidence), or language matters (the nature and value of bilingualism). Through the themes, the curriculum tries to build familiarity with the community, an understanding of culture from a multicultural perspective, background knowledge related to topics in question, and strategies for day-to-day communication with English speakers.

Process

At the beginning of a teaching cycle and as the sessions progress, coordinators and teachers brainstorm together to generate themes for the classes. These themes may include issues of interest to the community or topics that the students wanted to discuss in the past. Themes are then developed into "problem posing modules" that follow a five step sequence.

Five step sequence

- Initial inquiry introduces the theme and encourages group dialogue to explore ideas, opinions, and concerns that students might have

- Learning activity promotes confidence and competence in using English with a primary emphasis on expressing and understanding meaning and a secondary focus on language (vocabulary, language functions)

- Language experience links oral language and literacy with a special focus on writing

- Reading in context promotes different kinds of reading experiences, including silent, echo, choral, and round robin reading of a wide range of texts

- Home assignment links in-class activities with learners' lives beyond the classroom

These modules are then available for teachers to use in the classroom as appropriate. As learners provide input and teachers reflect on what best suits their classes, available modules are modified or new ones are created.[41]

The negotiated curriculum

Traditionally the conventional curriculum has focused on the acquisition of skills and knowledge and has prided itself in its objectivity and efficiency. The main function of instruction has been "instrumental," that is, leading to specific goal attainment which could be measured by tests of mastery.

The alternative curriculum, on the other hand, has long been regarded as "wishy-washy" and non-rigorous in its approach. Proponents have sometimes been accused of advocating a "so what do you want to learn today" approach to teaching, and many teacher trainers have pronounced the approach too complex for new teachers to implement.

As the official curriculum runs up against the reality of the classroom, distinctions between pre-specified objectives and emerging content often become blurred. For example, teachers in CBE programs increasingly use variations of the language experience approach (LEA), a holistic model that cannot be reduced to a set of behavioral objectives. Teachers who reject CBE as too simplistic and reductionist often teach de facto competencies, such as chart reading or form filling, particularly in response to student requests. Similarly, items on checklists of whole language reading and writing strategies (such as "can predict meaning from context" or "uses a variety of text aids") often have more in common with competencies than they do with the decontextualized skills taught in some basic literacy programs.

In innovative programs, curriculum development is iterative, that is, it moves back and forth between what a program intends and what classrooms can deliver. On the one hand, there is a conceptual framework, specified or implicit, that shapes content and guides teaching. On the other hand, there are teachers and learners who breathe life into the curriculum and give it meaning. As administrators know, only the teachers and learners know for sure what goes on behind classroom doors. For every teacher who enacts the curriculum as envisioned by the program, there is another who reconceptualizes it or commits "creative treason" while teaching. This is especially true in contexts where teachers do not have input into the official curriculum and therefore tend to practice "curriculum by subversion."[42]

It has been said that the true curriculum exists in the hearts and minds of the teachers, yet this information is rarely accessible to others. If ESL literacy teachers are to be professionals, what exists in their hearts and minds needs to be made public and examined. Only in that way can we find a common ground between the "curriculum as intended" by the program and the curriculum as enacted in the classroom.

Summary

As more and more ESL literacy programs are explicitly acknowledging the social nature of literacy, they are seeking to develop a literacy curriculum that allows them to integrate the various student goals and teacher interests with the social, academic, and/or economic focus the program has chosen to support. In a field in which curriculum has often been defined as a list of topics, grammar points, and functions to be taught, this signals a significant change. It means that issues related to the planning, implementation, and evaluation of literacy activities are now seen within a larger framework that links definitions of literacy and educational philosophies with teaching, staff development, and assessment. While the curriculum as a product to be delivered by teachers to students is still the dominant model in ESL and in literacy education, more and more programs are seeking ways of effectively combining product and process models.

Reflections: Making curriculum decisions

This chapter suggests that curriculum decisions are often political decisions that reflect certain values and represent certain orientations. It also suggests that pure ideological models often lose their purity when enacted in the classroom and that there may be a gap between the official curriculum and the operationalized version. The following questions are designed to help programs examine the realities of their curriculum and decide on changes where appropriate:

1. What orientations does your program support, either explicitly or implicitly? Why? Does your curriculum exemplify strong or weak forms of a particular approach? Why?

2. What are the goals of your program? Is there an "official curriculum" that spells out these goals or a guiding philosophy that shapes teaching? What is it?

3. Whose vision of language and literacy is represented in the curriculum? The funders'? The administrators'? The teachers'? The learners'? Why are some voices louder than others?

4. In many programs, some questions that should be asked are never asked and certain agendas are never examined. Some educators call this the "null curriculum." In your program, is there such a "null curriculum"? If so, what questions are never asked and why?

5. In your program, is there a good match between the official curriculum and the curriculum as it is operationalized in the classroom? Are there hidden agendas that subvert the official curriculum? Does the official curriculum present a "sanitized" version of what is really going on? If so, why?

6. To what extent is your curriculum pre-specified and to what extent is it emergent? In which direction would you like to move?

7. In your program, is there a curriculum framework that ties together goals, content, approaches, materials, assessment, and staff development? If so, what are the strengths and weaknesses of this framework?

Endnotes

1. See *An introduction to curriculum research and development* by Stenhouse, 1975.

2. There a great many educational and philosophical taxonomies that can help guide language, literacy, and learning. The model provided here is one of many, based on the work of Eisner & Vallance, 1974; Schubert, 1986; Giroux, 1983 and others. The categories are not written in stone, but are merely represented as a starting point for reflection and discussion.

3. For further discussion, see Aronowitz & Giroux, 1988; Eisner & Vallance, 1974; Delpit, 1988.

4.   See Crandall & Imel, 1991.

5.   For further discussions on competency-based education, see Alamprese et al., [1987]; Savage, in press.

6.   While not necessarily questioning the life skills curriculum per se or the value of teaching competencies, some educators maintain that competencies often are externally developed and may not be relevant to the needs of a particular group. Weinstein-Shr relates the story of her own experiences with a competency-based survival curriculum. She writes

> *[I] dutifully taught a class of older Hmong women to read supermarket labels, only to discover that the women bought their meat wholesale from a butcher and grew their own vegetables. After having them practice filling out forms, observations in family settings made it clear that the older children who had a facility with literacy did the family form-filling.* (Weinstein-Shr, 1989, p. 15)

7.   See Sheils, 1988.

8.   See Auerbach & Burgess, 1987.

9.   See Tollefson, 1991; Tollefson, 1989; Tollefson, 1986; Tollefson, 1985.

10.   For a discussion, see Jurmo, 1989; Sarmiento, 1989; Sarmiento & Kay, 1990; Ilsley, 1989; Collins et al., 1989.

11.   See Ilsley, 1989 and Sarmiento & Kay, 1990. Ilsley criticizes current programs by saying

> *... A comprehensive program should focus on an individual's needs, not those of his or her boss. Rather than directly benefiting the quality of life of illiterates, funds earmarked to educate non-reading adults are used, instead, to help corporations prosper. Learning to read the company rules may not be enough .* (Ilsley, 1989, p. 9)

12.   See de Beaugrande, 1980; Neisser, 1976; Rumelhart, 1985; and Smith, 1982a.

13.   For a full discussion on schema-theoretic approaches and interactive reading, see the chapter on approaches.

14.   See Rogers, 1969.

15.   See Maslow, 1954.

16.   See Knowles, 1980.

17.   See Giroux, 1981; Auerbach, 1990 citing Taylor, 1983.

18.   See Lytle, et al., 1986.

19.   See Lytle et al., 1986, citing Fingeret 1984, p. 26.

20. This view is often shared by funders. Yet many learners count changes in self-confidence and increases in self-worth as one of the most significant outcomes that have resulted from their participation in literacy programs.

21. See Apple, 1979 and Giroux, 1983.

22. See Auerbach & Burgess, 1987 and Tollefson, 1989.

23. For further discussion, see Auerbach, 1989; Freire, 1970; Shor, 1987; Spener, 1990; and Wallerstein, 1983.

24. See Delpit, 1988, p. 85.

25. See Tyler, 1949.

26. See Tyler, 1949. Literacy curricula based on this orientation often include computerized program management components that assess students, move them through an instructional sequence, and track their progress. For example, in some technology-based curricula, the computer program generates information about each lesson that the student has attempted and reports on several aspects of student achievement and effort (or lack thereof). Students who move too fast through an instructional set and, in the process, get all the answers wrong may get reported as "not trying hard enough;" similarly, if students take too much time between answers (talking to their friends or daydreaming, perhaps), the computer will report that insufficient time was spent "on task." [Examples are taken from the computer program entitled *Basic Adult Skills Education* (BASE).]

27. Examples are taken from the computer program entitled *Basic Adult Skills Education* (BASE).

28. See Auerbach, 1986 and Collins, 1983.

29. For example, see Spener, 1990; Moriarty & Wallerstein, 1979; and the curriculum module by Maria Malagamba-Roddy in this volume, for a discussion on how aspects of a Freirean approach can be used in a CBE program.

30. See also Maley, 1984.

31. These types of questions go back as far as Ralph Tyler's *Basic principles of curriculum and instruction* (1949).

32. See MELT, 1985.

33. Alamprese et al., 1987 citing National Center for Educational Statistics, 1982, p. 80

34. While most programs use either checklists or standardized tests, such as the BEST or CASAS to measure competency attainment, the model supports any valid and reliable evaluation measure as long as it is performance based. In fact, the MELT resource guide mentions a number of alternative assessments: simulations, in which places such as a bank or a grocery store are replicated in the classroom, role plays in which a student might pretend to be an employee calling in sick or a secretary taking the call, contact assignments

in which students go out into the real world to accomplish a given task such as ordering from the menu in a restaurant, or an actual performance such as following the instructions on a bag of micro-wave popcorn.

35.   In "Literacy through a CBE approach," K. Lynn Savage shows how competency-based curriculum can foster both survival and academic literacy and how it can be used to teach the three types of literacy which will serve as a basis for the National Adult Literacy Survey: prose literacy, document literacy, and quantitative literacy.

36.   For a full description of the curriculum, see Guth & Wrigley, 1992.

37.   See Auerbach, 1990 .

38.   Research cited in Stenhouse, 1975; when Popham, the father of the behavioral objective in teaching was told that real teachers don't teach by objectives, he replied, "Maybe they ought to."

39.   For further discussions and examples, see Isserlis, 1990; Auerbach, 1990 and Nash et al, 1989.

40.   For a full description of the El Paso LEA literacy curriculum, see Guth & Wrigley, 1992.

41.   The El Paso five step model also provides the foundation for the college's workplace literacy program, although one significant change has occurred. The program used videos of workplace situations as a background for discussion and language and literacy development. Since the videos necessarily constitute pre-established materials, the initial inquiry phase has been replaced by a "language input" stage that provides background for discussions and language development.

42.   See also *Green Card English: Curriculum Making as Politics* by Heide Spruck Wrigley (Wrigley, forthcoming).

References

Alamprese, J. A., Hemphill, D., Ramirez, S., Rickard, P., Tibbetts, J., & Wise, J. ([1987]). *CBAE evaluation study report. Investigating in change: Competency-based adult education in California.* Sacramento: California State Department of Education.

Apple, M. W. (1979). *Ideology and curriculum.* New York: Routledge and Kegan Paul.

Aronowitz, S., & Giroux, H. A. (1988). Schooling, culture, and literacy in the age of broken dreams: A review of Bloom and Hirch. *Harvard Educational Review, 58*(2), 172-192.

Auerbach, E. R. (1986). Competency-based ESL: One step forward or two steps back? *TESOL Quarterly, 20*(3), 411-429.

Auerbach, E. R. (1989). Toward a social-contextual approach to family literacy. *Harvard Educational Review, 59*(2), 165-181.

Auerbach, E. R. (1990). *Making meaning, making change: A guide to participatory curriculum development for adult ESL and family literacy.* Boston: University of Massachusetts [in press (1992), Regents Prentice Hall/Center for Applied Linguistics].

Auerbach, E. R., & Burgess, D. (1987). The hidden curriculum of survival ESL. In I. Shor (Ed.), *Freire for the classroom: A sourcebook for liberatory teaching* (pp. 150-169). Portsmouth, NH: Boynton/Cook/Heinemann.

Collins, M. (1983). A critical analysis of competency-based systems in adult education. *Adult Education Quarterly, 33*(3), 174-183.

Collins, S. D., Balmuth, M., & Jean, P. (1989). So we can use our own names, and write the laws by which we live: Educating the new U.S. labor force. *Harvard Educational Review, 59*(4), 454-469.

Crandall, J., & Imel, S. (1991). Issues in adult literacy education. *The ERIC Review, 1*(2), 2-8.

de Beaugrande, R. (1980). *Text, discourse, and process: Toward a multidisciplinary science of texts.* Norwood, NJ: Ablex.

Delpit, L. D. (1988). The silenced dialogue: Power and pedagogy in educating other people's children. *Harvard Educational Review, 58*(3), 280-298.

Eisner, E. W., & Vallance, E. (Editors). (1974). *Conflicting conceptions of curriculum.* Berkeley, CA: McCutchan.

Freire, P. (1970). The adult literacy process as cultural action for freedom. *Harvard Educational Review, 40*(2), 205-225.

Giroux, H. A. (1981). Literacy, ideology and the politics of schooling. *Humanities in Society, 4*(4), 335-361.

Giroux, H. A. (1983). *Theory and resistance in education: A pedagogy for the opposition.* South Hadley, MA: Bergin and Garvey.

Guth, G. J. A., & Wrigley, H. S. (1992). *Adult ESL literacy: Programs and practices.* San Mateo, CA: Aguirre International. (Available from the U.S. Department of Education, Clearinghouse on Adult Education and Literacy).

Ilsley, P. J. (1989). The language of adult literacy. *Thresholds in Education, XV*(4), 6-10.

Isserlis, J. (1990). Using action research for ESL evaluation and assessment. *TESL Talk, 20*(1), 305-316.

Jurmo, P. (1989). The case for participatory literacy education. In A. Fingeret, & P. Jurmo (Eds.), *Participatory literacy education* (pp. 17-28). San Francisco: Jossey-Bass.

Knowles, M. (1980). *The modern practice of adult education: From pedagogy to andragogy.* Chicago, IL: Association Press/Follett.

Lytle, S., Marmor, T., & and Penner, F. H. (1986, April). *Literacy theory in practice: Assessing reading and writing of low-literate adult.* Paper presented at the annual meeting of the American Educational Research Association (AERA), San Francisco.

Maley, A. (1984). "I got religion"- Evangelism in language teaching. In S. J. Savignon, & M. S. Berns (Ed.), *Initiatives in communicative language teaching* (pp. 79-87). Reading, MA: Addison-Wesley.

Maslow, A. H. (1954). *Motivation and personality.* New York: Harper & Row.

Mainstream English language training (MELT) resource package. (1985). Washington, DC: U.S. Department of Health and Human Services, Office of Refugee Resettlement.

Moriarty, P., & Wallerstein, N. (1979). Student/ teacher/ learner: A Freire approach to ABE/ ESL. *Adult Literacy and Basic Education, Fall,* 193-201.

Nash, A., Cason, A., Rhum, M., McGrail, L., & Gomez-Sanford, R. (1989). *Talking shop: A curriculum sourcebook for participatory adult ESL.* Boston: University of Massachusetts, English Family Literacy Project [in press (1992), Regents Prentice Hall/Center for Applied Linguistics].

Neisser, U. (1976). *Cognition and reality: Principles and implications of cognitive psychology.* San Francisco: W.H. Freeman and Company.

Rogers, C. (1969). *Freedom to learn.* Westerville, OH: Merrill.

Rumelhart, D. E. (1985). Toward an interactive model of reading. In H. Singer & R. B. Ruddell (Eds.), *Theoretical models and processes of reading* (pp. 722-750). Newark, DE: International Reading Association.

Sarmiento, T. (1989, September). *A labor perspective on basic skills.* Paper presented at the Conference on Workplace Basic Skills: A Labor-Management Approach, Columbus, OH: Columbus Area Labor Management Committee.

Sarmiento, A. R., & Kay, A. (1990). *Worker-centered learning: A union guide to workplace literacy.* Washington, DC: AFL-CIO Human Resources Development Institute.

Savage, K. L. (in press). Literacy through a CBE approach. In J. A. Crandall (Ed.), *Approaches to adult ESL literacy instruction.* Englewood Cliffs, NJ: Prentice Hall Regents/Center for Applied Linguistics.

Schubert, W. H. (1986). *Curriculum: Perspective, paradigm, and possibility.* New York: Macmillan.

Sheils, J. (1988). *Communication in the modern languages classroom.* Strasbourg: Council of Europe, Council for Cultural Co-operation.

Shor, I. (1987). Monday morning fever: Critical literacy and the generative theme of "work." In I. Shor (Ed.), *Freire for the classroom: A sourcebook for liberatory teaching* (pp. 104-121). Portsmouth, NH: Boynton/Cook/Heinemann.

Smith, F. (1982). *Understanding reading.* New York: Holt, Rinehart, & Winston.

Spener, D. (1990). *NCLE Q & A: The Freirean approach to adult literacy education.* Washington, DC: Center for Applied Linguistics, National Clearinghouse on Literacy Education.

Stenhouse, L. (1975). *An introduction to curriculum research and development.* London: Heinemann.

Tollefson, J. W. (1985). Research on refugee resettlement: Implications for instructional programs. *TESOL Quarterly, 19*(4), 753-764.

Tollefson, J. W. (1986). Functional competencies in the U.S. refugee program: Theoretical and practical problems. *TESOL Quarterly, 20*(4), 649-664.

Tollefson, J. W. (1989). *Alien winds: The reeducation of America's Indochinese refugees.* New York: Praeger.

Tollefson, J. (1991). *Planning language, planning inequality: Language policy in the community.* New York: Longman.

Tyler, R. W. (1949). *Basic principles of curriculum and instruction.* Chicago: University of Chicago Press.

Wallerstein, N. (1983). The teaching approach of Paulo Freire. In J. W. Oller, & P. A. Richard-Amato (Eds.), *Methods that work: A smorgasbord of ideas for language teachers* (pp. 190-213). Rowley, MA: Newbury House.

Weinstein-Shr, G. (1989, March). *Literacy and social process: A community in transition.* Unpublished paper. Philadelphia: Temple University, College of Education.

Wrigley, H. S. (forthcoming). *Green card English: Curriculum making as politics.* Unpublished doctoral dissertation, University of Southern California.

Chapter 8

Staff Development and Program Issues

A commitment to teachers is in a real sense a commitment to students.

— Karen Griswold[1]

Teaching adult English as a second language (ESL) literacy effectively is a difficult and demanding job, a job that requires special knowledge, skills, and practice. Staff development helps teachers grow, strengthens programs overall, and improves teaching. It is particularly needed at times of change and when new needs arise. For ESL adult literacy, this is such a time as programs are confronted with a burgeoning number of language minority adults seeking literacy services.

Staff development takes a variety of forms. These may include conferences, workshops, institutes, staff meetings, classroom observations, informal dialogue with colleagues, and participation in courses or a certificate program. It is often focused on teachers, but as the name implies, can include other staff as well.

This chapter is divided into three sections, "Background: Issues in Staffing and Professional Development," "Practice: Examples of Staff Development," and "Reflections: Questions about Staff Development." The "Background" section explores the barriers to staff development and the related issues of funding, advocacy, professionalism, and the diversity of needs among ESL literacy teachers. The "Practice" section outlines and discusses three major models for delivering staff development, and, through "Cases in Point," illustrates how these models are used in the field. The "Practice" section also presents a framework for determining content in ESL literacy staff development and outlines key points for delivering effective staff development. The "Reflections" section is a guide to help teachers decide which staff development issues they would like to see addressed in their program.

Background: Issues in staffing and professional development

Providing staff development opportunities is not a task that has received priority in adult education. According to a recent report, staff development is considered to be one of the major weaknesses in adult basic education, English as a second language, and literacy programs. The report states,

> Minimal training for adult education teachers and literacy professionals consists largely of voluntary attendance at workshops, conferences or seminars. At best, adult education programs usually offer one or two half-days per year of training and much of that time is devoted to administrative concerns and procedures or to motivational presentations. In addition, these programs are not likely to offer release time or monetary incentives for staff to participate in training activities.[2]

This state of affairs is no different for ESL literacy education, a new field where educational theories, teaching models, and classroom practices are just starting to coalesce. Some of the difficulties in delivering effective staff development to ESL literacy programs relate to the special nature of the field and the constraints faced by programs and teachers.

In this section, we will address the issue of professionalism, discuss the constraints that programs face in delivering effective staff development, and summarize the debate over qualifications versus credentials. We will also discuss the characteristics of ESL literacy teachers and outline the challenges that need to be addressed if the field wants a professional workforce.

Constraints on the delivery of staff development

Most ESL literacy programs are operating on shoestring budgets. They often feel that they do not have the resources, time, or funds required to sustain an ongoing staff development program. In addition, funding for adult ESL literacy is often short-term and subject to shift with the political winds.[3] As a result, teachers often find themselves in a quandary: how to find a balance between their own views of responsible and appropriate literacy education and the requirements and expectation of the funding source (or other stakeholders). For example, teachers who support a Freirean approach may find themselves teaching in a program that requires that certain prescribed and predetermined competencies must be taught.

Staff development can help teachers articulate their views and help them discover ways of educating funders. In cases where negotiating with funders is not possible, staff development can explore strategies for implementing a program that is educationally sound and socially responsible within the limits set by the funding agency.

Responding to the need for advocacy

In adult ESL literacy, staff development also needs to deal with the desire of teachers to act as advocates for their students. Many literacy educators feel that such an advocacy-oriented stance is necessary to correct misperceptions that society holds of literacy learners and counterbalance some of the disabling attitudes that language minority adults face. Such advocacy can take several forms: it can ask for a better understanding of the special characteristics of ESL literacy learners, increased resources to meet learner needs, and greater responsiveness by mainstream institutions (e.g., schools, health departments, housing authorities, places of employment) to the needs of language minority adults.

Teachers who take an advocacy stance often try to influence language attitudes. For example, they may point out that schools and funders should consider the positive aspects of learning literacy in the native language, as well as learning ESL, and not focus primarily on negative attributes, such as "limited English proficiency." In many such programs, advocacy is seen less as a political stance than a professional responsibility to act in the best interest of one's clients, in this case, the literacy learners.[4]

The role of the "teacher as advocate" remains controversial, however. A number of programs, particularly workplace programs that receive company funds, feel that well-meaning, well-intentioned teachers might end up hurting the program in an effort to help the students. Staff development programs can provide a forum to help ESL literacy teachers explore the need for advocacy and help them decide which form such advocacy might take.

Addressing the need for full-time jobs

Another challenge deals with the lack of full-time positions for teachers. Adult ESL literacy teaching is currently provided largely by part-time staff who receive very few benefits. Most teachers hold down part-time positions in a related field or patch together several part-time positions in order to earn a living wage.

Even if the programs have resources available, it is very difficult to provide rich staff development efforts if part-time teachers cannot participate because of other commitments. Since effective staff development requires coherent and consistent efforts, successful staff development will be difficult as long as there is no support from funders, programs, and practitioners themselves for an employment structure that includes full-time positions for qualified teachers.[5]

Given budget constraints, districts and programs often have to make a difficult choice. They must choose between spending money on developing a professional workforce with access to full-time positions or using available funds to serve more students. While some literacy programs have made the decision early on to hire only skilled teachers who work full-time, others are using a combination of full-time staff who receive benefits (largely administrators and coordinators), contract teachers who work full-time and receive few benefits, and part-time teachers who only teach a few hours and receive no benefits. In other programs, directors are continuously trying to create full-time employment by offering teachers a combination of assignments. Thus, an individual might teach two or more courses, assist students several hours a week in a learning center, and spend some time working on a funded curriculum project.

Balancing qualification and certification

The adult ESL literacy field faces an additional challenge related to the professionalism of the workforce: deciding who is qualified to teach ESL adult literacy. On the one hand, there are concerns about professionalizing ESL literacy teaching by insisting on strong academic credentials, such as certificates in ABE or TESL or a Masters degree in ESL. On the other hand, credentialed teachers who understand literacy issues and have experience teaching language minority adults are difficult to find. As a result, the field is grappling with the issue of how to ensure competence and foster professionalism without establishing rigid certification requirements that deny professional opportunities for good teachers who may lack academic credentials.

The issue of teacher qualifications has split the field. At present, states, districts, and programs differ greatly in their requirements for ESL literacy teachers. While some funding agencies insist teachers have academic credentials, others have not established any standards for teachers.

There are two major positions in this debate. Some educators maintain that adult education teachers will not be treated like professionals unless the field establishes strong prerequisites for teaching. Others criticize the politics of requiring credentials and maintain that experience in teaching and working with the community should be of equal importance. Those who support the latter position emphasize the need to find teachers who share the language of the learners and come from the communities that a program serves. They hold that it is important not to exclude teachers with strong backgrounds solely on the basis of credentials and to recognize that there are ways of gaining knowledge that do not depend on formal education.[6]

One proposed solution to this dilemma is to define "professional" and "skilled" in terms of qualifications that may include certification but do not depend on it. Thus, an ESL literacy professional could be someone who has

- acquired a knowledge base in the field in which s/he teaches

- demonstrated experience in the field

- maintains high standards of professional conduct

- participates in ongoing professional development

- can provide evidence that s/he is capable of teaching ESL literacy in ways that are educationally sound, socially responsible, and responsive to the needs of ESL literacy learners.

Some educators point out that different skills are needed in different contexts and propose that programs take a holistic approach to hiring and staff development. This means that programs should collectively look at their staff and other resources and decide what needs they should fill based on their particular context. Thus, a program may determine that it needs teachers who have strong academic backgrounds for some classes and teachers who speak the native language of the learners, or who come from the community of learners, for others. A program may then hire different people with different qualifications to fill their needs and not feel constrained by concerns about uniform qualifications.

Taking a holistic view, these educators suggest that states and programs look at employment requirements that are based on student populations and try to determine what qualifications are needed in a particular context. For example, an adult ESL literacy program in which learners come from the same community, share a common language, and are non-literate in their native language might be best served by a team approach. For example, one teacher might be bilingual with experience with working with adults, and another may have a strong academic background in second language acquisition or reading.

Whenever such a team approach to qualifications is implemented, it becomes necessary to take the differential needs of the teachers into account. Some of these needs are outlined below.

Adult ESL literacy teachers: Meeting the needs of a diverse group

ESL literacy teachers who work in adult education are a highly diverse group with diverse staff development needs. They differ widely in respect to personal background, educational training, professional experience, interest in language and literacy, and enthusiasm for teaching. They may teach in community colleges, in public schools, at the worksite, in union halls, or community centers, or they may tutor in libraries, prisons, churches and synagogues, or in housing projects. Some have degrees in teaching English as a second language, educational linguistics, adult education, or a related field but may not have a great deal of experience working with adults from non-traditional backgrounds. Others have been certified as teachers but may not have had experience teaching language minority adults. Others share the language and culture of the students and have years of experience working with adult learners but may lack academic training and certification.

Individual language and literacy teachers may define their professional goals in different ways and therefore need different kinds of support. They may regard themselves foremost as academic instructors of language and literacy, interpreting the teacher-student relationship as an association between a professional and a client. They may see themselves as "co-learners" and "facilitators" whose main purpose is to support students' efforts to gain greater control over the circumstances of their lives. In spite of discussions that emphasize an ideological rift between linguistic/academic perspectives and community orientations, most teachers seek to emphasize both professionalism in teaching and humanistic concern for their students.

Teachers also differ in their orientation towards language teaching and learning. Some put a strong emphasis on direct teaching, focusing on clearly outlined objectives of what is to be taught by the instructor and mastered by the students. Others take a more developmental approach. By working with their students to devise opportunities for reading, writing, and face-to-face communication, they allow learning to emerge naturally out of various literacy events. Aware of the debate in the literature, many of these teachers are looking for ways to balance traditional approaches (by which they themselves may have been taught) with the alternative approaches that are gaining in prominence.

Summary of background issues

In spite of their differences in background and goals, ESL literacy teachers have common needs both inside and outside of the classroom. They also have the right to have their voices heard by programs and funders.[7] In many cases, staff development can provide a forum for addressing the concerns of teachers, including their concerns about full time employment and teaching qualifications. Staff development can also help to meet the differential needs of teachers by encouraging them to explore their own views of teaching.

Practice: Examples of staff development

Three organizing principles govern the delivery of staff development in adult ESL and literacy programs: context, process, and content. Context refers to the environment in which staff development takes place, process explores the different modes of delivery, and content refers to what is taught. This section will first discuss three models used in the process of delivering staff development and then outline a framework for deciding on the specific content that staff development for adult ESL literacy might include.

Models of staff development

Over the years, staff developers and teacher educators have designed a number of approaches for staff development. For ease of understanding, we have collapsed these approaches into three broad models: the craft model, the applied science model, and the inquiry model[8]. The following section describes these models and provides examples of the different ways adult ESL literacy programs in the field have modified these models.

Craft model

The craft model, sometimes referred to as the mentor model, relies on the knowledge of the experienced practitioner to mentor less experienced practitioners. These experienced teachers (or "charismatic master-practitioners"[9]) often serve as master teachers. They may conduct workshops or act as mentors within their own programs. Master teachers may discuss or demonstrate teaching techniques or observe teachers in the classroom and provide feedback on their teaching. Besides asking experienced teachers to conduct workshops, adult ESL literacy programs frequently invite professionals from other disciplines (public schools, health departments, the courts, or industry) to share their experiences and provide information for teachers who may be unfamiliar with the social issues that concern their students.

In many ESL literacy programs, the master teacher role is filled by a coordinator who has a strong background in teaching ESL literacy to adults and shares strategies with teachers who lack this experience. In many cases the coordinator, usually a full-time employee, outlines lessons or develops tests that part-time teachers then use in their classes. In some programs, experienced teachers are certified as "trainers" who then deliver staff development to teachers in other programs. Many times, the receiving programs are in outlying areas where access to staff development is limited.

In applying the craft model, the content of the staff development depends on the group receiving the training. For example, in a program staffed primarily by interns and volunteers, a master teacher may develop information packets, orient the volunteers to the program, provide background on teaching language and literacy, and show them how to use methods commonly used in the program, such as the Language Experience Approach or Total Physical Response. Staff development is adjusted to address the special needs and talents of interns or volunteers, such as when interns are former students or bilingual.

In a program staffed by full-time, experienced teachers, the staff development based on the craft model focuses on issues of particular concerns to teachers or on special needs that have arisen. Topics may include integrating math into the literacy curriculum, fostering learner participation, and ensuring validity and reliability in alternative assessment.

Discussion of the craft model

The success of the craft model depends essentially on the expertise of the master teacher or coordinator and the ability of the teacher to examine the expert advice in light of her own classroom. Three dangers are inherent in this model:

1. The master teacher may not be aware of new developments in the field (e.g., advances made by socio-linguistics) and may not be able to move new teachers beyond the limits of the master teacher's own experience and training.

2. Master teachers and mentors may have been chosen for the "wrong" reasons, such as popularity, rather than teaching expertise.

3. Master teachers often present techniques without explaining the theory behind the techniques. As a result, techniques may be overgeneralized or misapplied when teachers try to use them.

To overcome the shortcomings of the craft model, most programs use master teachers and coordinators in some roles but supplement their staff development efforts with other approaches.

◆ *Case in point: Coordinators lead the teaching team*

Staff development at El Paso Literacy Education Action combines various approaches to staff development. The program offers workshops and conferences in which literacy educators train coordinators and teachers. On occasion, staff present conference workshops on innovative aspects of the curriculum (e.g., a video-based workplace literacy program). Some aspects of the El Paso staff development reflect features of the craft model. In weekly four-hour sharing and planning sessions, a coordinator, who is a literacy specialist, works with teachers, called facilitators. Together they develop a joint curriculum and plan assessment strategies. In collaboration with the coordinator, the facilitators develop lessons that follow a five step plan, originally designed by an educator/researcher. (See the curriculum chapter for details.) Facilitators in the program benefit in two ways: the five step approach acts as an overall framework that guides them in curriculum development and the experience of the coordinators facilitates decision making.

Applied science model

The applied science model is designed to link relevant research in the field with teaching practice. Designed to link theory and practice, it is most often used in teacher education programs at universities or colleges, teacher training institutes, and staff development conferences.

Typically, a professor, educational expert, or trainer provides the scientific or conceptual knowledge needed to deal with particular teaching problems and then suggests that teachers apply that knowledge to their own contexts. In some university-based programs, the teacher educator provides only a general discussion of teaching processes, and the teachers (or teachers-to-be) are expected to translate the knowledge they have gained into their own teaching practice. In other programs, theory and practice is linked more closely. Trainers or teacher educators may ask teachers to demonstrate what they have learned in a lab setting or try out various approaches at their own programs and report the results back to the group.

Research has shown that the applied science model is most effective when there is a strong link between theory and practice, since very little transfer to teaching occurs if teachers hear about an approach only from a theoretical perspective.[10] As a result of this shortcoming, many ESL programs now prefer an approach that starts with theory, then moves on to demonstration and observation of effective practices, and ends with hands-on application by the teachers.[11]

The applied science model often follows this sequence:

1.   Through workshops or demonstration lessons, teachers see how an experienced practitioner uses literacy activities and have an opportunity to discuss their observations.

2.   Teachers practice the strategies they first observed at the training site in their own classrooms, where they get feedback from a colleague or a resource person.

3.   At the home site, such practice is sometimes supported by peer coaching and additional reflection.[12]

Variations of the applied science model can be found in staff development for ESL, literacy, and ESL literacy. The following examples present some of these variations.

Attending conferences and workshops

Programs send their staff to conference presentations and workshops. They sometimes offer reimbursement for registration and mileage. As teachers return, they are asked to discuss what they learned at the conference or share ideas about new strategies for teaching ESL literacy with other teachers who did not attend.[13]

Presenting at conferences

Programs encourage teachers to give presentations at conferences that link theory with practice. These presentations not only highlight what the program is trying to do, they also give the practitioner a chance to think about her teaching and connect it to the ideas of others. In addition, participation at conferences help teachers feel part of the large community of literacy educators.

Using outside experts

Programs bring in researchers, consultants, or university-based educators to work with program staff. In some cases, the outside expert presents workshops on a particular area of ESL literacy. In other cases, they work with the program on an ongoing basis, provide feedback on curriculum development or assessment, and/or conduct external evaluations.

Teacher training institutes

Programs work together with teacher training institutes to build the capacity of their ESL literacy teachers.[14] These institutes set up regional workshops that teachers and teacher-trainers attend, or they send expert facilitators to the program itself to provide on-site training. In some cases, institutes present a series of workshops where teachers practice certain skills between sessions and then attend follow-up meetings throughout the year.

Teacher training videos

Programs develop staff capacity by using teacher training videos as a starting point for discussions. Teachers watch and then analyze the video in light of their own practice.[15]

Literacy centers

Programs work together with literacy centers, who assist in capacity building for programs and provide staff development for teachers. Often, these centers act as clearinghouses for materials and keep teachers up-to-date on issues and developments in the literacy field.[16] Some centers also conduct research.

Setting up conferences

Some programs set up their own local or regional conferences to which they invite speakers, practitioners, and workshop leaders. These conferences are designed to build the capacity of both the program itself as well as that of teachers in similar programs. In many cases, such conferences are built around a particular context, such as workplace literacy, family literacy, or community literacy.

Discussion of the applied science model

Since the applied science model is essentially a top-down model (although modified through teacher feedback), it has met with some criticism. First, the experience of the "trainer" can be very different from that of the practitioner, and often the complexity of actual teaching situations is not acknowledged. Second, the "trainer" may be wedded to one particular approach, and practitioners who have opposing views may feel put off.[17] Third, alternative models of teaching ESL literacy, such as whole language or participatory education, are slow to find their way into the training, and staff development courses that are a long time in the making are sometimes irrelevant by time they reach programs. Finally, the strong "how to" component of the model may stifle creativity and keep teachers from exploring their own alternatives.

◆ Case in point: Three types of training

As is the case in most adult ESL literacy programs, staff development at the REEP literacy/ESL program in Arlington, Virginia, combines various approaches. For example, the project encourages peer observations (teachers visit each other's classrooms, while a coordinator takes over a class) and promotes "action research" (teachers receive inservice credit for each action research project that is completed). Staff development at REEP also includes aspects of the applied science model.[18] Based on an assessment of staff training needs, the program provides three types of trainings:

- access to training in ten basic ESL techniques (through participation in an ESL Teacher Training Institute); these include dialogue and drills, role play, information gap activities, life skills reading, and cooperative learning

- additional "supertrainings" on the latest topics of interest to the staff (e.g., evaluating learner progress in achieving competencies)

- paid inservice training (one 3-hour training per teaching cycle), based on the needs identified by instructional staff; inservice has included teaching literacy across the curriculum and using instructional technologies.

Programs such as REEP have found that the applied science model will address some of their needs and leave others unmet. Many times, teachers report that although they gain a great deal from attending institutes that link theory and practice, they learn most from ongoing discussions with informed colleagues and experienced coordinators. The inquiry model, discussed on the next page seeks to address this need for collaboration and reflection.

Inquiry model

The inquiry model, also called the reflective teaching model, has two manifestations: (1) teachers work individually to reflect on their own practice by keeping journals or by developing an individual action research project, and (2) teachers work collaboratively in pairs or groups to make program decisions, develop curriculum, discuss classroom issues, and develop new strategies for interaction with learners. This model allows teachers to develop their own theories of teaching and to come to a greater understanding of the nature of decision making in the classroom. The inquiry model starts with problems that arise out of practice and then gives teachers the opportunity to explore solutions. Two major features of the inquiry model are peer observations and action research.

Peer observation

In peer observation, teachers work together, often in pairs, to strengthen their teaching. Typically, peer observation follows a five step process. Pairs or groups of teachers

- observe each other and identify key elements of the class with respect to both teacher behavior and learner responses

- comment on both intended and unintended outcomes

- discuss the class with an emphasis on what did and did not work

- make a plan to modify certain aspects of the class

- put this plan into action and discuss the changes that have or have not occurred as a result.

Through a process of observation and conversation, teachers gain insight into their teaching and support from fellow teachers whose experience is similar to their own.

Discussion of peer observation

The approach needs to be used with caution. Many educators feel that peer observation is not effective if used with unskilled teachers, since these teachers may not be sure what to look for in the classroom.[19] Pairing inexperienced teachers may also reinforce negative literacy strategies, such as an over-reliance on skill and drill activities. There is general agreement that peer observation is most effective as part of a wider staff development effort.

Action research

The inquiry model finds its strongest realization in action research, a process that links teacher practice with relevant theory in the field. Unlike the applied science model, however, action research begins with a classroom issue that has been identified by a teacher or a learner.[20] In action research, teams of teachers are brought together to identify an issue or a problem that has arisen out of their own teaching experience and to propose a way of addressing this problem. The action research process often involves examining and discussing research articles that speak to the problem, formulating a research question that focuses on a particular aspect of the class, and proposing an appropriate "intervention." Through a cyclical process of reflection, observation, action, and reflection, teachers effect change in their classes and in the program overall.

Discussion of action research

Action research is sometimes criticized as "not real research" since it is based on the personal experiences of the "researchers," includes only a small number of "subjects," is not subject to outside review, and does not yield replicable results. Educators have responded to these criticisms with two suggestions. First, some suggest action research be designated as "small r" research to distinguish it from more academically rigorous ("capital R") research. Second, they suggest action researchers work with a university-based educator or ethnographer who could help teachers conduct classroom-based research in a larger social science context. A recent report on staff development responds to the issue by saying

> It must be remembered that it is conducted for much more restricted purposes than most "academic" research and therefore must be judged by somewhat different standards. Within the context for which it is intended, some action research is good research, some is not ... Any process which encourages teachers and improves their ability to question their own practice is apt to be good staff development.[21]

♦ *Case in point: Action research*

The ESL literacy program at the International Institute of Rhode Island in Providence has used an action research project to develop a learner evaluation tool.[22] Working in collaboration with other practitioners, the two full-time ESL literacy specialists set up an action research project to help them gain greater understanding of the literacy students in their classes. Through a process of planning, action, observation, and reflection, they developed categories in which literacy change could be observed. These categories became the basis for a learner evaluation grid to be used as an alternative assessment tool (see assessment chapter for the grid itself).

The action research assessment project included evaluating existing tests, listening attentively to students, observing literacy behaviors in the classroom and on video, documenting what happened in each class, formulating preliminary drafts of assessment categories, and seeking input from other teachers. In observing the learners in their classes, the teacher/researchers asked themselves questions such as who sought help, was willing to help other students, wanted to go to the blackboard and write, or translated the facilitator's instructions to his/her co-learners. Answers to these questions and observations were developed into a written narrative and analyzed by the teachers. The evaluation grid developed out of this analysis.

As is the case with most action research projects, the process did not move from problem to solution in a straightforward, linear fashion. Rather it was a cyclical, recursive process in which ideas emerged and were developed through a process of trial, error, and refinement.[23]

The collaborative nature of the inquiry model encourages teachers to work together, consult with each other and with program administrators, and act as a source of information for other teachers. It reflects the recommendations made by advocates of school restructuring that teachers spend more time with their peers both inside and outside of the classroom.

♦ *Case in point: Teacher sharing*

As is the case with other programs, staff development at the Haitian Multi-Service Center (HMSC) in Dorchester, Massachusetts, combines features of different models of staff development. For example, master teachers work with interns in developing processes for teaching literacy in the native language (in this case Haitian Creole).   In these workshops, interns also learn how to read and write Creole, a language that does not have a strong written tradition.

Staff development at the Haitian Multi-Service Center strongly reflects certain aspects of the inquiry model. The program takes part in a collaborative staff development project developed by the Bilingual Community Literacy Training Project at the University of Massachusetts, Boston.[24] This staff development includes formal teacher sharing sessions in which teachers from the community discuss their experiences once a week and reflect on their teaching. The discussions are facilitated by an educator from the University of Massachusetts. Out of these discussions, themes emerge which are then further explored. Examples of such themes include using translation in class (how, when, how much) and how to handle error correction. Teachers have also experimented with keeping teaching logs and teaching journals.

To aid the teachers/interns in their reflections and document a participatory staff development process, the project has kept minutes of all the staff meetings. These minutes show how the teachers' thinking evolved over the course of a cycle and provide concrete evidence of what has or has not worked in the classroom. The Bilingual Community Literacy Training Project uses these minutes for three purposes: to (1) provide a permanent record and act as a collective memory of the staff development process, (2) provide the basis for longitudinal research, and (3) help guide future work.

Since the staff development at the HMSC includes interns, the program faces a challenge that other community-based organizations face as well: how to support a staff that has a strong understanding of the community and its language but has not had a great deal of formal training in teaching literacy and/or English as a Second Language. To build both confidence and competence in its teachers, the program practices what it preaches. It offers a participatory model that starts with the classroom experiences of the staff and extends these experiences through dialogue, discussions, and exchange of information and ideas.

The staff development at the Haitian Multi-Service Center also includes other aspects of the craft model (e.g., master teachers work with interns from the community who teach Creole literacy).

Discussion of teacher control

Many teacher educators agree that teachers should play a major role in their own professional development. There is consensus in the field[25] that staff development needs to be based, at least in part, on the goals and interests of teachers and that training is most successful if it can take teachers from where they are and move them to the next level of understanding. Yet, some teacher educators have expressed concerns about involving novice teachers in all staff development decisions. As Willig points out,

> It must be acknowledged that the degree of involvement of staff often follows a developmental course, depending on the level of awareness and knowledge of the staff concerning relevant topics. The less we know about a topic, the less we are aware of what we need to know. Teachers who have no prior training or experience teaching ESL literacy students and have little awareness of the range of topics that address the needs of language minority adults. These teachers may find it difficult to identify essential components for their own staff development. Those who have more experience and knowledge in the area will be able to participate to a greater degree in developing such plans.[26]

In recognition of the fact that staff development should be teacher-centered (i.e., respond to the concerns of teachers), although not totally teacher-driven (i.e. controlled by teachers), most programs have developed their own approaches to staff development. In doing so, they provide their teachers with access to current research and relevant theories, while making it possible for staff to determine the direction their teaching should take.

Content for staff development in adult ESL literacy

What staff development content can help ESL literacy teachers become more effective? Three areas should be included in most staff development. These areas are knowledge and understanding of

- social contexts of adult ESL literacy

- second language learning and literacy development

- teaching processes that support language learning and literacy development.

The following lists of topics can help programs, teachers, and staff developers discuss and explore what content to include in their staff development.

Social contexts of ESL literacy

Staff development in adult ESL literacy should help teachers gain an awareness of

- the lives of the learners, including their interests, goals, and special strengths in respect to education in general and English literacy in particular

- the role of languages in the community, including the role of oral and written English and the role of the native language(s)

- the functions and uses of English and literacy in the learners' lives

- the relationship between culture, experience, and literacy and the importance of linking literacy to the lives of the learners

- cultural, ethnic, and economic diversity in the community and its relationship to ESL literacy

- relationships between the program, public schools, employers, and community agencies that serve ESL literacy adults

- differences and similarities in the cultures of the learners

- social issues of concerns to the learners.

Adult learning, second language acquisition, and literacy development

Staff development in adult ESL literacy should help teachers acquire knowledge and understanding of

- the critical aspects of adult learning, including differences in learning how to learn

- the importance of learner participation in making decisions about their own learning

- the complexity of second language acquisition, including the concept that errors are a natural part of language development

- differences and similarities in learning to read and write in a first and second language

- the relationship between oral language and literacy and how they can be mutually supportive

- the importance of meaning in learning language and literacy

  the role that phonics can play in literacy learning

- multiple definitions of literacy and the various dimensions of literacy, including the socio-political, cultural, affective, and cognitive dimensions

- different modes of learning among literate and non-literate adults

- relationship between literacy in the native language and learning literacy in a second language

- the difference between acquiring oral communication skills and functional literacy and learning the academic skills needed for success in mainstream educational and vocational programs

- appropriate ways of assessing program success, including the role of standardized tests and alternative assessments.

Teaching processes that support language and literacy development

Staff development should show programs and teachers how to work with the learners in order to

- get to know the community and its languages through a community needs assessment

- develop a literacy framework, decide on the goals for the program, and set objectives

- find out more about the learners in the program, including their experiences with literacy and schooling, the way they use literacy in their lives, their goals, interests, strengths, and weaknesses in using English and literacy

- find a match between available approaches to ESL literacy, the literacy framework, and learner needs and goals

- develop themes and topics that link literacy with the interests of the learners and build relevant background knowledge

- set up projects and develop literacy activities that allow learners to use literacy for meaning-making, problem solving, and decision making

- organize literacy lessons or literacy events in such a way that learners can understand the purpose and see "the big picture"

- find a balance between a focus on meaning and communication and a focus on skill development (phonics, grammar, and vocabulary)

- design groupings so that individuals can learn from each other, support each other, and challenge each other

- integrate all four language modes (listening, speaking, reading, and writing) while providing special support in those areas that need development

- mix opportunities for using "practical English" with opportunities for developing literacy for self-expression, cognitive development, and/or social change

- build language awareness and a sense of "correct" English without impairing communication and meaning-making

- assess learner progress in language and literacy in ways that match the program focus and base assessment on learner strengths.

Promising practices

The following section presents promising practices in staff development for adult ESL literacy.

◻ Teacher sharing

These teacher sharing sessions are made public through minutes that are kept of each meeting. The minutes reflect (1) the problems and issues of concern of the staff, (2) the suggestions that were made in respect to a problem, (3) arguments and discussions regarding these suggestions, and (4) feedback given as new ideas were tried in the classroom. These minutes represent a permanent record, not only of the program's staff development efforts, but of the growth of the teachers as well.

◻ Collaborations with other professionals

Increasingly, adult ESL literacy teachers make efforts to extend their own knowledge and understanding about the communities they serve. To assist them, programs may bring in professionals that provide information and answer questions.

At ReWA in Seattle, a lawyer comes to talk to staff and learners about issues of domestic violence. Discussions include the legal recourse available to victims of domestic violence. Since the lawyer is from the community of the learners, she is also aware of the cultural dimensions of domestic violence and is able to sensitize the staff to these issues.

In a Hmong refugee program, a community officer from the police force has discussed hunting laws, and a public health nurse talks to teachers about the need to discuss immunizations with students.

In some amnesty programs, teachers forged strong relationships with community lawyers who provided information on changing legal requirements of amnesty.

◻ Teachers learn the students' language

In some programs, teachers and staff are given the opportunity to learn one of the languages that the learners speak. Some family literacy programs offer language classes to teachers, secretaries, and administrators, and some workplace education programs offer Spanish to supervisors. These programs have several goals in mind: to help teaching staff develop elementary proficiency in the language of the learners and to facilitate everyday communication skills. Language classes are also designed to help participants develop an awareness of what it is like to struggle with a foreign language.

In a volunteer program in Santa Cruz, new tutors are given an introduction to Norwegian to help them understand the strategies they use in trying to make sense out of a language they don't speak. Other programs use different alphabets (Cyrillic, for example) to help the teaching staff gain greater awareness.

Tips for staff development

Although different models of staff development may be appropriate for different contexts, the field seems clear on the following tips:

☞ Regular staff development should be incorporated into the program design.

☞ Programs should pay staff to participate in staff development.

☞ Staff development should begin by meeting the needs of teachers and responding to their concerns about day-to-day teaching and then move on to broader issues.

☞ Mentor or master teachers should be selected through a collaborative process that includes all teachers. Such selections need to be made on the basis of experience and respect for the teacher's competence and not on the basis of popularity.

☞ One time workshops are not enough for most teachers to learn and grow. Effective staff development needs to be delivered as part of a comprehensive, integrated system.[27]

☞ Multiple forms of staff development help meet the varied needs of teachers at different times of their development. Individual staff development efforts must complement each other, reflect common goals, and be based on assumptions that have been made explicit.

☞ Effective staff development links theory and practice and enables teachers to try out new strategies in their own classrooms. Teachers should be aware that, while there is no single unified theory of adult learning, there are viable theories and approaches in linguistics and education that can guide the teaching of ESL and literacy to adults.

☞ Program change is facilitated through collaborative models that include participation by administrators, teachers, and learners in both planning and implementation. Strong teacher involvement results in greater program-wide interest and commitment to learners.

☞ ESL literacy teachers need targeted staff development that focuses on issues of concern to teachers both inside and outside of the classroom.

☞ Staff development topics should be identified through a local needs assessment (written surveys, phone interviews, personal interviews, focus groups) and through information gleaned from writings, talks, and discussions with other educators.

☞ Staff development must take into consideration the needs of both the novice teacher and the experienced practitioner and recognize that teachers have different needs at different stages of their careers. Effective staff development should draw on the experiences of teachers and build on their strengths. Teachers should be encouraged to discuss both their successes and failures and have opportunities to talk about the decision making processes they use in the classroom.

☞ Effectiveness of staff development efforts needs to be evaluated by teachers and administrators who share a common understanding of the purpose of staff development and the expected outcomes.

☞ Staff development can help teachers articulate their views and help them discover ways of educating funders. In cases where negotiating with funders is not possible, staff development can explore strategies for implementing a program that is educationally sound and socially responsible within the limits set by the funding agency.

Reflections

Effective staff development is based to a large extent on the expressed and perceived needs of teachers. Teachers thinking about their own students may want to consider the following questions in deciding on their staff development needs.

Professional development

What are your own priorities regarding your own professional development? Do you feel strongly about issues such as working conditions, career paths in ESL, responding to funding requirements, advocacy for students, and teacher qualifications? How can staff development help you and your fellow teachers address these issues?

Models of staff development

1. What model would help you the most in your professional development: the craft model, the applied science model, or the inquiry model? Why?

2. What combination of these might be most effective given the staffing in your program?

3. If your program were to implement an action research project at your site, which issues would you investigate? What kind of support would you need?

Content for staff development

This chapter has discussed the importance of knowledge and understanding in three key areas of adult ESL literacy: social context, second language learning and literacy development, and teaching processes. In which areas do you consider yourself particularly strong? In which areas are you weak?

If you could develop staff development content that reflects the literacy issues in your classroom, what topics would you address? To be more effective, what would you need to know in each of the following areas?

- social contexts that influence literacy development for my students

- second language learning and literacy development in adults

- supporting the language and literacy development of my students.

Are there any areas of adult ESL literacy that you are particularly interested in, such as teaching initial literacy, setting up group work, or using alternative assessment?

Endnotes

1. See Griswold, 1989.

2. See Tibbetts et al., 1991.

3. Funding for ESL literacy programs comes from a variety of sources including the federal government (for workplace literacy, family literacy, amnesty, and refugee programs), private foundations, state departments of education, or a combination of federal and state funds.

   Funding for staff development also varies for these programs. In some cases, programs use federal or state funds earmarked for staff development (e.g., monies offered under section 353 of the Adult Education Act) or use "321" funds designed to supplement adult education programs. In other cases, the monies come out of the local budget. Programs receiving federal monies directly often negotiate funds for staff development as part of the contract with the federal government. Occasionally, programs submit proposals to foundations or state and federal agencies and receive "mini-grants" for special staff development projects.

4. See Hamayan, 1990.

5. See Tibbetts et al., 1991.

6. See Auerbach, 1990.

7. See also "Practitioners' Bill of Rights" in *Making Meaning, Making Change* by Auerbach, 1990 and "Language and literacy teachers: Diverse backgrounds, common concerns" by Wrigley, 1991.

8.   These terms, "craft model", "applied science model" and "reflective model" are borrowed from a taxonomy developed by Wallace. See Wallace, M.J. (1991) *Training foreign language teachers: a reflective approach.* New York: Cambridge University Press.   The description of the models   provided here differs slightly from the descriptions used by Wallace.

9.   Program administrators and teachers often meet these individuals at conferences and invite them to conduct staff development at their programs. While some of these charismatic master practitioners are trained teachers, others may have little experience and may not fully meet the staff development needs of the program (K. L. Savage, personal communication, November 8, 1991).

10.   See Joyce & Showers, 1982.

11.   Training provided by the ESL Teacher Training Institute in California is based on this model.

12.   Ideally, discussions between peers about what was effective and ineffective in the classroom can lead to reformulation of the theories that underlie second language teaching and can generate new practice.

13.   Quite often coordinators bring back the names of educators to be used as consultants in program-sponsored workshops (K. L. Savage, personal communication, November 8, 1991).

14.   For examples of teacher training institutes contact the ESL Teacher Training Institute in California; the Illinois ESL Adult Education Service Center; and Statewide Adult Basic Education System (SABES) in Massachusetts.

15.   For examples, see the following video series: *Teacher training through video* (Savage, 1991) and *Teacher to teacher,* 1988.

16.   In some states, such as California, resource information is available online. See the Outreach and Technical Assistance Network (OTAN); an example of a resource center that offers program and staff development, serves as a clearinghouse, and acts as a research center is the Statewide Adult Basic Education System (SABES) in Massachusetts; as part of that system, the Adult Literacy Resource Institute provides assistance in ESL literacy.

17.   D. Terdy, personal communication, January 31, 1991.

18.   See also site report in Guth & Wrigley, 1992.

19.   K. L. Savage, personal communication, November 8, 1991. The point has also been made by other teacher educators.

20.   See Stenhouse, 1975.

21.   See Tibbetts et al., 1991.

22.   See also site report in Guth & Wrigley, 1992.

23.   For a description of the process, see Isserlis, 1990.

24.   See site report in Guth & Wrigley, 1992.

25.   L. Savage, personal communication, November 8, 1991; D. Terdy, personal communication, January 31, 1991; see also Tibbetts et al., 1991.

26.   See Willig, 1990, pp.394-395, "Response" to "Preparing mainstream teachers for teaching potentially English proficient students," by Hamayan, 1990.

27.   See also Tibbetts et al., 1991.

References

Auerbach, E. R. (1990). *Making meaning, making change: A guide to participatory curriculum development for adult ESL and family literacy.* Boston: University of Massachusetts [in press (1992), Regents Prentice Hall/Center for Applied Linguistics].

Griswold, K. (1989). Collaborative work groups: A strategy for staff and program development. *Information Update*, *5*(3), 2-4, 9. New York: Literacy Assistance Center.

Guth, G. J. A., & Wrigley, H. S. (1992). *Adult ESL literacy programs and practices: A report on a national research study.* San Mateo, CA: Aguirre International. (Available from the U.S. Department of Education, Clearinghouse on Adult Education and Literacy).

Hamayan, E. (1990). Preparing mainstream teachers for teaching potentially English proficient students. In C. Simich-Dudgeon (Ed.), *Proceedings of the first research symposium on limited English proficient students' issues* (pp. 1-22). Washington, DC: U.S. Department of Education, Office of Bilingual Education and Minority Languages Affairs.

Isserlis, J. (1990). Using action research for ESL evaluation and assessment. *TESL Talk*, *20*(1), 305-316.

Joyce, B., & Showers, B. (1982). The coaching of teaching. *Educational Leadership*, *40*(1), 4-10.

Savage, K. L. (Editor). (1991). *Teacher training through video.* [Video series]. White Plains, NY: Longman.

Stenhouse, L. (1975). *An introduction to curriculum research and development.* London: Heinemann.

Teacher to teacher. (1988). [Video series]. Syracuse, NY: New Readers Press.

Tibbetts, J., Kutner, M., Hemphill, D., & Jones, E. (1991, July). *Study of ABE/ESL instructor training approaches: The delivery and content of training for adult education teachers and volunteer instructors.* Washington, DC: Pelavin Associates.

Willig, A. (1990). [Response to "Preparing mainstream teachers for teaching potentially English proficient students"]. In C. Simich-Dudgeon (Ed.), *Proceedings of the first research symposium on limited English proficient students' issues* (pp. 394-398). Washington, DC: U.S. Department of Education, Office of Bilingual Education and Minority Languages Affairs.

Wrigley, H. S. (1991). Language and literacy teachers: Diverse backgrounds, common concerns. *TESOL Adult Education Newsletter, XVI*(1), 1, 4.

Chapter 9

Curriculum modules

This chapter presents ten curriculum modules, or units written by experienced teachers of adult ESL literacy. These units demonstrate examples of meaning-based teaching that can be used in a variety of contexts, including workplace, family literacy, and community literacy. These units illustrate a variety of teaching strategies, including how to teach initial literacy, how to create and use learner-generated materials, how to link literacy with a discussion of social issues, how to conduct research in the community, how to integrate phonics into a meaning-based curriculum, and how to teach context-specific vocabulary and life skills. Two of the modules present examples of teaching literacy in a bilingual context. The following modules are included in this chapter:

Co-constructing the foundations: a bilingual curriculum on housing
Celestino Cotto Medina and Deidre Freeman

Resolving family conflicts
Ana Huerta-Macias

Aids in our community
Maria E. Malagamba-Roddy

Spanish language literacy breaking the literacy barrier with a song
Peggy Dean

Keeping in touch
Nancy Hampson

Beginning learners write for each other: the news
Janet Isserlis

Using the stories of new writers
Gail Weinstein-Shr

Phonics in context: using grapho/phonemic cues in a learner-centered ESI literacy classroom
Lynellyn Long and Marilyn Gillespie

Environmental print
Pat Rigg

In a workplace ESL literacy class
Laima Maria Schnell

CO-CONSTRUCTING THE FOUNDATIONS:
A BILINGUAL CURRICULUM ON HOUSING

by

Celestino Cotto Medina

&

Deidre Freeman

This lesson is composed of two parts: a native (Spanish) language component and an English as a Second Language (ESL) component.

INTRODUCTION

This lesson is dedicated to the group of learners who are in the ESL class and are no longer able to take its Spanish counterpart because of budget cuts. They have taught us a lot about the need for having native language literacy classes and post-literacy classes in combination with English as a Second Language instruction. The activities included in this lesson are the result of their initiatives, needs, and expectations.

BACKGROUND

Students: This group of learners is comprised of 15 latino/a participants, the majority of whom come to the program from Spanish East Harlem and the South Bronx community. The majority (58%) are of Puerto Rican origin while 29% are of Dominican origin and 13% are from Central and South American. Most of them are women with children. Some have grandchildren. They are between the ages of 30 and 70 and have been in this country from 6 to 36 years. Most of the participants are receiving some kind of public assistance. They all have around a fifth grade level of reading and writing in Spanish. Their ability in oral English varies from a group of students who have difficulty communicating in English to a smaller group of students who have fairly good communication skills. Reading and writing skills in English also vary.

Part I: Constructing the Foundations the Native Language Component

by Celestino Cotto Medina

Approach: This is an integrated lesson plan. It integrates linguistic, science, and math skills. Since El Barrio Popular Education Program enhances bilingual skills, one of the purposes of this unit is to allow students to develop their native language education and to build the foundations to second language acquisition.

Throughout the development and implementation of this unit, students are expected to learn to: **listen** to instructions, arguments, and debates; **comment** on and discuss readings and research findings; **write** about class discussions and research topics; **read** articles, tables, charts, and graphs; and **interpret** graphs, research findings, and charts.

Goals:

- Develop awareness and critical consciousness on the housing problems confronted by members of our community, particularly our students

- Develop literacy skills needed to be independent learners

Objectives:

- To list/mention housing problems related to housing conditions in their communities

- To indicated possible alternative solutions to their most urgent housing related problems

- To work cooperatively in small groups

- To research some aspects of the housing situation in the community

- To organize data into meaningful structures (i.e., charts, tables, graphs)

- To transform collected data into graphs

- To write a composition based on research findings and/or ideas discussed in class.

Context: Prior to the development and implementation of this unit, students were brainstorming and discussing major problems confronted by them and the people of their communities.

LITERACY IN ACTION

A. Getting Things Started

Materials: Graph paper, small notebook to take notes and write down collected data, color pencils, blackboard, and twelve inch rulers.

Classroom Set-Up: Students are organized into small groups and encouraged to work cooperatively. They are seated around three tables arranged in a rectangle facing each other. A small blackboard sits in the empty side of the rectangle.

Classroom Environment: Students are comfortable and relaxed. The free exchange of ideas is encouraged. The learning environment is student-centered and oriented toward cooperative learning.

B. Making It Happen

The facilitator/teacher starts the lesson by writing down on the board the generative word "housing" which students themselves had previously generated. S/he encourages students to think about housing and housing related problems. Key relevant words, phrases, and ideas are written on the blackboard to fuel the thinking process. After introductory brainstorming and general discussion, students are ready for small group cooperative work.

LITERACY ACTIVITIES

Activity Set I

This activity requires a two-hour class period. The students are asked to form small cooperative learning groups. While working in groups they will discuss those housing problems which affect them most, their families, and their immediate relatives. A group list of housing related problems and possible alternative solutions will be prepared. When the small group discussion is finished, the group selects a representative responsible of reporting to the class. The following set of instructions (in Spanish) were given to each student:

1. Reunete con dos o tres companeras (os) para que discutas con ellas (os) los problemas relacionados con el problema de la vivienda que mas te afecta a ti y a tu familia. Estos podrian ser: las condiciones de la planta fisica, plomo en las paredes, alquiler muy elevado, etc. (Trata de pensar en otros que, segun tu criterio, afectan las condiciones de vida de tu familia.

2. Prepara una lista de los problemas discutidos por el grupo.

3. Una vez tenga la lista de problemas preparada, discute con tus companeras (os) posibles soluciones a esos problemas y enumeralos. Esto se podria hacer preparando una tabla de informacion. Pidele al maestro/facilitador que te explique como hacer una tabla si nadie en tu grupo sabe.

4. Elige junto a tus companeras (os), el representante del grupo. Esta persona dara un informe a la clase sobre los problemas y medidas para combatirlos que tu grupo discutio.

5. Entregale al maestro/facilitador una copia del informe que tu grupo preparo.

Activity Set II

This activity set requires two two-hour class periods. During the first two-hour class period, the students will do community research in the immediate neighborhood. Data collection takes approximately one hour. All data will be written down on a table previously drawn by the teacher/facilitator on the blackboard so that all students will be able to copy it. The class will be divided into ten pairs and each pair will be responsible for the collection of data in a previously assigned sector of the neighborhood.

The following set of instruction is given in Spanish to each pair of researchers:

1. Esta actividad requiere que caminemos un poco. Haremos una visita a nuestra comunidad con la intencion de llevar a cabo una investigacion.

2. El proposito de la investigacion, es averiguar cuantos edificios abandonados y cuantos edificios ocupados hay en el sector de El Barrio que cubre desde la calle 100 hasta la calle 110, entre las avenidas Park y Primera.

3. Iras con un companero o companera a lo largo de una calle contando los edificios abandonados y los edificios ocupados. Uno de ustedes contara los abandonados y el otro contara los ocupados.

4. El maestro/facilitador ha preparado un formulario para que puedas anotar el numero de edificios que tu contastes.

5. Cuando hayas terminado el conteo, debes regresar al salon y apuntar en una tabla que el maestro habra preparado en la pizarra, el numero de edificios abandonados y ocupados que tu y tu companera (o) contaron.

6. Con la informacion obtenida, prapararas una GRAFICA de los edificios ocupados. El companero maestro te dara instrucciones de como preparar la grafica.

Activity Set II: Second Part

The second part of Activity Set II includes making graphs, tables, and charts to present research findings and answer questions. The following instructions are given in Spanish to the students:

1. Termina de preparar una segunda grafica, usando esta vez, las cantidades dadas para los edificios abandonados. Sigue el mismo procedimiento que en la grafica anterior.

2. Construye una tercera grafica combinando ambos reglones de informacion, (el numero de edificios ocupados y el numero de edificios abandonados.) El maestro/facilitador te explicara como construir dicha grafica.

3. Una vez hayas preparado la grafica, debes de contestar las siguientes preguntas:

   a. Que ventajas tu le ves al uso de la grafica?
   b. Que calle o calles tienen la cantidad mas alta de edificios abandonados? De edificios ocupados?

   c. Que tu crees que se puede hacer con estos edificios?

   d. Que otro tipo de problemas se puede ilustrar con graficas? Discutelos con tus companeros y mencionalos.

   e. Que otro tipo de investigacion se puede hacer en la comunidad? Si es posible, prepara una lista de cosas que segun tu criterio, se pueden investigar.

Winding Down: Hold an open discussion on the research findings; interpretation and analysis of data; what the learners liked and did not like about the different activities; and how to improve class activities.

COMMENTS

Assessment and Evaluation: Class participation, oral and written reports, written compositions, and interpretations of graphs are all part of an on-going process of assessment and evaluation.

Follow Up: Students will be asked to do the following:

- Make a list of additional research they would like to do in the community.

- Write/send letters to local, state and, federal representatives requesting immediate action in helping to deal with the most urgent housing problems in the community.

Part II: Co-constructing the Foundations
The ESL Component

by Deidre Freeman

Approach: I use a variety of approaches that combine whole language and problem posing methods. Each lesson starts with speaking and listening and moves to reading and writing. Sometimes this may vary. The lesson is almost always in the context of a theme of interest to the learners and is initiated by them. As in this lesson, we begin with a brainstorming exercise which generates language and content that will then define the life skills activities as well as the action research, determined and carried out by the learners. Another determining factor in my approach is to coordinate and reinforce what the participants are learning in their native language class.

The **goals** of this lesson are to build on and reinforce the literacy skills that students are learning in their Spanish class and to help them transfer those skills to English. These skills include:

- expressing ideas and opinions in oral and written form
- collecting and interpreting data and information
- posing questions and forming hypothesis
- reflecting on what was learned and connecting it to previous knowledge.

Students also work on building their English vocabulary. In this particular lesson learning will be contextualized in the topic of housing.

Context: The class has been working on their "Tree of Life," an activity created by the Nationwide Women's Program of The American Friends Service Committee. In this activity, learners plot out three generations of their family tree, focusing on the family's economic history. The Trees of Life have been an on-going project for this group. During one class, I asked the students to add housing information for three generations to their trees. They added the answers to the following questions to their trees: What kind of housing did the different generations live in? Did they own or rent the dwellings?

ESL LITERACY IN ACTION

A. Getting Things Started

The classroom is set up with tables in a horseshoe shape so that everyone can see each other and the chalkboard. Getting the class ready requires making sure students are prepared to listen to each other.

B. Making It Happen

We begin every class by checking in as a whole group. Some of the questions we've used to open the class are: "How do you feel today?" As the weeks go by, we begin to focus more on the homework as a way of making the transition into the lesson, so the question becomes "What did you learn yesterday?" or "What did you learn in Spanish class?"

The participants will have begun a discussion on the topic of housing through a brainstorming exercise around the generative word "housing." In the native language component of this class, they have already identified the biggest problems that affect their housing. We will spend some time going over what they discussed and learned about in the Spanish component of the class in order to build a working vocabulary on the topic of housing and begin communication in English.

LITERACY ACTIVITIES

Activity Set I

This activity requires two, two-hour class periods. The following instructions are given to the students in English:

1. On the card I give you, write down the biggest problem you and your family have with housing. Write only a few words or a sentence.

2. Now, I want you to stand up and show each other your cards. Find people who have the same problem. As you find them stay together and find any other people with the same problem. When you have everyone who has the same problem, stand together in a group.

3. Now, in your groups, I want you to talk about the problem and come up with a short drama that shows the rest of the class that problem in the ways you have experienced it. Your skit should be about 2 to 3 minutes.

After each group preforms its skit, I ask the rest the following questions:

- What happened?
- What is (are) the problem(s)?
- Could the person have handled the problem a different way?

At this point the group re-enacts the scene and the audience cuts in when it feels something could have been done differently.

Then I ask the following:

- What happened?
- What did the person do/say?
- What other possibilities do we have?
- Why do you think this problem exists?

When the possibilities have been exhausted, I ask if anyone has any questions about this situation. We record the questions and use them for further investigations.

For homework, I ask students to write about why they think the housing problems talked about in class exist.

Activity Set II: The West Side Story

This activity builds on the Activity Set II of the native language component of this class. In the native language class, students investigated how many buildings were occupied or abandoned in their neighborhood and did a number of follow-up activities using graphs. The ESL activity, like its native language counterpart, will take two two-hour class periods. Here our goal will be to build on what the participants learned in the first investigation and to do a comparative study of the same streets on the West Side (rather than the East Side) of Central Park, an economically more affluent neighborhood.

We begin with a discussion of what they learned in their investigation of the East Harlem neighborhood. I ask students to summarize their findings in English. Then I give the following instructions:

1. We are going to do another investigation, similar to the one you did in your Spanish class. But this time, we are going to do an investigation of abandoned and occupied buildings on 100th to 110th Streets from Central Park West to Riverside Drive.

2. Before we go out, let's try to predict what you think we will find. In groups of three or four, try to come up with a few ideas of what you think we will find on the West Side. You have five minutes. After five minutes, one person from each group will report what they discussed with the class.

Using newsprint, the teacher notes down what the groups predict. After the investigation and analysis of their findings, the group will compare the findings with their predictions.

3. Like in the other investigation, you will go with a classmate to the street. How did you do the first investigation?

Solicit from class that one person counted the abandoned buildings and another one counted the occupied buildings. Also solicit that they recorded their findings on a page that the other teacher had prepared for them.

4. We will go together. We will take the bus to the other side of the Park. Then each of you will go to the your assigned street. We will meet in an hour at 105th Street and Broadway, have a cup of coffee, and return to class together.

5. When we get back to our classroom, we will write down our findings on the chalkboard. What information will we put on the chalkboard?

The facilitator tries to elicit from the group that they will write down the number of abandoned and occupied buildings per street.

6. In your first investigation what did you do after you wrote down the number of abandoned and occupied buildings?

The facilitator elicits from the group that they created three bar graphs: one with all the abandoned buildings, then one with the occupied buildings, and finally, one comparing the two for each street. We discuss labeling axises to get the group going. We do only a combination graph showing the occupied and abandoned buildings per street on the West Side. Later we will make another graph showing the East Side as compared to the West Side.

7. Now we are going to make a graph which shows the number of abandoned and occupied buildings on the west side of 100th Street and the number of abandoned and occupied buildings on the east side of 100th Street. How would we do that on the graph?

The teacher elicits various opinions about labeling the axises of the graphs and the placement of the information. The group figures out what presentation represent the data most effectively. Different groups may decide to try different methods.

Once the second graph is prepared, the groups discuss the following questions:

-   On the West Side, on which street are there more abandoned buildings?

-   On which streets are there more occupied buildings?

-   Are there more abandoned buildings on the West Side or on the East Side? Why? Name three or more reasons why you think there are more abandoned buildings in that neighborhood?

-   Did you notice any difference in the types of building on the East Side and West Side?

-   Let's look at our predictions. Were our predictions accurate? How were they the same? How were they different?

-   What questions do you have as a result of this investigation?

Winding Down: The questions that the students have as the results of this investigation will be listed on newsprint. The students will generate the next theme for the class based on these questions. The findings from the present investigation, together with the graphs from the native language findings will be posted on the school bulletin board and included in our end-of-the-year publication.

COMMENTS

Assessment and Evaluation: What clues me into whether the learners are "getting it" is how they participate in the activity and if they are on target with the activity at hand. I interpret participation in the broad sense, since each learner participates in different ways. The homework also gives me an idea of how they understand things and where I need to be more clear or model more or take more time in explaining. Some of the evidence is recorded in their written work. Other information can not be recorded, such as participation and changes in participation at the personal, program, and community level.

Saving the Day: We mainly work with the whole group using pair and small group activities. One successful pair strategy is to pair higher English language proficient students with less proficient students, and have the higher level students help the lower level ones. On some occasions, students are grouped by ability. For the most part, I have found that mixed level small groups (3 to 4 students) with a clear, structured activity work best.

Follow Up: As mentioned before, future activities emerge from the questions students raise based on the results of this unit. We will develop curriculum about the most pressing issues students discuss: tenants' rights, housing court, etc. Other activities are initiated in the native language component of the class and given follow-up in the ESL component. Such activities include writing letters to politicians, landlords, and social service agencies.

ABOUT THE AUTHORS

Celestino Cotto Medina has worked at El Barrio Popular Education Program for the past two years. He is completing his Ph.D. in Geography at Columbia University and is a published writer of short stories. He has used participatory education in New York and in Puerto Rico.

Deidre Freeman has worked in the field of Adult ESL for six years as a teacher, curriculum developer, and coordinator, primarily for labor unions and workplace programs. She recently returned to teaching as her primary focus and is working with ESL literacy in the classroom on a daily basis.

RESOLVING FAMILY CONFLICTS

by

Ana Huerta-Macias

INTRODUCTION

Lo más importante para mí es mi familia. (My family is the most important thing for me.)

— Literacy student

Keeping the family together and in harmony is of utmost concern among many of our adult literacy parents. Thus, it is imperative that family issues be included as part of the content in any ESL adult literacy course which teaches language via the teaching of survival skills, whole life skills, and/or parenting skills.

BACKGROUND

This lesson would be taught as part of a course for students who are able to engage in simple conversations in English utilizing vocabulary which is common to everyday life. Their proficiency levels vary from advanced beginner to intermediate. Note, however, that this same lesson is easily adaptable for a more advanced group. The literacy levels in the native language vary; some may have gone through six years of schooling in their native language while others may have as many as ten or twelve years of schooling. Most of the adults are parents with children of varying ages, from toddlers to high school students or even older. All have expressed needs with respect to learning parenting skills, particularly in the areas of discipline and family conflicts which arise from a variety of situations. Finally, the lesson is designed for a small group of approximately twelve or fifteen students.

Language is best learned when the content is meaningful, interesting, and relevant. Thus, a participatory, whole language, learner-centered approach is used in this lesson. Much of the time is spent in whole class and/or group discussions of various family "problems." Problem posing is used at the beginning of the lesson in order to generate discussion. Language experience is used during the writing portion of the lesson. The lesson, furthermore, is divided into five steps which include oral language, reading, and writing activities.

ESL LITERACY IN ACTION

The purpose of the lesson is to teach the parents, through discussion and sharing of ideas and experiences, how to use various strategies for resolving conflicts that arise in families.

This lesson fits into a series of lessons with a "Family" theme. Previous to this lesson the students will have had lessons on the following topics: *Different Types of Families* (including, for example, extended families, single parent families, adopted families, etc.), *Family Meals, Communication Skills, Communication with School Personnel, Reading a Report Card*, and *Communication in the Family*. A follow-up lesson to this lesson, *Resolving Family Conflicts*, could be *Communicating with Teen-agers*. The latter would focus on those "communication gap" problems which tend to arise specifically with children in their teens. Each lesson is designed for a two-hour time block.

A. Getting Things Started

A classroom with movable chairs is essential. The classroom should be large enough to accommodate the group of students. An assistant is desirable, although not imperative. The classroom environment should be warm and informal. Students should always feel free to speak up. Large colored pictures/posters placed around the room of different families or individuals communicating with each other will help set the tone.

Supplementary reading materials should be selected and/or adapted from a variety of books, magazines, and pamphlets prior to the lesson. The selections should be brief (see examples in appendix). "Problems" for group discussion and/or "situations" for role play should also be selected and/or composed prior to the lesson. A vocabulary list with words that might come up in a discussion of family conflicts is also put on the board before the lesson. These are not to be memorized or used in isolation but rather are there to refer to as they come up naturally or as the need occurs during the lesson, particularly during the discussions.

B. Making Things Happen

The following outlines the five steps which form the framework for this lesson as well as all other lessons that would be taught in the series. The five steps are initial inquiry, learning activity, reading activity, writing activity and home activity/tutorial

Step One: The initial inquiry is a discussion which takes place with the group as a whole. The instructor acts as a facilitator as s/he guides the discussion through open-ended, problem posing questions designed to generate a variety of responses from the students. It is important that the instructor let the students do most of the talking and let them guide the discussion through their responses and additional questions. The instructor might begin the discussion by sharing a brief, personal anecdote describing a family conflict/problem which often arises in his/her family. This would be followed by a variety of other questions which might look like the following:

- What types of conflicts/problems occur among members of your family?
- Do your children fight a lot? Over what?
- What happens when two of your teen-agers want to use the bathroom at the same time?
- How about when one of them wants to use the car at a time or for an activity which you don't feel is a good one?
- What do you say? How does s/he react?
- What might have been an alternative?
- Have some of you experienced similar problems?
- What advice can you share?
- What do you do when your little one has a temper tantrum?
- Is there an easy way to say no?
- Do you ever feel that your "homemaking services" are taken for granted?
- How do you get other family members to help with chores?
- What happens when they don't do what they are supposed to?

Step two of the lesson is the learning activity. In this step the students get an opportunity to do group or individual work (depending on the lesson) on the theme as they engage in concrete, hands-on activities and/or an application of what was discussed in step one. In this case the students will be doing small group, problem solving discussions and, if time allows, role-play.

The instructor divides the class into groups of three or four students. Each group is presented with a problem to solve (these may be on strips of paper or written on the board). The groups brainstorm on some solutions or strategies to help solve the problem. The brainstorming should answer three basic questions (also on paper or on the board): 1) What, in simple terms, is the problem? 2) Who is/are the person(s) involved in the problem? 3) What are at least two ideas/strategies — with pros and cons for each — for solving this problem? (See appendix for examples of problems.)

After fifteen or twenty minutes, a member or two from each group share their problem and solutions with the rest of the group. Brief role-plays may also be done at this time by the groups to exemplify their solutions.

Step three, the reading activity, gives the students an opportunity to do some in-class silent reading on the topic of family conflicts. The instructor presents several passages (see appendix for examples) and allows the students to choose one or two they are most interested in. Approximately fifteen minutes is allowed for this activity. The instructor is available for help as s/he monitors the class during the reading. The information is briefly shared/discussed after everyone is finished reading.

Step four is the writing activity. During this step, the students write about something related to the theme of the lesson. Ideas for this come from the previous activities. The writing may be totally free or guided. In this case, the writing is guided.

The instructor asks the students to write out their responses to the problem which was discussed in groups during step two. That is, they should briefly describe the problem, the people involved, and at least one solution.

An alternative for the students is also presented. Instead of writing the responses to the group discussion, they can write about something related to the passage they read in step three, such as what they learned, reactions, or applications of the reading passage.

The writing passages are collected and <u>holistically</u> reviewed by the instructor. Feedback is provided at a later time by way of constructive comments and/or suggestions. Each instructor sets up his/her own system for providing feedback and rewriting where appropriate.

Step five of the lesson is not an in-class activity but rather provides suggestions for follow-activities to do at home or with a tutor when one is available. Choices are always provided. Each student may do one or more than one activity. Suggestions for this lesson might be as follows:

- Do some additional reading on a related subject by looking through books, magazines, and brochures which are available to you.

- Take a specific problem/conflict which has occurred in your family in the recent past and do an analysis and "write-up" of the problem similar to what was done in class during step two. Follow up on one of the solutions during the week and see what happens.

- Reflect and write about how communication occurs or does not occur in your family. Devise some strategies to improve the situation.

- Do some additional study on the vocabulary list provided in class. Look up the words in the dictionary; look for them in additional reading selections; use them in your writing.

COMMENTS

A holistic assessment is used for all of the students' work done during the class and at home. All students should participate in the discussions to varying degrees. Look to see that they are comprehending the questions and responses, and that they are engaged in the discussion. Help out with vocabulary and phrases as needed. Simplify the vocabulary where needed so that the language is comprehensible to the students. Each instructor should develop his/her own system for the evaluation of written work. Typically, this would be a point scale (e.g., 1 - 5), accompanied with descriptions for each rating, which would allow the instructor to evaluate each piece of writing holistically. A system for providing feedback should also be set up which allows for one-on-one conferencing several times throughout the course.

As mentioned above, the vocabulary should be simplified as necessary if the students are having difficulty comprehending the discussion. Help is provided by the instructor or other students when individuals have trouble finding just the right word or phrase. If necessary, the vocabulary list might be reviewed before step one as an aid for the students.

Follow-up activities are described in step five of the lesson. Additional lessons might focus on specific areas in resolving family problems; such as discipline with young children, coping with teen-agers, or with the students' own, elderly parents. Specific topics will depend on the particular group's needs and interests.

ABOUT THE AUTHOR

Ana Huerta-Macias received her Ph.D. in Applied Linguistics from the University of Texas at Austin in 1978. Since then she has been active in the fields of ESL, bilingual education, bilingualism, and literacy. Most recently, she was the coordinator of an intergenerational family literacy project funded by Title VII (OBEMLA) of the U.S. Department of Education.

AIDS IN OUR COMMUNITY

by

Maria E. Malagamba-Roddy

INTRODUCTION

I became involved in creating things in the classroom — in learning from the experience of the students. My students and I resembled a community much more than a class, and I enjoyed being with them. We worked together in an open environment which often spilled out the school building into the streets, the neighborhood, and the city itself.

— Herb Kohl

BACKGROUND

Background of the group: Our Basic ESL (literacy) classes are held at night for three hours. The lesson presented here involved students whose English skills were minimal. Most were illiterate in Spanish, their native language, and only a minority had attended first or second grade. Seventy percent of the students were young men from rural Mexico. Many students work as gardeners and maids in affluent, suburban San Mateo County, California.

Approach: Our program follows a Competency Based Approach that includes a cross-cultural perspective and a learner-centered orientation. The ESL Basic staff uses whole language, language experience, and problem posing methods. These teaching methods have enabled our students to immediately apply what they have learned in the classroom to their everyday lives and to rapidly improve their English language skills. Our program believes that literacy is a developmental process that requires a holistic, non-linear, problem-centered approach. The ESL literacy curriculum was developed in response to students' main concerns: health, nutrition, shopping, housing, employment, and transportation.

Lesson goals:

- Students will become familiar with printed information on AIDS.

- Students will be able to learn, identify, and use key words in the AIDS information pamphlet.

- They will be able to discuss the following: what to do, where to go, who to see or talk to, and how to help themselves and others with regards to the AIDS problem.

- They will be able to write an AIDS prevention prescription to use in educating friends and family.

Context: The Health Unit is an extensive one in our curriculum. We expand it as students' needs arise. The AIDS lesson was created as the result of a problem posing activity. A student responded to a question about mental health in the community with the following: "AIDS is a big problem. It's a health problem and it's a mental health problem too. We don't talk about it. We need to know more about AIDS."

I asked the class for ideas on how to address this topic, and wrote their suggestions on the board. Several students suggested talking to a professional, so we invited a speaker from the AIDS Project to visit and talk to our class. In this manner, we added a new lesson to our health unit.

ESL LITERACY IN ACTION

The guest speaker provided pamphlets both in English and Spanish, a short film, and condoms. She delivered a short informative lecture. Students asked questions, while I listened and developed the English vocabulary to be used later in class.

During the 15 minute coffee break, students were able to approach the guest speaker individually and ask her further questions.

A. Getting Things Started

Materials: I created a code using an enlarged picture from the AIDS information pamphlet showing a young Hispanic couple embracing. Condoms fall from his open wallet and her open purse. This code will be used for problem posing and to illustrate students' written prescription "AIDS prevention." Other materials include lined practice paper for print writing, an overhead projector and transparencies of the code.

Seating arrangements: To facilitate conversation and problem posing, have students sit in a circle. For reading activities, have them sit in pairs. For writing activities, have students work either individually or in groups of three or more.

Classroom environment: The classroom environment should be cooperative, and students should be respectful of each other's opinions and work.

B. Making It Happen

Step 1: I asked students if they had found the guest speaker's presentation interesting and informative. They replied that they had. I proceeded to show the code on the overhead projector and asked in English:

- What do you see?
- What is happening?
- Where can you find this picture?
- What is the picture about?
- What is the message?
- How can you use this picture?
- Who gets AIDS in our community? How? Why?

Step 2: As students responded, I wrote student-generated vocabulary on the overhead projector: couple, AIDS, information, danger, dangerous, sex, kill, clinic, help, use, urgent, everybody, problem, death.

Then I wrote the teacher-generated vocabulary on the overhead projector: pamphlet, prevention, prevent, safe, safe sex, silence, condoms, AIDS Project counselor, AIDS phone number, fatal, no cure, need, right away, call, ask, die.

I also wrote some of their best answers on the overhead projector. Students copied words in their notebooks.

Step 3: We read vocabulary and sentences together as a group. I called on a few students to read them out loud.

Step 4: I continued with my problem posing questioning strategy by asking the following questions:

- What can you do to get help?
- Where can you go for help?
- Who can you talk to for help?
- How can you protect yourself?
- How can you help inform others, your relatives, your friends?
- What can you do right away?

I wrote the best answers on the board and students copied them into their notebooks.

Step 5: I asked students to sit in pairs and I distributed the AIDS Information pamphlets in English. I asked them to find the words we had just studied and to underline them.

Step 6: I gave students the code pasted on lined paper and asked them to sit in groups of four facing the board. I asked them to write the prescription "AIDS prevention" in a collaborative manner, and then to turn in their prescriptions to be shared next class. I told them they could use some of the answers we had discussed as a class. I modeled a few examples for them.

Students corrected their own work during the follow-up lesson. They were proud of their work. I asked them if writing had helped them organize the newly acquired information so they could, in turn, explain to others (relatives and friends) how to protect themselves against AIDS. They all respond affirmatively and enthusiastically. Here is one student's written work:

> "AIDS is a big problem in our community. Everybody can get AIDS. We need to talk about AIDS. We need information about AIDS prevention. We can call the AIDS telephone number and talk to a counselor in Spanish. AIDS has no cure. It is fatal. People die. We need to have safe sex. We need to use condoms. We need to help friends and relatives. Silence about AIDS kills."

COMMENTS

Assessment/Evaluation: I asked students to vote and rate the lesson. It turned out to be one of their favorites. They showed interest, respect and involvement. Everybody participated in the activities. English was generated throughout the lesson. During the next class students mentioned talking to relatives and friends about AIDS. They were proud of their written product (the prescription) and shared it with the class. A follow-up lesson (Drug Use and AIDS Transmission) expanded the topic of AIDS prevention.

ABOUT THE AUTHOR

Maria Malgamba-Roddy has been a literacy teacher for seventeen years. She started in Mexico as a volunteer in 1974, and has been an ESL literacy practitioner since 1985. At present she is a reading instructor at Hartnell College and a Family Literacy consultant for Alisal Elementary School District in Salinas, California.

SPANISH NATIVE LANGUAGE LITERACY
BREAKING THE LITERACY BARRIER WITH A SONG

by

Peggy Dean

INTRODUCTION

Building literacy in native language is like making improvements on your own home. The results compliment the learner/worker and reflect personal accomplishments. The lesson included in this module offers a popular Mexican song, "La Bamba," as an effective tool for building native language literacy skills. This song acts like an old friend who introduces a new, positive experience in print.

BACKGROUND

A salient characteristic of the adult Spanish literacy class is diversity. Students come from a variety of educational and experiential backgrounds, ranging from no prior education to approximately three years of primary school. While one student may have extensive urban work experience and demonstrate considerable oral English, another may have been farm/home bound and lack even basic arithmetic concepts.

Their common bond is a strong desire to learn to read and write in order to get a better job and/or help their children succeed in school. Eventually, almost all of the students say that they want to learn English. Many have made various attempts at ESL classes but dropped out in frustration after only a few months because they can't handle the double load of literacy and English. For these individuals, the key to success in English lies in native language literacy.

Keeping in mind the multilevel character of the Spanish literacy class and the open entry-exit policy that is prevalent among the majority of programs, an eclectic approach can best meet the students' needs. Elements of a Whole Language Approach and Freirean methodology are brought together to support the student at an appropriate level of development. Through this combination, the phonetic reliability of Spanish is coupled with a strong contextual base.

The goal of this learning module is to incorporate each student into the literacy continuum at a point appropriate to his/her abilities and facilitate progress as effectively as possible. Individualization and small group work help students maximize learning and maintain sound progress. Extensions of the activities for home practice play a significant part in the materials.

LITERACY IN ACTION

The entire class will be conducted in Spanish.

A. Getting Started

"La Bamba" can initially be presented in a variety of ways. The main goal is to generate dialogue among the students, involving them in the learning process. The specific direction the exchange will take depends upon on the students themselves. Some points of departure are:

- Play the 1950's recording of "La Bamba" by Richie Valenz along with one or two more recent recordings made by groups in Mexico. Identify minor changes in lyrics and contrasts in music styles.

- Discuss the words and what they mean.

- Have students sing or someone play the song as they first learned it.

- Ask students to recall when they first heard the song. What were they doing? Where were they? What was their life like then?

- Introduce the idea that "La Bamba" is a song from Veracruz, Mexico. Ask if anyone has visited there and what it is like? Locate the city on a map.

- Talk about the life of Richie Valenz/Valenzuela, the young man who arranged and sang the U.S. recording of this song. He went from migrant farm laborer to recording star in less than 5 years. Is that type of success still possible? Ask students for success stories they have heard.

After the dialogue and when the students feel comfortable with the words of the song, begin by writing the first verse on the board. Indicate each word as you read it slowly, various times. Single out individual words and ask that students read them. Even the lowest level students should be able to recognize a few words due to their knowledge of the song. More advanced learners can be grouped and proceed to the following verses to decode them and continue on with the exercises. Be sure that each student is clear on the tasks they are to perform.

LA BAMBA

Lea cada verso e identifique las palabras.

Para bailar la bamba,
para bailar la bamba se necesita
una poca de gracia,
una poca de gracia y una cosita.

Ay! Arriba y arriba,
ay! arriba y arriba y arriba iré,
yo no soy marinero,
yo no soy marinero por ti seré
por ti seré, por ti seré

Para subir al cielo,
para subir al cielo se necesita
una escalera grande,
una escalera grande y otra chiquita.

Una vez que te dije,
una vez que te dije que eras
bonita, se te puso la cara,
se te puso la cara coloradita.

En mi casa me dicen,
en mi casa me dicen el inocente
porque tengo muchachas,
porque tengo muchachas de a
quince veinte.

Types of questions/directions to use with basic level students:

- How many times does the letter "a" appear in the first line? Second line? Circle them.

- How many words begin with the letter "p" in the first verse? The letter "b"? Underline them.

- What words begin with a "b" in the first verse? Where are they?

Have students work first with the verse on the board and then repeat the same set of directions having them use work sheets at their desks. This repetition will serve as a check for understanding.

Estudio de silabas

<u>marinero</u>

ma ri ne ro

ma	ra	na	ra		No + ra = Nora			mi + ra = mira		
me	re	ne	re		Mo + na = Mona			ra + na = rana		
mi	ri	ni	ri		Ro + ma = Roma			mi + na = mina		
mo	ro	no	ro		mo + no = mono			ri + ma = rima		
mu	ru	nu	ru		ma + no = mano					

COPIE:

<u>Mira la rama.</u>   _____

<u>Nora mira a Mona.</u>   _____

Sound discrimination and association are important first steps in literacy. Too often we overlook the fact that some students must be carefully introduced to sound differences before they can begin to link a certain sound to a letter or set of letters.

Develop vowel and consonant sounds using a generative word like "marinero" and activities similar to the following:

Ask students to give words that begin with the sound "ma", like **mapa**, **masa**, **mano**, etc. Contrast this with "me" words like **mesa**, **menos**, and **meta**. Write the two syllables on the board in different places. Pronounce a series of words that begin with one or another of the targeted syllables and ask that they point to the first syllable of the word they hear.

Once syllables are identified, meaningful combination can take place. Decoding skills for some students develop rapidly using this approach. Deal with capital letter and punctuation questions as they arise in a natural, developmental way.

Writing practice should be integrated into word and syllable study. Most students will have had some previous practice at writing their name and personal information. This skill depends on hand-eye coordination and for most students will only improve with considerable practice. Provide many practice sheets and encourage students to work at home. Make sure that every student knows the words that they are copying.

Escriba en letra de molde o en manuscrito:

la bamba   arriba

_____   _____

casa   para

_____   _____

Fill-in exercises demonstrate a minimal, but important step forward in literacy. With the support offered by the learner's familiarity with the words of the song, active deciphering skills can be introduced and used. Students can create practice items to exchange with others or present to the class, based on this form. Carefully review each verse as it is targeted. Try to consistently ensure student success. Motivation comes from positive feedback.

Llene los espacios con las palabras dadas.

Para _____ la bamba,

para _____ la bamba, se _____

una _____ de gracia,

bailar	necesit a
poca	bailar

Sentence joining increases the reading load significantly. It nevertheless is a manageable task because it faithfully mirrors the given lyrics. It is a confidence builder in itself and can spark some interesting comments from the nonsensical mismatches that are grammatically correct.

Marque una línea entre las dos frases correctas.

Para bailar la bamba　　　por ti sere.

En mi casa　　　se necesita una poca de gracia.

Yo no soy marinero　　　me dicen el inocente.

Sentence construction items advance quickly into semi-independent or guided writing. The first of these exercises requires only that the student put the words in order. No conjugation nor word addition is necessary. The projected first word is capitalized, giving some students a needed point of departure.

Escriba las palabras en orden.

Yo/no/bailar/sé

_____

Se/necesita/escalera/una/grande

_____

On a more demanding level, the sentence skeletons require that the students create their own sentences. The given words must be supplemented, verbs conjugated, and punctuation and capitalization used appropriately. Have students initially work in pairs and orally plan their sentences before writing each one. Reading and reacting to the sentences written by another group is an exercise in self esteem for everyone.

Escriba su propia frase.

no/subir/escalera _____

muchacha/bonita/baile_____

COMMENTS

The logical follow-up for this sequence is a Language Experience paragraph. A single student or a small group dictates their ideas concerning some aspect of the discussion concerning the song. Practice items like those offered here can be written to accompany the student story. With minor editing and supplements, these paragraphs and their work sheets become part of the class materials. The opportunities for peer tutoring are obvious as the author of a Language Experience paragraph helps a classmate read it.

The role of teacher in a multilevel literacy class seems to fluctuate between instructor, facilitator, and evaluator. As each student or group is set into motion, the teacher goes from one to another assessing progress and identifying needs. While at the most basic levels considerable time is dedicated to direct instruction, as students progress, monitoring and facilitating groups becomes a priority.

ABOUT THE AUTHOR

Peggy Dean is a consultant with the Adult Learning Resource Center of Northern Illinois. She works principally with the native Spanish programs literacy/ABE/GED. She co-authored a Spanish literacy workbook, *Leer y escribir hoy*, in 1990.

KEEPING IN TOUCH

By

Nancy Hampson

INTRODUCTION

We know that language acquisition is supported in a classroom environment which is "student-centered," and has a "low affective filter." We also know that students' literacy improves when lessons are connected to "authentic" reading and writing tasks that help adults function in their life roles. Look what can happen when the instructor turns classroom management over to the students.

BACKGROUND

In this beginning level ESL classroom, the instructor teaches a series of lessons integrating speaking, listening, reading, and writing applied to a life skill competency. The continuing application of the lesson is to assign classroom monitor tasks that require students to *use* the language and literacy skills on a daily basis.

Background of the group: Students are placed into the ESL program of this large metropolitan adult school district based on an oral interview to assess speaking and listening skills. This lesson was designed for low literate, beginning, ESL students whose speaking and listening skills are at the "Comprehension-Early Production-Speech Emergence" stages of language acquisition, as described in *The Natural Approach: Language Acquisition in the Classroom* (S. Krashen and T. Terrell, 1983).

Four of the twenty-four students were in the "Silent Period;" eight were experimenting with "Early Production," naming and using two-word sentences; and twelve were communicating in short phrases and simple sentences. In terms of first language literacy, none were preliterate (from a culture in which literacy is rare or non-existent); eight were non-literate (from a literate culture, but whose education is not above an elementary level); and six were literate in their first language, but not literate in the Roman alphabet.

The class was held in a multi-ethnic community in San Diego, California. Nationalities represented were Vietnamese (6), Cambodian (2), Lao (3), Ethiopian (2), Salvadoran (2), Russian (1), and Eritrian (1). All were refugees who had arrived in the United States within the past year. The age range was 19 to 72, with the majority of students in their 30's. Four were over 65 years old and three were under 20. Most lived with family or extended family and were supported by welfare. The class was half male and half female.

Approach or method: Because these students are at the beginning level of language acquisition and literacy, instruction is quite controlled by the teacher. The ESL program's instructional approach is competency-based, student-centered, communicative, and integrated with life skills, so the instructor plans activities which encourage interaction and practice within authentic contexts. Lesson objectives are expressed in terms of what the students can *do*, i.e., how they can apply what is learned in the classroom to their real lives, living in an English speaking culture.

Goal of the lesson: The long range goal of this series of lessons is that students be able to address a postcard and write a "get well" message to a classmate. Other objectives of the lesson are for students to:

- read and write personal information (name, address, city, state)

- identify postal items and services

- use the language function of expressing concern for an absent friend

- identify and follow culturally appropriate behavior for communicating with a public school.

Context: The previous competency component was Health. Students had learned to write a note of excuse. Forms were subsequently used for students to write the reason for an absence when they returned to class. The teacher sent postcards to students who were absent so that several students had the experience of receiving a "get well" postcard from the class. The outcome of this series of lessons is that a classroom "secretary" be identified to send postcards to students who are absent for two days.

The teacher uses classroom "monitors" as a way to extend the competency lessons and simulate work experiences in the United States. The monitors have duties related to the competency lessons and through these jobs, help manage the classroom. After each unit of instruction, a monitor position is identified. The monitor positions in this class included attendance clerk, welcoming committee, treasurer, shopper, host/ess, news team, supply clerk, and custodian. Students use their developing literacy and communications skills to participate in authentic communicative tasks related to the management of the classroom. Positions change frequently so all students have the opportunity to be monitors. Through the monitor system, the class is jointly managed by students and teacher, enhancing the feeling of class ownership and community.

ESL LITERACY IN ACTION

A. Getting Things Started

Since the classroom is managed by students and instructor, the social and learning environment is interdependent. Periodically the instructor includes team building activities into the lesson to make new students aware that this class is different than the authoritarian approach that they might have experienced in other schools.

Preparation and set up: The first few minutes of class are a bustle of activity as students assist in getting ready for the lesson. Students clock in, locate their name cards, set up equipment, prepare the refreshment table, set up activity stations, welcome fellow students, orient new students, and setting out supplies and materials at the direction of the teacher.

Students are seated by table groups ("teams") which are heterogenous by stage of language acquisition and literacy level. Students on each team are assigned numbers (1,2,3,4). Some learning activities will be heterogenous (1,2,3,4,) and some will be homogenous (1's, 2's, 3's, 4's).

Some classroom tasks are assigned by number in the group, for example, number 1's may comprise the welcoming committee for new students. They greet new students, ask what their primary language is, and assign a buddy to acquaint the new student with class routines. Number 3's may be assigned to post butcher paper "stations" on the walls behind each of the six groups.

The teacher prepares and assembles the following materials for this lesson:

- Realia - postcards, stamps, "get well" card
- Visuals from the Health unit
- Name cards which included students' addresses
- Number card packets for non-literate students
- Sentence strips of postcard message — 1 set each table group
- Flashcards of words from the postcard message

- 2 sets of colored letter cards for "Concentration" (different colors for upper and lower case)
- Listening post with Language Master flashcard reader and headphones
- Yes/no answer form for comprehension check
- Copies of two previous dialogues for review

B. Making Things Happen

The objective of this lesson is that students will be able to address a postcard to themselves. The language focus is reading and writing, but because there are non-literate and students in the "silent period" of language acquisition, the learning activities will include TPR, listening and questioning strategies requiring no oral response.

Warm up: The opening activity encourages students to interact by using language previously taught.

Step 1: As a review of the previous health unit, students will be directed to ask classmates "How are you?" and respond "I am fine" or "Not so good."

Step 2: As a review of yesterday's lesson, the teacher will hold up realia of items related to the post office and have students name them and answer yes/no questions.

Step 3: The teacher will call on numbers 1 and 2 in the teams to respond to "What's your name?" and "What's your address?" Students can use their name cards as a prompt. Number 1's will come to the board write their name on the board and spell it, pointing to the letters.

Literacy Activities: The instructor focuses the students' attention on the new lesson, states the lesson objective and relates it to the previous learning. The instructor then presents the new information, checks comprehension, and prepares students for the homogenous practice of reading and writing.

Step 1: Teacher models a review dialogue, playing both parts.

A: "Where were you yesterday?"
B: "I was at home."

A: "What was the matter?"
B: "I was sick. I had a fever."

A: "We missed you."

Step 2: Number 1's are invited to the front to demonstrate the dialogue. The new line "We missed you" is modeled and acted out. The teacher pantomimes sending a card. The teacher and number 1's do a substitution drill and change the location (work, hospital, etc.)

Step 3: As a transition to the new lesson and to provide comprehensible input, the teacher models writing a postcard on the overhead projector.

```
1.  Dear Truc,

2.  We miss you very much.

3.  Please come back soon.


4.          Your friend,
```

```
1.  City Adult School
2.  462 Tait St.
3.  San Diego, CA.  92111

    4.    Mr. Truc Nguyen
    5.    145 White St.
    6.    San Diego, CA  92106
```

Step 4: Following her model, the class reads with the teacher. She delivers the cards to the students. The class reads with her.

Step 5: The teacher checks student comprehension by asking yes/no questions, or when and who questions. Table groups confer and give one answer. If mistakes are made, the teacher rereads or emphasizes the visual clues the students are holding.

Step 6: Activities to relate the spoken word to the written word.

- Sentence strips are read and distributed to table groups to match to the model on the overhead; table groups order sentence strips on their table.

- Teacher directs number 2's in the groups to read the message.

- Strips are scrambled. Table groups are directed to go to the butcher paper stations and order the sentence strips to make a postcard.

- Teacher conducts a sight word lesson with flashcards from the sentence strips. Number 1's read the first line of the message; 2's arrange the words in order; 1's check; 3's and 4's listen.

Step 7: Students are regrouped homogeneously by literacy level to practice reading readiness, and reading development and writing skills. The teacher sets up one activity with one group (more literate) while that group practices, the teacher moves to the other group (less literate) to give instructions.

1's & 2's (more literate)	3's & 4's (less literate)
Teacher (Sets up pair work)	Pairs
Spelling lesson: Sight words from message; rhyming pattern — <u>we</u>, <u>be</u>, <u>he</u>, <u>she</u> (Sets up spelling worksheet and reviews dialogue to be read with a partner.)	Concentration game to match capital and lower case letters. Language master review of personal information words — name, address, city, state, zip code.
Pairs	Teacher
Practice spelling Practice reading dialogue: "What's your name?" "Please spell that."	Listening to and sequencing numbers as in addresses and zip codes. From a packet of numerals, students order dictated numbers.

Heterogenous Groups
TPR (Total Physical Response) activity: using students' name cards which include their addresses: Point to your last name; point to your first name; point to your city, etc. **Listening activity**: All students are directed to stand. if they can answer "yes" to the teacher's questions, they remain standing. If they answer "no," they sit down. For example, I live in the U.S. (all remain standing). My zip code is 92105 (all those who do not live in that zip code, sit down).

Step 8: Number 3's from each group distribute blank postcards to their tables. Ones and 2's are directed to address the postcards to themselves and copy the message from their butcher paper model. Number 3's and 4's copy their name and address from their name cards onto the postcard. Students put stamps on their postcards. The teacher collects the postcards to be filed in a box and sent by the class secretary to absent students. They will be asked to bring the card to class, read it with their table group, and post it on the bulletin board.

Winding Down: At the end of each class, the student monitors from each table group follow commands to put away all the classroom equipment, supplies, and materials. The commands are given by the students who have held that position in the past. Student monitors may ask table mates to "give me a hand." Students who are new to the class or not as proficient in speaking have the opportunity to learn the routine by helping another student with the job. The attendance clerk announces who was absent. The teacher involves the class in planning the next lesson and asking "tomorrow?" Students indicate thumbs up or thumbs down. Announcements or news are given. As students leave the class, they must give a parting remark to three classmates who are not at their table. They are encouraged to use past dialogues or something that was practiced in the lesson, e.g., "what's your name?" or "where do you live?"

REFLECTIONS AND COMMENTS

At the beginning levels of ESL, teacher judgement is the major evaluation tool. Because cooperative learning is used, many times the reports back from students are arrived at by group consensus. However, the teacher has the opportunity to note group interaction and to observe individual progress when the homogeneous groups meet for skill practice. Because the class is so interactive and student-centered, students are interested and eagerly participate. Problems that arise are referred back to the students for consideration. The tasks built into the shared classroom management require that students review and practice key phrases and expressions that they will encounter frequently in their English speaking environment. As they gain confidence in the use of their new language, they are more likely to take the risks of communicating outside the safety of the classroom.

ABOUT THE AUTHOR

Nancy Hampson is the Resource Instructor for Literacy for the Continuing Education Centers of the San Diego Community College District. She has been an instructor of beginning ESL for the past thirteen years. She has presented workshops at national, state, and local conferences, has authored a "Tutor Training Manual" for volunteer tutors, trained adult literacy volunteers, and served as Chair of the San Diego County Literacy Network. She leads Staff Development workshops for CASAS, the ESL Institute, and the Adult Literacy Instructor's Training (ALIT) Institute.

BEGINNING LEARNERS WRITE FOR EACH OTHER: THE NEWS

by

Janet Isserlis

INTRODUCTION

The News, written weekly, is a one page collection of learner-generated information that facilitates the development of reading and writing skills among learners with a wide range of abilities.[1] The generation of the News is also an organizing component of the curriculum and materials development process.

BACKGROUND

The News is essentially an extension of the language experience approach (LEA). Used on a regular basis, it elicits meaningful content for literacy and language work in a learner-centered classroom.

Background of the group: The activity was developed with low level literacy/ESL learners of mixed nationality, age, gender, and varying degrees of oral/aural competence. Class size averages between twelve and fifteen learners, and is comprised of recently arrived refugees and immigrants, as well as those who have been in the country for many years. Many of the learners work, or have worked, and many are married with children. The News began as an extended collection of LEA stories generated by learners in a class which meets four times weekly for two hours a day. All the learners have an understanding of what reading is and vary in their abilities to decode and encode print. All are able to participate in generating the news.

Approach: The News incorporates, expands upon, and reflects a whole language philosophy in which meaningful whole units of language are elicited, written, and read by learners. Reading and writing skills are developed within the context of meaningful communication. The class may also engage in problem-posing or life skills activities based on topics learners contribute to the News.

Purpose: The overarching purpose of the activity is to enable learners to share information that they find interesting and important, and to use this information to generate and read language in a meaningful context. The process of generating and reading class news enables learners to work collaboratively, and builds community through the sharing of high-interest information. By focusing on information which students choose to share, text is created and learners soon work together to write and read the News.

ESL LITERACY IN ACTION

Generally, the News is generated once a week. The day itself is flexible, depending on whatever other events may be going on in the class. The process of generating the news is extended to the following day when learners read a typed version of the News. Up to two two-hour sessions are required for the News, although in smaller groups, less time may be required.

A. Getting Things Started

Set Up: A single teacher can generate the News. The necessary items for this activity are newsprint, markers and/or a large blackboard or white board.

Warm Up: Prior to actually generating the News, the teacher might write something like *Last weekend, I* .... on the blackboard, and then ask each learner to write one thing he or she did. Similarly, the teacher might use an open-ended sentence such as:

> *On Saturday, I like to......*
> or,
> *In my country, many people like to.......*

These sentences can tie into ongoing discussions, or can be used as a warm up to writing. Through this activity, learners become comfortable going to the blackboard to write, and everyone has an opportunity to read about each other's activities. Learners collaborate to complete this writing by contributing suggestions for spelling or asking for help. Soon, learners begin to do the writing for each other. They not only begin to make the grammatical transformations from first to third person, they also learn each other's names and about each other's lives. The more open-ended format of the News evolves from these warm up and/or topic-related writing exercises.

Once this routine has been established, little, if any warm up is needed. The facilitator can begin the session by offering chalk/marker to a "known" writer and asking if anyone has any news. Learners then take turns writing each other's news, calling on one another to read and reread.

B. Making It Happen

Literacy Activities: Initially, the facilitator asks learners what news items they have to contribute. This process follows the language experience approach where the teacher transcribes learners' statements, using the learners' own words. At the most beginning level, learners may be asked very specific questions, such as "What did you do before school today?" or "What did you have for lunch?" Their responses can be recorded to form the basis of a very brief news item. When the news is typed up and read the next day, the responses, "Today I cooked soup" and "I ate chicken," become the news item, "Sok cooked soup yesterday. She ate chicken."

Although the facilitator is the first scribe for the group and may record learners' reports during the first few sessions, learners are encouraged to become scribes for their classmates once they become familiar with the process. Even very reticent writers will act as scribes with encouragement from the rest of the group.

The News uses the same process as other language experience activities that normally occur in a classroom, such as writing short paragraphs about a new student, visitors to the class, celebrations, and unusual events. In addition, the topics of different writing activities often become subjects for future news items.

Learners are often able to facilitate the entire process by themselves. This is particularly true in mixed ability groups. All of the students have the oral/aural capacity to share their information, and the more proficient writers can act as scribes for the others. This process encourages students to access each other in ascertaining information, seeking clarification, and asking questions. Additionally, the use of learners' names and experiences increases their awareness of each other as well as validating their experiences and increasing reading and writing abilities overall.

Using the News: The News can be read and processed in a variety of ways. Students may read silently, aloud in small groups, or aloud to the whole class. Students can complete interactive activities individually or in collaboration with other students. The facilitator may ask who wants to read (a general invitation) or ask a particular student if s/he wants to read her/his story. In addition, the News can be adapted for classroom exercises like any other text. Finally, learners may circulate their News to other groups within the school, who in turn may exchange copies of their own News.

REFLECTIONS AND COMMENTS

On "slow" news days, the facilitator may add news items like a weather report, or word activities such as the following:

- Word count — "How many times did you read 'to' in today's news? Please circle 'to.'"

- Cloze exercise — "Today is ____ / yesterday was ____ / tomorrow will be ____."

- Information seeking exercise — "Who's at school today? How many men are in the room?"

Writing activity — "This weekend, I want to _____."

These exercises help increase learners' interaction with the paper and with each other. Reading, rereading and interactive activities can also follow, such as:

- "Circle the "b" words, underline _____."

The more the News format assumes and maintains some regularity (e.g., the date is always in the same place on the page), the greater the chance that learners will engage in predictive reading patterns. Predictive reading could include scanning for the weather report, the calendar, or looking for their own and each other's names in **bold** or underlined type at the beginning of a news item. The use of regular and predictable features in the News simulates the reading of real newspapers, which have predictable formats. At more advanced levels, as time and resources permit, learners can also become engaged in the production process, typing, laying out, and xeroxing.

ABOUT THE AUTHOR

Janet Isserlis is a literacy specialist at the International Institute of Rhode Island. She has worked as an ESL facilitator and literacy practitioner with immigrants and refugees in community based and worksite settings since 1980.

Endnote

1. The News can be used with any level group, and can be used to summarize the week's events, or to review particular happenings in a class. (For more on using text for review of classroom activity, summarizing, etc., see Nash, Talking Shop, 1989, pp. 71-73 .)

USING THE STORIES OF NEW WRITERS

By

Gail Weinstein-Shr

INTRODUCTION

This module is to celebrate the human tapestry, woven deeper and more colorful with each tale told in a gathering of travellers.

BACKGROUND

Who: I first became interested in the power of learner tales at Community College of Philadelphia, where a copy of *New Sounds, New Visions* was placed without explanation in my mailbox. This collection contained stories from the College's ESL students, ranging from three sentences to three pages in length. A simple story about fishing in Cambodia moved me; I read it to my nearly-mute "zero-beginners" on a whim. As if by magic, my silent companions suddenly had much to say, with previously-hidden resources for saying it. Since then, I have never come upon a group of any level or background who were indifferent to the tales of those who have come before them. Here in China (where this module is being written), the directors of chemistry research institutes who gather with me to improve their English readily admit their notion that "if it doesn't hurt it's not learning." Even these older scientists, hardened by years of rote learning (the head of the institute learned English by memorizing an entire dictionary!), are unable to resist the stories I've brought with me as told by immigrants struggling with parents and children, tradition and change, beauty and horror, and the whole range of human experience that we all share one way or another.

To what end: At first, when I stumbled onto learner stories, I was satisfied that they were compelling; these snatches of language provided something worth understanding by listening or reading, as well as the inspiration for something worth saying or writing. Learner tales provided a catalyst for engaging in communication beyond the mechanical displays that we profess to hate but elicit in our classrooms nonetheless. As time goes on, I am beginning to see the ends more broadly, as I see the ends of ESL teaching itself more broadly. I have one story written by a Chinese woman about her frustration, now that she is unable to help her children with their homework because of her limited English. A Puerto Rican woman, whose children are getting "sassy" as they control more of the household's communication with the English-speaking world, may feel a kinship with an Asian woman who once seemed impossibly different. She may also see that her loss of control is not a personal failing, but rather an understandable result of the shift in language resources typical of the immigrant experience. By comparing experiences, that is, by placing them in social and historical context, it becomes possible to make sense of them collectively. It also becomes possible to act on that new sense if we wish.

In sum, my goals for using learner stories are to engage both the learners and me in material that is moving or otherwise compelling, to promote discussion and writing that does not bore us off our gourds, and ultimately, to create opportunities for comparing experiences, for reflecting collectively, and for creating a community that can support one another in striving for both linguistic and non-linguistic goals.

ESL LITERACY IN ACTION

A. Getting Things Started

Learner stories can be found from a variety of sources. For stories close to home, collections like the one compiled by Community College of Philadelphia are ideal. Student newsletters (see Janet Isserlis, this handbook) can also provide terrific materials. In the absence of organized collections, it is always possible to use compositions from the class itself (with permission of the author), or to ask the cooperation of a class from the next level to select and share some of their stories. I personally enjoy finding ways to collaborate with my colleagues, and I've found that new users of English are very happy to be placed in the role of "mentor" by sharing their stories with even newer users.

For stories from further and wider, there is a growing wealth of regional and national sources. One of my favorites is *Voices* magazine, in which the stories of new writers are published along with a large photograph of the author.[1] The folks at *Voices* are making efforts to include the writings of more non-native writers, as well as to expand the number of short, simple pieces that will appeal to new readers. Building a library with materials from within the class or school and from outside can become a gratifying class project.

Stories can be selected by teachers at first, and then by students themselves. As learners skim the stories, check out titles and pictures, and make guesses to choose one for reading, they are doing what good readers do in preparation for approaching a text. In settling on a group process for selection, learners can practice the arts of negotiation, persuasion, turn-taking or voting, modelling citizenship practices along the way.

B. Making Things Happen

When I teach a story, I usually proceed with four general steps, each with its own set of language and literacy activities. These are to read and react to the story; to play with (and master) the language in the story; to generate language beyond the story (elicit new stories); and to compare experiences for reflection and/or action. Below, I describe each with some examples.

Step 1: Read and react.

Before reading a story, I usually ask students to make guesses about the story, such as "What do you think this story is about?" "What do you think will happen"? If there is a photo of the author, I might ask "What can you guess about the author?" "Do you think she is like you? Why or why not?" For new learners, the questions can be very simple. "Does the author look happy or sad? Do you think the story will be happy or sad?" I experiment with ways of reading. Sometimes I let students read silently, sometimes I invite a confident learner to read it out loud as others look on.

I like to give learners a chance to react, even before they've understood completely. Any reading can elicit some kind of feeling or hunch. I usually stay away from comprehension questions that display whether or not the readers have understood correctly.
I figure that if we discuss reactions and feelings, I'll know how much they understood at first, and they will slowly come to understand more. I want learners in my classroom to come to trust their hunches, and to be reminded of how much they do know, rather than having to display what they didn't get.

Step 2: Mastering the language of the story.

One way to become familiar with language is to play with it with others. Unscrambling sentences can be done as a paper and pencil exercise, or they can be cut into "strips" for a group to put together correctly. "Hot Music," by Martha Gonzalez of New York City[2] works well with new learners:

Put the sentences in the right order.

_____   I felt happy because we loved each other,

_____   I remember when I was twenty years old.

_____   My husband sang these songs in those times.

_____   but now I feel sad because he is dead.

__1__   I think the Mexican music I heard on Jose's cassette is romantic.

For short stories like this one, copying the sentences in the correct order after completing the task gives one more opportunity to become familiar with story language.

I also like to scramble words. This is my butchery of a poem by Mika Higachi, a Japanese learner in Chicago:

a. _____
           sky   Blue

b. _____
           grasses   Many

c. _____
           air   Clear

d. _____
  to   deep   Want   breaths   take

e. _____
  bit   A   cold   little

f. _____
    sleepy   bit   little   A

g. _____
  beautiful   But   season   very

h. _____
  keep   I   can't   quiet

Finally, there are a thousand ways to make a cloze exercise and adapt it to the right level. The traditional technique is to leave out every seventh word. To challenge more restless learners, sometimes I leave out every fifth word. To support more tentative learners, I often provide a list of the missing words from which to choose the answers. A second way to support the less confident learner is to do the cloze as a "dictation," allowing the learner to listen, read along, and write in the appropriate place.

Another variation is to leave out a specific part of speech in order to teach a grammar point. Depending on the level of the students, I do or do not supply a "grammar box" with a list of the needed words.

I Help My Kids, My Kids Help Me[3]

```
┌─────────────────────────────────┐
│     I, me, my,  they, them      │
└─────────────────────────────────┘
```

_____ help _____ kids.

_____ teach _____ good things.

_____ play with _____ .

_____ protect _____ and _____ correct _____ .

_____ kids help _____ too.

_____ bring _____ things.

_____ teach _____ English.

_____ kids make _____ happy.

Maybe _____ will take care of _____ when _____ grow old.

To make any of the exercises more challenging, they can be done before reading the story. The difficulty of the task can also be adjusted for small group work in multilevel classrooms.

Step 3: Generating new language, telling new stories.

As I see it, each story is a catalyst. Reading the story and mastering it's language are, in my view, the warm up. The heart of the task is to provide opportunities for learners to hijack the language for their own meanings and their own purposes.

I believe it is easy to underestimate the possibilities for inviting new learners to make their own meanings. An invitation to start a conversation can be as simple as circling yes or no:

a	I like to listen to music in the morning.	Yes	No
b.	I like to listen to music in the evening.	Yes	No
c.	I like to listen to music when I feel happy.	Yes	No
d.	I like to listen to music when I feel sad.	Yes	No
e.	I like to listen to music from my homeland.	Yes	No
f.	I like to listen to American music.	Yes	No
g.	I like to listen to loud music.	Yes	No
h.	I like to listen to soft music.	Yes	No

If the invitation has worked, as soon as participants compare their answers, stories are ready to ooze out the cracks. Once the seeds for new tales have been sewn, learners can be invited to generate their own language through simple pair interviews ("What is your favorite music?," "When do you like to listen to music?") to be followed by partner reports to the group.

Sentence completion is another kind of invitation that can be generated from the theme of the catalyst story:

I feel happy when _____.

I feel sad when _____.

From new users of English to native-speaking workshop participants, this form of invitation often makes it easy to get started. Yes/No questions, simple private writing and pair interviews all make it possible to try out the language of the new story before going public. By the time an interesting tale has emerged, it becomes harder to worry about "losing face" and more compelling to get the tale told.

Step 4: Comparing experience for reflection and/or action

"I love my grandchildren very much. I am learning English so I can talk to my grandchildren. But I also want them to understand a little Chinese. I think every language is useful!"

— Susan Yin, age 74

If you substitute the word "Yiddish" for "Chinese," this could have been my own great grandmother after the family's long journey from Poland. As my mother tells it, my great grandmother lived in her house for nearly a decade. Her parents (my grandparents) wanted the children to learn English as quickly as possible, and so avoided the use of Yiddish. Grandmother and grandchildren did not know how to talk with one another, and she died as a stranger in her own home. Both my mother and her sister still speak with enormous regret of the loss of their grandmother even before she died. Could Susan Yin's story, read with time for reflection and discussion, have helped some family member to see what was happening and have averted disaster? I can't help but wonder.

A simple chart can be an invitation to see patterns in the march of the generations. My favorite way of using this chart is when there are mixed ages in the group who can help one another understand the story from another angle.

Name	Age	Relation	Favorite Language

I aim for my classrooms to become safe places where language use is a topic of discussion and reflection. I might ask learners to complete sentences like these:

a. I like to use English when_____.

b. I like to use my language when _____.

I often use the stories of others to invite learners to talk about how language is used in their own families. It is my hope that the experiences of those who have come before will help learners to recognize the value in what they have brought with them, and to make decisions that reflect that understanding.

Some stories provide a natural invitation to reflect and then act. Pijian Liang, a Chinese woman from Massachusetts, wrote this story:

> My next door neighbors are Black people. They have two children. They are friendly. Everytime we meet I say "hi." They say "hi" back to me and they always smile. Sometimes they lend eggs to us. Sometimes I borrow milk from them.
>
> They are nice people but we haven't talked much because my English isn't very good.

One invitation for reflection and <u>individual action</u> might look something like this:

   a. Do you know your neighbors?
   b. What are your neighbors like?   (Tell 2 things you know.)
   c. What do you want to know about them?   (Write 2 questions.)
   d. How can you get to know them better?   (Write 2 ideas.)

After brainstorming in small groups and then as a class, I have students each choose one of the ideas to test out. After approaching their neighbors, learners come back and report their experiences to one another.

I believe that learner stories can also provide the stimulus for <u>collective action</u>. I found that the escape story of a Vietnamese woman provided material for inviting learners to see their situation collectively. We begin by documenting individual experience:

   a. (Tell why) I came to America because _____

   b. (Tell how) I came to America _____

We proceed by compiling and synthesizing that information by making two class lists on the blackboard: Why/How we came to America, as preparation for a group story with two paragraphs that start like this:

We came to America for many reasons. Some of us ....

We came in many ways. Some of us ....

One follow-up activity is to collect individual stories for a book, using the group story as an introduction. The learners can decide together who should read the book: neighbors? children's teachers? the children themselves? community leaders? politicians? Telling a collective story is part of creating a collective voice.

Another follow-up activity is to interview other immigrants or refugees (recent or long-time) about why and how they came to America. It is often striking for people on both sides of the conversation to see past their differences and find threads of sameness. As learners investigate themselves and others, whether the theme is about coming to America or about anything else, it becomes possible to envision the larger possibilities for community both within and beyond the language classroom.

COMMENTS

The creation of a portfolio, in which learners and teachers can look together at a body of text that the learner has produced, is probably one of the best ways to invite examination of language development. Depending on the focus of the program and or the objectives of the learners, the materials can be examined for any number of specific linguistic features.

I believe that assessment efforts should also reflect that people use language to serve non-linguistic ends. Reading and creating learner stories can be part of a process of collecting and reading a wide range of materials, documenting reactions, learning about one another, and becoming more connected to the new world outside the classroom. Each of these dimensions are ones that can be assessed by learners and teachers through a variety of formal and informal ways.

Learner stories provide a way to invite students to learn about, react to and ultimately shape their new world. As a closing thought, I invite my colleagues to think about our own changing professional world and our own need for connections beyond our classrooms. I'm beginning to believe that everytime we invite our students to read, react and write, we should be doing the same thing! In a sense, we are all learners, both the new users of English and us.

ABOUT THE AUTHOR

Gail Weinstein-Shr, a cultural anthropologist at heart, has done research on the functions and uses of literacy in Philadelphia's Hmong refugee community. She is interested in the potential of the ESL classroom for building community among learners and teachers. She has just become a faculty member at San Francisco State University, where she looks forward to inviting future ESL teachers to join her in exploring the possibilities.

Endnotes

1. Available from 9260-140 St, Surrey, B.C. Canada, V3V 524.

2. From *Voices* magazine

3. By Gebre Goso, quoted in Auerbach, E., *Making Meaning, Making Change.*

PHONICS IN CONTEXT:
USING GRAPHO/PHONEMIC CUES IN
A LEARNER-CENTERED ESL LITERACY CLASSROOM

By

Lynellyn Long

&

Marilyn Gillespie

INTRODUCTION

Within the field of reading, the debate continues between those who advocate teaching reading by emphasizing the relationships between letters and sounds — or phonics — and those who advocate the use of whole texts to stress reading as a meaning-making process. This module describes how phonics-related activities (or, to be more accurate, "grapho/phonemic cuing systems") can be usefully integrated into lessons built around social themes that have meaning to adult students.

BACKGROUND

Our experience has suggested that there is no single best approach to teaching reading. A learner-centered teacher employs a variety of reading and writing techniques, always keeping in mind the central concern that the content addressed in the classroom be meaningful to students. By meaningful, reading and writing needs to reflect both the immediate and larger concerns and literacy activities of the learners. Finding out what those concerns and activities are requires going into the learners' communities and actively watching, listening, and asking questions over an extended period of time. The teacher needs to be an applied ethnographer and he or she needs to ask the learners to be their own applied ethnographers as well. This understanding can then be blended with what we know about how reading is learned and how it can best be taught.

Over the past two or three decades researchers have learned a great deal about the process of learning to read by closely examining what effective readers do. Good readers, they found, construct meaning during the reading process, drawing on prior knowledge and experience to understand the text. Using what they already know (the context) they make predictions about what they will read, confirming them as they go along.

Readers use three kinds of language cues to predict meaning from text. They use "semantic cues" to predict a word that is meaningful in context and "syntactic cues" to predict a word that is grammatically acceptable. When they come to a word they cannot predict using these cues, they may then slow down to use "grapho/phonemic" cues to sound out the word. In fact, all these cuing systems work together virtually simultaneously during the process of making sense of text. According to a growing group of reading specialists, the issue of phonics has to do not so much with whether it should be taught, but when and how. They see phonics not as a "method" of reading in and of itself but one cuing system. It is usually more efficient (and less time consuming) to predict a word from the context, but, when that is not possible, some basic phonics knowledge can be invaluable. For this reason, many believe some basic symbol/sound relations should be taught, especially for single consonants, consonant digraphs (e.g., "ch" and "th"), and consonant clusters (e.g., "st" and "bl").

This understanding of reading provides yet another compelling rationale for learner-centered adult education. Reading (and writing) the kinds of whole texts adults use in their everyday lives provide adult students with chances to try out using all of the cuing systems together in ways that fragmented exercises cannot. What's more, materials that are of immediate interest and concern to learners will also be easier to read because they are predictable. Adults, for example, can use what they know about families to guess how the following sentence might be completed. "Juan is my son and Maria is my _____."

For many adult learners this way of seeing reading will be quite new. Many may come to the classroom with the belief that reading *is* sounding out words. It makes common sense that in order to read, they must first learn all the sounds of the letters and how to pronounce them. Phonics is the "missing key" and if they haven't learned to read before, they may believe that it is because they just haven't learned the "laws" of phonics. In many societies, the traditional way of teaching reading may have focused on memorizing religious texts, reading aloud, and decoding skills. Learners may also have been taught to read slowly and methodically, one word at a time, stopping themselves if they come to a word they don't know (but often losing the "sense" of what they read in the process). They may even believe its "cheating" to guess at a word they can't sound out.

Adult learners need special help to understand that reading is more than pronouncing words. One way to help them to begin this process is to ask students to discuss (possibly with an interpreter and/or in the native language) how people learn to read in their cultures. For example, do literacy activities traditionally take place on temple grounds through menomic chants? Are these activities individually or collectively accomplished? Who traditionally imparts this knowledge? Who is expected to learn to read and write? What happens when one learns to read and write? Students may then want to talk more about someone they know who is a good reader and what makes that person a good reader. A process for doing this is called the Burke Reading Interview (see Weaver, 1988).

Another way to increase students' awareness of language is to help them to brainstorm reading strategies, clues people use to help them figure out the meaning of words. Teachers can help learners to explore how they already employ strategies such as using what they know about a topic to predict a word; relying on illustrations, photos, and titles; using what they have already read to guess what comes next; using the words around the word that don't know to make guesses; and using analogies or "rhyming words" to make guesses.

Students can also be helped to get phonics "know how" both directly and indirectly. With guided observation, learners can internalize many correspondences and patterns well enough to apply them. Teachers can discuss some of the prominent sound features in texts students are reading. They may want to begin with consonants for which there is a single sound, followed by consonant blends. Generally, beginning sounds are taught first and then ending sounds. Many reading specialists believe that it is less useful to teach vowels sounds, although frequently consonant-vowel-consonant clusters, consonant-vowel or consonant-vowel-consonant-silent "e" clusters will be introduced. Especially with vowel patterns, researchers have found that there are too many exceptions for the teaching of particular "rules" to be useful. Some specialists claim explicit teaching of all but a few rules is not necessary since most new readers will unconsciously induce the common patterns given plenty of opportunities to read environmental print and predictable materials and to write using invented spelling. Using rhymes, songs and stories in which various sound elements are prominent is one way to develop the awareness of the system of letter/sound relationships.

Involving students in writing is another way. Teachers can comment on letter/sound relationships as they help students to write letters for words they want to represent. In helping students to take the risk of using invented spelling it may also be helpful to teach a short lesson on history of English.

Later on in the learning process, teachers can show students how many words in English are not phonetically regular and describe the many linguistic roots of common words (e.g., that "kn" as in "know," "knew," and "knee" come from our Danish roots, and "gnaw" and "gnat" come from our Greek roots). Learning about homophones (words that mean different things but sound the same like "main" and "Maine") and homographs (words that sound different but have the same spelling, like "read" and "read" and "desert" and "desert") can also help illustrate the fact that the "magic key" of phonics may not unlock all the doors to reading.

As with so many other learning issues, the challenges of learning to read are compounded for ESL learners. Each of the cuing systems presents difficulties. Grapho/phonemic cues presuppose that the learner knows the sounds of the language to start with, something we as ESL literacy teachers know is not always the case. Not only must the initial consonants "r," "l," and "w" be taught, but students will often need to learn to discriminate between the three sounds. ESL learners may also find it harder to use syntactic or grammar-related cues when they don't understand the syntax of English sentences or semantic cues when they don't understand the meaning of the words in English. The ability to predict can only improve as the learners' second language proficiency improves. But this is all the more reason for learner-centered lessons around themes which have been found to have deep meaning to students. Not only do they engage their hearts and minds, but they provide a rich resource for predictable texts.

In what follows, we outline a process for both the teacher and the learners which is reflected in a lesson plan format. While one could take this lesson and try to use it, the actual content may or may not be relevant to your class and it is bound not to be relevant to at least some of the learners. The point in outlining a series of activities is to suggest a process, not an actual plan. The topic chosen, "parenting," reflects the concerns of many adult learners in various classes we have taught.

ESL LITERACY IN ACTION

A. Getting Things Started

Let's assume that you live and work in the community and/or one way or another have spent a lot of time there. You have spent some time doing applied ethnographic research and have been invited to visit various learners in their homes at various times of the day, see the places where they work, attend their religious and social activities, and join various community organizations. You have developed a rapport with the community and think that you are beginning to know the language and ways of its place.

In the course of your work, you notice that parents are complaining that their children are not well-behaved, that children do not have enough respect for their elders, and that the parents are at a loss to know how they can and should "discipline" their children. A recent incident — a social worker has charged parents who hit their teenage son with child abuse — has generated some debate and concern about "American ways." The learners in your class are worried. Some wonder if by following their customary practices of disciplining the child, they could be arrested for child abuse.

This is a loaded issue so you may not want to address the particular incident initially. The discussion which follows about "parenting" and the particular questions asked may seem simplistic, but by keeping the questions simple, it gives all involved the chance to decide how much they want to discuss, analyze and ultimately, address on this issue.

Before the class begins, you suggest that the theme for the next class could be "parents." You write the word on the board and people agree or have already agreed that it is a worthwhile topic. (Through translation, you have reached an understanding that the learners have the final say in the content of the topics to be addressed in class.) You then ask the class to bring in photographs of their own parents and their children, letters and documents they write for their children or children write on their behalf (e.g., notes to school), and any other written material related to parenting.

Within the context of previous lessons, students had become familiar with many of the initial consonant sounds. You had also used the Glass Word Analysis technique to help students to see patterns of initial consonant and vowel-consonant sounds. Most students can now use these grapho/phonemic cues to identify words with which they are unfamiliar, although, from writing samples, you had noticed that some learners have trouble distinguishing "b" from "d." Since the class knows for the most part the consonant and short vowel sounds, you decide to be ready to pull out consonant-vowel-consonant patterns from language they will create in the upcoming lesson. Using various resource materials, you come up with a list of words you expect can be used during the class: dad, mom, at, fat, cat, sat, got, tot, lot, not, pot, had, bad, sad, mad, lad, etc. Note that you will practice only two short vowels (and their phonetic variations) in this list. The "bad" and "dad" provide a chance to highlight the difference between "b" and "d" and left to right orientation.

B. Making Things Happen

You begin the class with a few questions and with the word "parent" written on the board. "Who are your parents?" "Do they live with you?" Ask learners to show their photographs and use the photographs to write a few descriptive phrases or sentences (e.g., "Tuy's mother and father in Vietnam").

After you have generated a good discussion and written material on their parents, you decide to ask about their parenting. "Are you a parent?" At this point, write the words "child" and "children" on the board. "Do you have any children?" Point to the word. "How many?" "One child?" "Three children?" Write the words "father" and "mother" on the board. Ask "What do mothers do for their children?" "What do mothers do?" At this point, you can begin to generate stories to illustrate their photographs and discussions. Given the concerns and interests of the class, the discussion may lead to issues of children and discipline, i.e., "Can parents hit children?" The discussion could deepen by shifting into the learners' first languages (here the teacher would need to speak the first language(s) and/or involve an interpreter).

You can help the discussion themes move from oral to written expression by recording stories the learners recount and by summarizing the main points of the discussion in writing. You need to ensure that the writing remains in context and is comprehensible to the learners so that they can practice reading what they have written at home. One way of doing this is to write captions for photographs or drawings. You may also want to summarize in a chart format, like this:

Parents

	Our Parents	Us
	Father/ Mother	Father/Mother
Live		
Work		
Do with children		

Such charts provide cues for learners to decode the written language later. The phrases within the charts can be illustrated, and a narrative can be developed from the chart. You may want to have students copy the narrative so it can be used for further reading practice.

As you move from discussion to writing, you can work on introducing some of the c-v-c words that you want to practice. For example, when introducing "Father" and "Mother," you can also write "Dad" and "Mom" and let the learners decode these words themselves. When discussing issues of discipline, you can introduce words such as "bad," "sad," "had," and "mad," and again have the learners decode these words independently based on their prior knowledge of the sound system. (If you add the word "glad" you will probably need to assist them with the initial blend.)

You can then follow up with some recognition games. For example, the learners with flash cards of the various letters can form their own words from the given patterns [again using a Glass Word Analysis Technique]. They can also take turns dictating different words from a list of three possibilities (e.g., one learner dictates "bad" and the learners choose the word from a list of three words -- dad, bad, and bid). The purpose of such games is to practice the left to right orientation and to distinguish "b" from "d". In addition, the learners are gaining the experience in certain word patterns which will enable them to read and write these patterns independently.

Next, ask the learners to share the written materials they have brought about being parents (e.g., children's books, notices from school, letters, forms, etc.). Discuss what literacy strategies they use to negotiate writing and reading of these materials. "Who reads this book?" "Who answers this letter?" Help them to expand their repertoire by analyzing a form to determine which parts they may now be able to decode and answer. Point out where "parents" or "children" is located on several forms, for example, and the visual clues that suggest such questions (e.g., a list for children). If time allows, learners can also work together on other activities such as drafting a simple note to a teacher explaining that their "child is sick."

C. Winding Down

For homework and/or to review the material, you can prepare a list of questions about their narratives which allow students to practice both the word patterns and the language generated from their narratives. (You should use question words that have already been introduced and read the questions over with orally with the learners.) They can also dictate their own questions from the narratives.

During the course of the lesson, make copies of their work so you can analyze it in developing the patterns, structures, and themes for the next lesson. Finish the class with a brief discussion of subsequent topics and materials. For example, if from the discussion, issues about "children and school" emerged, that could be a theme for a later lesson.

COMMENTS

A. Assessment and Evaluation

As teachers, we use learners' writing samples to assess which themes and patterns need to be developed. The more experience we gain in both the learners' own contexts for reading and writing and with their particular linguistic systems, the more effectively we can be in analyzing their progress. We need to keep a vision of what it means to be an independent reader and writer and gradually move learners towards increasing levels of independence. Through this process, learners begin introducing more of their own questions and assist the teacher by being ethnographers themselves.

As teachers, we have also found that the introduction of relevant themes is also an interactive process. As in any learning process, themes emerge and re-emerge, often acquiring increasing levels of complexity. This spiralling process is an integral part of learning. Each theme will have several elaborations and increasing literacy content.

In addition to analyzing learners' texts, it is also useful to use miscue analysis techniques. In miscue analysis learners are asked to read a passage aloud while the teacher notes the kinds of errors they make. This can then be used to diagnose areas where further instruction is needed (see Weaver, 1988).

B. Resources

The following texts helped us in preparing this unit and may be useful to you in learning more about reading and the role of phonics and in planning your own lessons:

Celce-Murcia, M. (Ed.) (1991). *Teaching English as a Second or Foreign Language.* Second Edition. New York, NY: Newbury House.

Intended as a basic introduction to the profession of teaching English to speakers of other languages, this text contains several useful articles devoted to the teaching of reading in ESL. In *Teaching Children to Read in a Second Language*, Barbara Hawkins describes recent research on how second language learners become readers. The article overviews special considerations in the use of phonics and whole language approaches for ESL learners.

The Center for the Expansion of Language and Thinking (CELT) Crisis Hotline, (602) 929-0929, 325 E. Southern Avenue, Tempe, Arizona 85282.

Call this free hotline to obtain copies of short fact sheets on issues related to the use of phonics and whole language, the meaning of literacy, and issues in evaluation of students. Although most topics directed toward educators and parents of school-aged children, the same issues can be applied to working with adults.

Gillespie, M. (1989). *Many Literacies: Training Modules for Adult Beginning Readers and Tutors*. Center for International Education, 283 Hills House S., University of Massachusetts, Amherst, MA 01003.

The reading chapter describes a series of short activities to use with small groups of adult students, including activities to help students examine their own reading history, discuss their beliefs about what good readers and learn about reading strategies. There is also a description of the language experience approach and tips for deriving word recognition activities from student-written texts.

Long, L. and Spiegel-Podnecky, J. (1988). *In Print: Beginning Literacy Through Cultural Awareness*. Reading, MA: Addison-Wesley.

In Print is written especially for adult ESL students who are just beginning to learn to read and write. Each chapter is organized around a theme which reflects the lives and experiences of adult learners. In addition to a series of critical questions around the theme and the introduction of sight words, integrated into each lesson is a "Listen" section in which the learner works on phonics skills and an "Analyze" section in which focuses on structural analysis skills such as how to put syllables, prefixes, and suffixes together to form words. The Teacher's Guide describes the rationale for each activity.

Traub, N. & Bloom, F. (1983). *Recipe for Reading*. Cambridge, MA: Educators Publishing Service, Inc.

This traditional phonic texts provides a basic sequence of phonics activities and examples which can be used by teachers to design their own lessons. It also describes a series of phonics-related activities such as sound cards, word games, and sequence charts.

Weaver, C. (1988). *Reading Process and Practice: From Sociolinguistics to Whole Language*. Portsmouth, NH: Heinemann Educational Books.

This comprehensive text was designed to help teachers better understand the theory and practice of the reading process. It is an excellent resource for a general description of contrasting models of the reading process, including whole language and phonics-based approaches and for details on language cues, reading strategies and miscue analysis. Although the book is addressed to those who teach children, the basic principles also apply to instruction of adults.

ABOUT THE AUTHORS

Marilyn Gillespie is the Director of the National Clearinghouse on Literacy Education for Limited English Proficient Adults at the Center for Applied Linguistics in Washington, D.C. She has a special interest in learner-generated writing and is conducting a study on native language literacy.

Lynellyn Long works in the Office of Women in Development at the Agency for International Development and is an adjunct professor at the American University. She has recently completed *Ban Vinai*, a book on refugee camp life in Thailand.

ENVIRONMENTAL PRINT

by

Pat Rigg

INTRODUCTION

Even vegetarians can read **McDonald's** beneath the golden arches. Our environment indoors and out is full of signs, labels, cautions, and ads. We swim in print: much of it is readable because it is in rich context. We can build on our students' ability to read this in expanding their English conversation, reading, and writing.

BACKGROUND

Background of the group: This is for people who are just becoming literate in English. They may already be literate in other languages, or they may be reading and writing for the first time in their lives.

Approach: This is a holistic approach. Language is not fragmented, but is kept whole, and the social nature of language and of literacy is respected. Students' knowledge is the basis of the lesson. It can be used with a problem-posing approach: some examples of environmental print can be Freirean "codes:" some examples or categories can lead to an exploration of social issues. (See Follow-Up.)

Purpose: This lesson demonstrates to students

- that they already are reading in English, using context and prior knowledge
- that they can predict what print they'll see in many situations
- that this knowledge can increase their reading and writing.

Context: This easily ties into student exploration and examination of the physical contexts in which they live and work. The lesson can be used early in the term, as it helps build a sense of community as well as a sense of one's reading ability.

ESL LITERACY IN ACTION

A. Getting Things Started

The classroom should be arranged so that students face one another. Teacher and students should value collaborative learning. A file of photographs or slides which show examples of environmental print would be useful but it is not required.

B. Making It Happen

Warm up: Look around the room. There may be "no smoking" signs, "on/off" light switches, directions for what to do in the event of fire, brand names on pencils, student notebooks, and labels on clothes (Adidas, Levis), as well as snappy slogans on T-shirts and sweatshirts.

Literacy activities: First, as a class, see how many items of environmental print you can find in the room and list them on the board or overhead.

Second, leave the room, either as a group or in pairs. Walk through the school, or through a couple of streets, noting (by writing) everything there is to read on the street (license plates, bumper stickers, automobile insignia, tire insignia, street names, mail boxes, building names, no parking signs, bus stops.) If there are stores, note their names; on store doors note the VISA and MasterCard logos, the hours posted, Push/Pull on doors, and the advertisements in windows. Walk into a grocery, drugstore, or hardware store and list the first 50 or 100 things to read that you notice.

Third, compare those notes. Categorize the examples. The students can make one 3" x 5" card for each example, so that they can be manipulated and placed physically into one category or another. Making the cards requires the students to translate their perhaps skimpy notes into clearly readable examples. They probably will confer with each other to make sure that their spelling and capitalization are accurate. After one group has categorized several examples, have another group categorize the same examples. Then, both groups can talk about what they selected as distinctive features to form the categories they created.

COMMENTS

As with any lesson, student involvement and interest indicate a successful lesson.

Assessment/Evaluation: Students should be contributing examples, discussing them among themselves, and writing (using temporary spelling rather than conventional spelling if necessary). The list of examples of environmental print suggested by the students should increase (double or triple) in the first week of this lesson.

Saving the day: Occasionally a student will "block" and say he cannot read any environmental print because he feels unable to pronounce everything accurately. Try to convince the student that reading is not pronouncing words or letters but building meaning from print. Deciding that an ad for Camel cigarettes says "smoke cigarettes" instead of "Cool Character Camel" is real reading; so is reading "Exit" as "This way out."

Follow-up: Students can make a bulletin board of examples, design their own T-shirt slogans, bumper stickers, etc. Students can bring in lists of environmental print they've noticed and contribute it to a common class list on newsprint or on computer.

If someone has a camera and film, students can take pictures of environmental print. This gives them a chance to decide what sorts of environmental print they want to get examples of. They will need to discuss examples and types, and perhaps to draw and write illustrations to their discussions. They may write lists of what they want to shoot, with some sort of directions as to where these items are. All of this discussing and deciding involves the students' recalling specific pieces of print, a sort of mental "rereading."

Final Words: Environmental print is readable, easily obtainable, practically free, and involves both writing and reading. And it's fun.

ABOUT THE AUTHOR

Pat Rigg has a small consulting firm with a big name — American Language & Literacy — in Tucson, AZ. She has worked with and written about adults becoming literate in English for many years. She co-edited TESOL's *Children and ESL: Integrating Perspectives* and NCTE's *When They Don't All Speak English*.

USING TOTAL PHYSICAL RESPONSE (TPR) IN A WORKPLACE ESL LITERACY CLASS

by

Laima Maria Schnell,
Workplace Literacy Project/Adult Learning Resource Center

INTRODUCTION

Being a monolingual personnel manager in a factory where the majority of the workers speak virtually no English can be rather daunting. Having a worker speak to you for the first time saying "I so happy I speak you now" can be an encouraging sign of things to come. Workplace literacy, with its much-needed ESL component, is a welcome development in today's manufacturing world.

BACKGROUND

A lunchtime workplace literacy class at a uniform factory in Chicago brings together a group of sewing machine operators for an hour of eating and learning. This particular class consists of 10 women, mostly Korean, although a few other nationalities are represented as well.

The class is a beginning ESL class and, although the company has stressed the importance of improved oral communication between the workers and supervisors, reading and writing is also incorporated in each lesson. Perhaps, given the fact that the majority of the women come from another alphabetic writing system, reading and writing is rather threatening to them. Since most of the women live and work in a neighborhood of Chicago where the majority of the signs are written in Korean, they are exposed to relatively little English environmental print outside the worksite.

ESL LITERACY IN ACTION

An attempt is made to introduce reading and writing from sight words to simple sentences in bite-size, non-threatening lessons. Lessons begin with known oral material and move on to challenging written material.

Amidst lots of chatter, heating of food and delicious smells, the class finally settles down, and pencils replace chopsticks.

A. Getting Things Started

The company feels it is important for the sewing machine operators to know the names of the garments they sew. Classes focus on introducing the names of certain garments and describing them using work-relevant vocabulary, such as long sleeve, wide lapel, belted, and pleated. The teacher prepares a set of flashcards that has been used in a variety of oral activities. Most of the students can identify the garments either passively by pointing to the correct card or actively by pronouncing its name. Flashcards of the garments' names have also been prepared and used in reading exercises.

The first exercise begins with the teacher placing a dozen or so flashcards on the table facing the students and asking them what garment they are making today or what garment they have made. The students' task is to select a garment, name it in whatever context the question requires, and ask for the card. The teacher may use follow-up questions like "Is it this jacket with the round collar?" in order to elicit some description from the student. The teacher may give the student the incorrect card to elicit some objection and clarification.

The reading Total Physical Response (TPR) exercise begins when each student has one of the flashcards in front of her.

B. Making Things Happen

The students are familiar with oral TPR activities and the teacher explains that this is a reading TPR activity. The teacher stresses the importance of silence during the activity and promises to help if there's confusion. The teacher holds up a long piece of cardboard upon which word cards have been taped to form commands.

Give	the Baron jacket	to	Hwa

Students quietly read the command and the student who has the Baron jacket gives it to Hwa.

Using masking tape, the teacher quickly changes the command by changing one of the elements in the sentence.

Give	the Tux Dress	to	Hwa

or

Give	the Baron jacket	to	Myung

or

Take	the Baron jacket	from	Myung

or

Put	the Baron jacket	next to	the high-low pants

(Prepositions have been previously studied and similar oral activities have been previously performed.)

By now, the flashcards are unevenly distributed on the table or in the students' possession. The teacher assigns a student to collect the cards by saying "Where is the Tux Dress?" and "Where is the Baron jacket?" and eliciting responses such as "Here it is" or "I have the Tux Dress" or "On top of the pleated pants."

The second part of the lesson involves strip sentences. Each student is given an envelope containing slips of paper upon which individual words have been written. The student must independently line up the words to form two (or more) correct sentences. The sentences are similar to the commands practiced in the first part of the lesson.

Peer assistance is encouraged at this point as some students have a difficult time with this experience. They then compare their sentences with their neighbor's. The deck of flashcards is divided between two or three students and they again act out a few of the commands. The students are encouraged to write their sentences into their notebooks before the envelopes and flashcards are all collected.

A follow-up exercise, best done during a subsequent class as a review or reinforcement, involves a dictation. Students are given a sheet of paper with blanks where words will be written as they are dictated. The correct words are written underneath the lines. Students are told to cover up the answers as they write. After they are done with each sentence, they compare their words with the model. The last few sentences have no answers written beneath.

Give	the	Baron	jacket

to	Hwa

Take	the	Tux	dress

from	Myung

COMMENTS

The sewing machine operators at this factory do little reading and no writing at their jobs. Their work is shown to them through modeling, and conversation is discouraged throughout the work day. Despite this seeming lack of the need for language skills, the company is aware of the fact that there is little communication between supervisors and workers, and that this creates a fractionalized, unwelcoming environment.

What happens in the English classroom defines and sharpens the students' roles in the factory. The material they stitch together each day forms a garment that has a name and a written form. These garments can be talked about in communicative ways. Pride in each woman's work is quite evident as garments are described, compared, and discussed.

As a teacher, I sometimes wonder how and if what happens in the classroom really helps my students either in their job or other aspects of their lives. How useful to them is this particular lesson for example? And yet, the lesson provides the opportunity for personal interaction, a meaningful context for their long hours of labor, a slow but steady understanding and mastery of their environment, and the personal sense of satisfaction and empowerment that all learning provides.

ABOUT THE AUTHOR

Laima Maria Schnell has a B.A. in French and a M.A. in Applied Linguistics. A two-year assignment with the Peace Corps in Ecuador convinced her of the importance and the urgency of learning a language in the culture where it is spoken. For the last few years, she has been involved in teaching ESL to adults in both community-based and workplace programs.

Conclusion

Much of our research has focused on innovative practices, and the picture we have painted may not necessarily represent the realities of the average adult ESL literacy program. It must be acknowledged that most adult ESL literacy programs face tremendous challenges: they have to deal with unstable funding, find room in cramped quarters, and make do with limited resources. This is true for innovative as well as "ordinary" programs.

Most adult ESL literacy teachers face challenges as well. Many spend long hours designing materials and creating rich literacy activities for their students. A great many of these teachers also regularly contribute to the overall curriculum of the program. Yet these efforts are not always acknowledged, nor are they rewarded monetarily. Resources that other professionals take for granted, such as xerox machines or word processors, are often missing. For a large number of teachers, working in an adult ESL literacy program is a luxury they can ill afford, since it often means having to take a second job somewhere else in order to make a living wage. While some good teachers do burn out, many continue on because they love their students, and teaching ESL literacy is what they do.

We must also acknowledge that not all effective teaching takes place in innovative programs, nor are all good teachers necessarily innovative. Many provide good solid teaching by adapting available materials and using conventional teaching techniques. These teachers contribute to the field as well. They might contribute even more if greater access to resources and staff development targeted to their needs were available.

What has to happen for programs to continue their endeavors and for teachers to keep the faith? Stable funding and decent working conditions are needed, and so are rewards for excellence and an ongoing commitment to support good teaching. There must be recognition of the fact that many of the standards that quality programs have set for themselves are complex and rigorous and that the successes they have achieved are real, although they are not always measurable by standard means.

Besides sustained funding, commitment, and support, the greatest hope for the field might lie in collaborations: collaborations among teachers who are interested in ESL literacy and want to share materials and ideas; collaborations among programs who want to forge a common agenda and share resources and expertise; collaborations between students and teachers who want to work together and learn from each other; and finally, collaborations among learners and staff who want to share decision making.

Interdependency Hypothesis – skills learned in acquiring native language transfer when learning a 2nd language

Proficiency

Common Underlying Hypothesis – skills learned in acquiring native language transfer beyond learning language skills to more difficult cognitive skills.

Contains